THE SOCIALIST NETWORK

BY
NESTA H. WEBSTER
(MRS. ARTHUR WEBSTER)
AUTHOR OF
"THE FRENCH REVOLUTION," "WORLD REVOLUTION"
"SECRET SOCIETIES AND SUBVERSIVE MOVEMENTS"
ETC.

LONDON
1926

FOREWORD

The object of this book is not to provide a history of Socialism, but merely an account of the Socialist organisations of modern times. Hence no mention is made of isolated Socialist theorists, but only of people connected with, or giving rise to, concrete societies or groups. Secret or occult societies do not enter into the scope of the inquiry, which is not concerned with mysterious inner circles, invisibles or high initiates working in the dark, but only with open movements—societies with recognised headquarters, offices, executive committees, published lists of members, official organs, statements of aims, etc. Though such a presentation of the revolutionary movement is necessarily incomplete, and may fail to satisfy those who care to inquire into causes, it will appeal the more to practical people who are unwilling to consider anything they cannot see before their eyes.

It has seemed to me that a sort of guide-book of this kind, accompanied by a chart, might be useful, in view of the fact that the ramifications of the Socialist movement have now become so vast and complicated that it is almost impossible to follow them. The very difficulties with which I have been faced in the course of my work have encouraged me in this idea. Often I have been obliged to search for days in order to discover some simple fact, owing to the extraordinary vagueness with regard to dates and practical details which characterise Socialist publications—histories, pamphlets, year books and manuals alike. Long pages are devoted to the doctrines of some society, but when it was founded, where and by whom, may not perhaps once be mentioned. Again, one is confronted by conflicting evidence which has to be sifted in order to arrive at the truth.

What wonder, then, that the so-called " Capitalist Press " falls into the strangest blunders when dealing with the different phases of this movement, and that anti-Socialist writers, whose particular business it is to study the subject, from time to time commit inaccuracies which detract from the value of their work ?

In this little book I lay no claim to infallibility ; indeed, I do not believe it would be possible for a single human brain to master all the details of this bewildering network and to avoid going wrong on some point—an international committee of experts would be needed to achieve such a result. All I can claim is that I have spared no pains to find out the facts of the case by seeking my data in the Socialists' own literature, ranging from the pamphlets of Babeuf to those of the Komintern. If, then, inaccuracies of any importance occur, it will not be for want of long and arduous research, and in this case I shall be glad to have them pointed out to me with a view to correction in a further edition. My only concern is to find out the truth and make it known.

Aylesbury

CONTENTS

Foreword 5

CHAPTER I
Origins of Modern Socialism 9

CHAPTER II
Marxian Socialism (Pre-War Period) 11

CHAPTER III
Anarchism and Syndicalism 26

CHAPTER IV
The War and Pacifism 32

CHAPTER V
The Russian Revolution 40

CHAPTER VI
World Bolshevism. 48

CHAPTER VII
Bolshevism in Great Britain 62

CHAPTER VIII
The Capture of Trade Unionism 73

CHAPTER IX
The Bolshevisation of British Trade Unionism . . 84

CHAPTER X
Subsidiary Communist Organisations 95

CHAPTER XI
Pacifism (Post-War) 103

CHAPTER XII
Youth Movements 113

CHAPTER XIII
Socialism and Christianity 126

CHAPTER XIV
Conclusion 134
Diagram of the Moscow Organisation . . . 138
Abbreviations 140
Index of Persons 145
General Index 158
CHART OF SOCIALIST NETWORK . *In Pocket at End*

THE SOCIALIST NETWORK

CHAPTER I
ORIGINS OF MODERN SOCIALISM

ALTHOUGH the main doctrines of Socialism have manifested themselves at intervals throughout the whole history of civilisation, the present Socialist movement cannot be said to date back further than the eighteenth century. Until then attacks on the existing social order had taken the form only of sporadic outbreaks, but with the philosophers, the Encyclopædists and the Freemasons of France, the social revolution began, and since that period has never ceased to agitate the world. In a word, the revolution of which the 1789 explosion in France was the first outward expression is the same revolution we are living through to-day. This is proved conclusively by the chart here appended, where the unbroken continuity of the movement is shown in the form of a genealogical descent which admits of no dispute.

The Jacobins.—Beginning at the top right-hand corner, we find the first organised association of men and women formed for the purpose of overthrowing the existing social order—the Society of Jacobins. Starting as the Club Breton in 1789, the Jacobin Club soon formed a vast society with branches in every corner of France and with related groups in foreign countries. Although the doctrines of the Jacobins were not yet known under the name of Socialism, they, nevertheless, embodied certain Socialist ideas. To judge by the public speeches and writings of the leaders, these more closely resembled the theory professed by the small body of modern Socialists known as " Distributionists " than to that of Collectivism, yet in reality, according to the testimony of a contemporary, Marx's ideas on " class warfare " and " wage slavery " were already current among them.

" The plan of the Jacobins was to stir up the rich against the poor and the poor against the rich. To the latter they said : ' You have made a few sacrifices in favour of the Revolution, but fear, not patriotism, was the motive.' To the former they said : ' The rich man has no bowels of compassion ; under the pretext of feeding the poor by providing them with work he exercises over them a superiority contrary to the views of Nature and to Republican principles. Liberty will always be precarious *as long as one part of the nation lives on wages from the other.* In order to preserve its independence, it is necessary that every one should be rich or that every one should be poor'" (Fantin Desodoards, *Histoire philosophique de la Révolution Française,* IV. 344, published in 1807).

Babouvistes.—In 1795 however, after the fall of Robespierre, the complete theory of Communism as advocated by the modern Bolsheviks was formulated by François Noel Babeuf, who assumed the name of "Gracchus" and placed himself at the head of a conspiracy for the violent overthrow of the government and its replacement by a Communist State. The system advocated by Babeuf was in almost every detail identical with that of modern Communism—State control of industry and destruction of private enterprise, compulsory labour to be paid for not in money but in kind (as indicated by Bukharin, one of the present Soviet leaders, in his *Programme of the World Revolution*), the workers not to be allowed to choose their profession, but told off in gangs to do whatever work the State required (cf. *Russian Code of Labour Laws*), the nationalisation of children and destruction of family life, etc. The Bolsheviks of Russia thus rightly described themselves in their first Manifesto as the "direct successors" of Babeuf (*The New Communist Manifesto of the Third Internationale*, with preface by William Paul, published by the Socialist Labour Press, Glasgow, 1919).

Utopian Socialism.—After the suppression of the Babouviste rising and the execution of its leaders (in 1796), the doctrines of Babeuf and of his colleague, Buonarotti, continued to hold sway amongst the secret political societies of France during the first half of the nineteenth century. This period may be described as the "Golden Age" of Socialism ; Socialist doctrinaires, in many cases sincere idealists, such as Louis Blanc and Buchez in France and Robert Owen in England, followed each other in quick succession, and put forward every conceivable scheme for the reconstruction of society on a Collectivist basis. Several of these men proved their belief in their own theories by putting them into practice under the form of associations and settlements—all, however, unsuccessful. Of these, Robert Owen's "New Harmony" settlement, Fourier's "phalansteries," and Cabet's community in Texas are the best known. But the revolution of 1848 and the failure of the Socialist provisional government in France put an end to all such theorising, and by 1850 Socialism was generally regarded as dead —an exploded doctrine that could never be revived.

CHAPTER II

MARXIAN SOCIALISM (PRE-WAR PERIOD)

Marxism.—With the collapse of French Socialism the social revolution entered on a new phase. Although the Collectivist theories of Babeuf had persisted amongst the Utopian Socialists— as Marx described them—in France and England during the first half of the nineteenth century, the class war waged by the Jacobins and the Babouvistes had largely died down, and except amongst the followers of Blanqui pacific methods had been preferred to violence. Further, the militant atheism of the Jacobins had played no part in the Socialist but only in the Anarchist movement. But these characteristics were to be revived by the man who must be regarded as the pioneer of the modern Socialist movement, the German-Jew Karl Marx.

Whilst Utopian Socialism was still on its trial, in 1847 Karl Marx and his colleague, Friedrich Engels, published the famous " Communist Manifesto " which to this day forms the Credo of Bolshevism. The contention of certain Marxists to-day that the Bolsheviks in advocating violent revolution have misinterpreted the doctrine of the Prophet is effectually disproved by the concluding words of the Manifesto :

" The Communists disdain to conceal their views and aims. They openly declare that their ends can only be attained by the *forcible overthrow* [my italics] of existing social conditions. Let the ruling classes tremble at a Communistic revolution. The proletarians have nothing to lose but their chains. They have a world to win."

It was not until Marx obtained control of a concrete organisation that his theories were able to make considerable headway.

The 1st Internationale.—In 1862 a number of French working-men, pacific interpreters of Proudhon's syndicalist theories, had formed the " Working-men's Association " with a view to improving the conditions of labour. This was the organisation which Marx succeeded in capturing. At an inaugural meeting in St. Martin's Hall, London, on September 28, 1864, the French working-men's society became transformed into the International Working-men's Association—now known as the 1st Internationale. Before long the French leaders, Tolain and Fribourg; the English members, Cremer, Odger, Weston, Professor Beesley, and also the Mazziniste

Wolff, were gradually superseded by the German and Jewish clique —Karl Marx, Hermann Jung, Eccarius, Lessner, Moses Hertz, etc. The history of the 1st Internationale, like the history of the Jacobin Club, consisted mainly in a struggle between contending factions, from which the Marxists emerged triumphant. First came the struggle against the Mazzinistes, who were speedily eliminated. The Proudhonians held their ground until 1868, when at the Brussels Congress the Marxist theory gained the ascendant, and in 1869, at the fourth Congress, in Basle, so far prevailed that Fribourg declared " the Internationale of the French founders was dead, quite dead."

The Social Democratic Alliance.—Meanwhile the Anarchists had entered the lists. In 1864 the Russian Michel Bakunin had founded his "Alliance Sociale Democratique" on a secret society basis, for the purpose of violently overthrowing the existing social order, not in favour of Communism, but of complete Anarchy.

The difference between the two creeds is shown in the definition of Marx's system given by the Socialist Malon, member of the 1st Internationale, and by Bakunin's résumé of his own programme :

Marx : " The State Socialism of Marx was comprised in the conquest of political power, that is to say, of the State, by the working-class which has for its historic mission to put an end to the class war by the abolition of classes, and to the present economic miseries and contradictions by ' the nationalisation of production and distribution of wealth.' "

Bakunin : "Abolition of the State in all its religious, juristic, political, and social realisations ; reorganisation by the free initiative of free individuals in free groups."

It was this formula that became later that of Anarchism.

" I abominate Communism," declared Bakunin, " because it is a denial of freedom, and I cannot understand anything human without freedom." In their advocacy of the class war and of militant atheism the Bakuninistes were, however, at one with the Marxists, and in 1869 the " Alliance Sociale Democratique " was admitted to the 1st Internationale. Then the struggle between the Communists and Anarchists began, and in 1872 the latter were excluded, leaving the Marxists in possession of the field. The headquarters were then removed to New York, and four years later, in 1876, the 1st Internationale came to an end in Philadelphia.

The 2nd Internationale.—For thirteen years no Socialist Internationale existed. Then the idea was revived at Congresses in Paris and Brussels in 1889, the 2nd Internationale was founded " and constituted as a central International Socialist Bureau in 1900."

At the outbreak of the Great War :

"it included twenty-seven countries, with a membership of twelve millions. These were composed of the great Socialist or Labour Parties, which each pursued their particular activities in the various

MARXIAN SOCIALISM (PRE-WAR PERIOD) 13

countries along their own lines, and with virtual independence. At periodical intervals, usually of three years, the parties met in an International Socialist Congress to pass resolutions on Socialist policy and general questions. . . . In the intervening periods the International Socialist Bureau, consisting of three delegates from each national section, was entrusted with the work of carrying out the decisions of the Congresses and arranging for future Congresses. The International Socialist Bureau usually met once a year, and the continuous business was carried on by an executive composed of members of the Belgian section working with a secretariat at Brussels. This Executive consisted of Vandervelde (Chairman), Camille Huysmans (Secretary), and two other members of the Belgian section. The expenses of the Bureau were defrayed by contributions from the National Labour and Socialist organisations of the countries affiliated" (R. Palme Dutt, *The Two Internationals*, p. 1. 1920).

Adolphe Smith, of the Social Democratic Federation, who acted as Official Interpreter at the Congresses of the Internationale from the outset, expressed the opinion that by 1893 it had become completely Germanised. The representatives of the British Trade Unions, distinguished at home for their "great tenacity combined with moderation and common sense," abroad "displayed complete ignorance of racial differences, foreign history, customs and languages," and were therefore unable to hold their own in discussions with the Continental delegates. This "gave the Germans their chance," and "German ascendancy was demonstrated at the Zurich Congress of 1893, because it was then definitely decided that the British Trade Unions would no longer attend in their official capacity. From that time the British Trade Unions ceased to appoint delegates to the Congresses of the Internationale," although they helped the Congress of the Internationale to meet in London in 1896 (Adolphe Smith, *The Pan-German Internationale*, p. 7).

From the time of the 1st Internationale onwards we see, then, the Marxists gaining ground everywhere and Utopian Socialism retreating further into the background. We shall now follow the course of this movement in different countries.

SOCIALISM IN AMERICA

Beginning at the left-hand of the chart, we find Socialism in America to have been German in character from the outset. To quote the résumé given in the admirable Report of the Joint Legislative Committee in the Senate of the State of New York on Revolutionary Radicalism, under Senator Lusk (filed April 24, 1920), known usually as "The Lusk Report":

"The present Socialist movement in the United States must be distinguished from the early experiments in Utopian ideals, represented by the sectarian communities such as the Shakers, or the experiment in Communism made by the Owenites, or the Fourierists and the Icarian communities.

"The modern movement of organised Socialism may be dated from the formation of the Social Party of New York and vicinity which was organised in January, 1868, in the Germania Assembly rooms on the Bowery. The membership of this organisation, recruited solely from the German labour circles, and its policies and platform, were in accord with the principles then set down by the International Working-men's Association.

"In 1868 this party nominated an Independent ticket, but the number of votes which it secured was negligible. The organisation did not survive this defeat, but in the same year some of the leading spirits of this organisation organised what has been termed by Morris Hillquit 'The first strictly Marxian organisation of strength and influence on American soil,' which was known as the Allgemeiner Deutscher Arbeiter Verein.

"In 1869 this organisation was admitted to the National Labour Union No. 5 of New York, and in the following year joined the International Working-men's Association as Section I, New York. It should be noted that the pioneer element of the Radical and revolutionary movement in this country was German. . . .

"The movement was generally stimulated by the action taken in transferring the General Council of the International from London to New York. The general secretary of the council at this time was S. A. Sorge, who was an intimate friend of both Karl Marx and Friedrich Engels. He became the most active of the organisers in the new movement." (*Lusk Report*, I. 505, 506.)

Social Democratic Working-men's Party—Socialist Labour Party of North America.—In 1871 the Social Democratic Working-men's Party of North America was formed by dissident members of the International, and after the dissolution of the latter carried on the work of Socialism. At a convention held in Philadelphia in 1876 the North American Federation of the International Working-men's Association, the Social Democratic Working-men's Party of North America, the Labour Party of Illinois, and the Socio-Political Labour Unions of Cincinnati, were all consolidated into a new organisation known as the Working-men's Party of the United States, founded upon Marxian principles, which in the following year took the name of the Socialist Labour Party of North America. This was led by the Jewish Marxian, Daniel de Leon.

" For about twenty years the Socialist Labour Party was the dominant factor in the Socialist movement in this country. It was recruited largely from alien elements, and particularly under the influence of German leaders. It was wholly out of touch with American life and American principles. The despotic character and extremely narrow viewpoint of the party leadership finally resulted in alienating newly converted Socialists from the party, and a new party, known as the Social Democratic Party of America, came into being in 1899.

"An attempt to harmonise the difference was made in the following year and a convention was held in Indianapolis on July 29, 1901,

MARXIAN SOCIALISM (PRE-WAR PERIOD)

representing the various Socialist organisations with the exception of the New York faction of the Socialist Labour Party. The result of this convention was the formation of the Socialist Party of America, which has led the Socialist movement in this country since that time." (*Lusk Report*, I. 509, published in 1920.)

Intercollegiate Socialist Society.—In 1905 the Intercollegiate Socialist Society was organised in New York, ostensibly "for the purpose of promoting an intelligent interest in Socialism among college men and women," but in reality openly propagating Socialism (*Lusk Report*, I. 1119). Amongst the founders were A. J. Muste and a Russian Jew, Misca Hilkowicz, who had assumed the name of Morris Hillquit and later played a leading part in the Left Wing Socialist movement (*Congressional Record*, December 19, 1925, pp. 4 and 5). The Intercollegiate Socialist Society has now become the League for Industrial Democracy, under which name it carries on propaganda amongst the youth of America.

Rand School of Social Science.—In 1906 the American Socialist Society, a membership corporation with a board of directors elected annually, founded the Rand School of Social Science, which became a powerful centre of Socialist propaganda. In the years 1918–19 its registered students numbered over 5,000. But by this date the course of the revolutionary movement in America had largely veered towards Syndicalism, with which we shall deal in the following chapter.

SOCIALISM IN GREAT BRITAIN

Before 1881 no Socialist organisation of any kind existed in this country. The spirit of class warfare that the Jacobins of France had communicated to their allies in the British revolutionary societies had been extinguished in the wave of reaction that followed on the first French Revolution, theoretical Communism had ended with Robert Owen's fiasco in 1827, whilst the Chartist riots had roused the nation to the danger of popular violence. Only the little band of "Christian Socialists," led by Charles Kingsley and Frederick Maurice, continued to preach the necessity for a complete reconstruction of the social system, but without the spirit of class hatred, and also without any organisation at their disposal wherewith to bring pressure to bear on public opinion. Meanwhile, in the world of labour the growing strength of the Trade Union and the Co-operative movements, and in the political arena the humanitarian schemes of Lord Shaftesbury—always the opponent of Socialism—did much to counteract the work of agitators. During the thirty years that elapsed after Karl Marx and Friedrich Engels came to live in England (in 1849), their theories made little or no headway, and here, as on the Continent, it was not until another concrete organisation was formed that Marxism was able to gain a footing in this country.

The Democratic Federation.—In the autumn of 1880 "a few English members of the foreign Rose Street Club in Soho "—a district that has always been the haunt of alien agitators from Marat to the present-day Anarchists—" set to work on the difficult task of awakening the wage earners of this country to the truths of scientific Socialism and Social Democracy." We quote the words of H. W. Hyndman, leader of this group and the former ally of Mazzini, who in 1866 had formed his " Universal Republican Alliance " operating on the Continent, but with its Supreme Council in London. Hyndman had now passed under the influence of Marx, and so the Democratic Federation " propagating the Marxian doctrine of class war " (M. Beer, *A History of British Socialism*, II. 197. 1920) came to be founded.

The first conference was held at the Memorial Hall, Farringdon Street, on June 8, 1881. A few Radicals were present on this occasion, but most of these were scared away by the declaration of purely Socialist theories, and Hyndman with his Social Democratic followers were left in possession of the field.

Amongst the earliest members of the Democratic Federation were Herbert Burrows, the Radical and Freethinker Dr. G. B. Clark, the Irish historian Justin M'Carthy, the Positivist Professor Beesly of the 1st Internationale, Butler Johnstone for fifteen years Tory member for Canterbury, several journalists, including Morrison Davidson and Joseph Cowen, M.P., of the *Newcastle Chronicle*, a number of old Chartists—James and Charles Murray, Morgan, W. Townsend and S. Oliver—also John Williams, James (not Ramsay) Macdonald, Garcia, Helen Taylor, the stepdaughter of John Stuart Mill, and William Morris, the poet. In 1882 a band of "Christian Socialists"—J. L. Joynes, an Eton master, Frost, H. H. Champion, Royal Artillery, also Champion's disciple, George Lansbury, joined the movement.

The S.D.F.—The Democratic Federation soon developed, as Hyndman had hoped, "into a thoroughgoing revolutionary organisation," and on August 4, 1884, by way of emphasising its Socialist character, changed its name to the Social Democratic Federation. Many years afterwards—from 1908 to 1911—it was known as the Social Democratic Party.

Amongst the early members of the first S.D.F. were John Burns, Tom Mann, Annie Besant, Will Thorne, Guy Aldred, Harry Quelch and Ben Tillett.

The Socialist League.—But at the outset a split had taken place in the Federation. No sooner had the S.D.F. been formed than— to quote the words of Adolphe Smith, who became a leading member —Marx and his friends " made their descent upon the new movement. Marx died in 1883, but he or Engels deputed his daughter, Eleanor Marx, and her ' husband,' Dr. Aveling, to join." Then they brought in the Austrian Anarchist, Andreas Scheu, and Belfort Bax, and together they persuaded William Morris " to split away from the Social Democratic Federation and found the Socialist League, because Hyndman and the others would not follow the orders of Engels. . . . Eleanor Marx was the first to leave." She was followed by William Morris, Belfort Bax and Andreas Scheu. This was at the end of 1884. Hyndman now became the target of the German group. Already, in their letters to Sorge, Marx and Engels had described him as "the curse of Socialism in Great Britain"— an opinion which Hyndman observes was reaffirmed later by Keir Hardie, Ramsay Macdonald and Philip Snowden—and at the discussion which preceded the split off from the S.D.F., Hyndman relates that he was obliged to sit and listen "to the most virulent abuse" of himself "for three solid hours."

The Manifesto of the Socialist League, issued by William Morris and Belfort Bax, gives the following as its object:

"Socialism means that the land, the capital, the machinery, factories, mines, workshops, stores, means of transit, banking, all means of production and distribution of wealth must be declared and treated as the common property of all" (Dan Griffiths, *What is Socialism?* p. 99: Grant Richards, Ltd.).

The Socialist League only succeeded in enlisting a few hundred members, in spite of its energy in the circulation of Socialist literature. Its organ, *The Communist*, was edited by William Morris, who in 1890 wrote his famous description of a Socialist England under the name of *News from Nowhere*. But by this time Anarchist elements in the League had gained the upper hand, and in 1889 had deposed Morris as editor of *The Communist*, which they handed over to an Anarchist workman, Frank Kitz. Morris then recognised the advisability of returning to his allegiance to Hyndman, and after the collapse of the Socialist League in 1892 practically rejoined the S.D.F., to which the rest of the dissenters, Belfort Bax, Aveling, Eleanor Marx and Scheu, also returned. The programme of the present S.D.F. is comprised in the following formula:

"The establishment of the Socialist Commonwealth on a democratic basis; the common ownership of the means of production and distribution; the production of wealth for the use and enjoyment of all, instead of the production of commodities for the profit of the few."

The organ of the S.D.F. was *Justice*.

The Fabian Society.—In January 1884, just before the Democratic Federation changed its name to the Social Democratic Federation, the Fabian Society, named after Fabius Cunctator, the Roman General, came into existence, under the leadership of Professor Thomas Davidson, "an ethical Anarchist Communist," who aimed at "reconstructing human life on the principle of the highest morality" (Beer, II. 274). Davidson was quickly superseded by two young men who, a few months later, entered the movement—a journalist, George Bernard Shaw, and a clerk, Sidney Webb, son of a London hairdresser. Other early members of the Fabian Society were Graham Wallas, Hubert Bland and William Clarke, also Sydney Olivier and Annie Besant (now President of the Theosophical Society), who came over to it from the S.D.F. Later H. G. Wells became one of its leading members.

It is difficult for the lay mind to understand the antagonism that has always existed between the F.S. and the S.D.F. Both are fundamentally Marxian in their advocacy of the socialisation of land and industry, but the Fabians have always been essentially the "drawing-room Socialists" of England, disdaining street-corner oratory, recognising the right of non-manual labour to a place in the scheme of things, and professing disapproval of violent revolutionary methods for bringing about the Socialist paradise. Hyndman speaks of " the bureaucratic Fabian Society which has so assiduously promulgated the doctrines of middle-class permeation and high-toned intrigue " (*Reminiscences*, p. 310); yet it is probable that Fabianism, precisely by its method of middle-class permeation, notably in the Civil Service, has done more to accelerate the revolutionary movement than the cruder agitation of the S.D.F.

The programme of the Fabian Society is now as follows :

"The Fabian Society consists of Socialists. It therefore aims at the reorganisation of Society by the emancipation of Land and Industrial Capital from individual ownership, and the vesting of them in the community for the general benefit. In this way only can the natural and acquired advantages of the country be equitably shared by the whole people.

"The Society accordingly works for the extinction of private property in land, with equitable consideration of established expectations, and due provision as to the tenure of the home and the homestead ; for the transfer to the community by constitutional methods, of all such industries as can be conducted socially ; and for the establishment, as the governing consideration in the regulation of production, distribution and service, of the common good instead of private profit."
(*What is Socialism ?* p. 98.)

The offices of the Fabian Society are at 25 Tothill Street, London, S.W.1, and its official organ is the *Fabian News* (monthly).

Fabian Research Department.—A later development of the Fabian Society was the Fabian Research Department, founded in the autumn of 1912 by Mr. and Mrs. Sidney Webb, Major H. J. Gillespie, Emil Davies (a German), Mrs. Pember Reeves and G. D. H. Cole, then a Don of Magdalen College, Oxford. Another Fabian, Julius West, author of a book on Chartism, was first made secretary, and was succeeded a few months later by William Mellor, for many years Associate Editor of the *Daily Herald*, which was started as *The Herald* in the same year.

In the autumn of 1914 G. Bernard Shaw became the Chairman, and remained in this post till the end of the war. G. D. H. Cole

MARXIAN SOCIALISM (PRE-WAR PERIOD)

became Vice-Chairman, G. P. Blizard Honorary Secretary, Sidney Webb continued as Chairman of the Insurance Inquiry and Mrs. Webb as Chairman of the Inquiry into the Control of Industry. After the outbreak of war a further Committee was formed, to deal with the question of International relations, for which Leonard S. Woolf drew up a memorandum (R. Page Arnot, *History of the Labour Research Department*).

In 1918 the Fabian Research Department became the Labour Research Department, of which an account will be given later.

The I.L.P.—Although both the Fabian Society and the S.D.F. had adopted Marxian doctrines, neither appears to have been sufficiently Germanised to satisfy the man whom Mrs. Marx was wont to describe as her husband's " evil genius "—Friedrich Engels. Accordingly, some four years after the death of Marx, he set to work on a new movement, under the control of the Marx-Engels clique, consisting of himself, Eleanor Marx, known as "Tussy," Marx's youngest daughter, and her "husband," Dr. Aveling, to whom in reality she was never legally married. On May 4, 1887, Engels wrote to Sorge:

" Aveling is making a famous agitation in the East End of London . . . he and Tussy are hard at work. It is a matter of founding an English Labour Party with an independent class programme. This, if it goes well, will then force the Social Democratic Federation and the Socialist League into the background, which will be the best solution of the undecided quarrel " (*Briefe . . . an Sorge*, p. 263).

Marx's daughter was then deputed to gain a footing in the trade unions, and soon Engels was able to write complacently of the Gas Workers and General Labourers being "bossed by Tussy" (*die von Tussy gebossten* Gas Workers and General Labourers). In 1892 Engels wrote again : " We are making great progress here in England. Affairs advance splendidly. Next year there will be seen marching behind Germany not only Austria and France, but also England." Engels was right in his forecast, and in January of the following year, 1893, the Independent Labour Party was founded under the leadership of Engels' tool, Keir Hardie, whom he contemptuously described as an " over-sly Scot " (*einer uberschlauer Schotte*) and " a poor devil of a Scotch miner," running a weekly paper, the *Labour Leader*, which Engels declared to have been financed with Tory money (*Briefe an Sorge*, p. 414). The year of 1893 thus marked a double triumph for the Germans—the exclusion of British trade union influence from the Continental Internationale and the penetration of the trade unions in England by German influence through the foundation of the I.L.P., under the guidance of the Marx-Engels clique in London. The plan of the I.L.P. had already been mooted in 1888 in a Manifesto to the workers of Scotland by members of the Scottish Labour Party, led by Keir Hardie, Cunningham Graham, Dr. Stirling Robertson and George Gerrie, and the way further paved by the Labour Union of Bradford, founded in 1890 by Ben Tillett, Robert Blatchford (editor of *The Clarion*, founded 1891) and Joseph Burgess.

The inaugural meeting of the I.L.P. at Bradford was attended by about 120 delegates, five from the S.D.F., twelve from the F.S., including Bernard Shaw. "No difference could be detected between the programmes of the I.L.P. and the S.D.F., but marked divergences existed between them in their attitude towards the trade unions and in the tone of their propaganda " (Beer, II. 304).

The Programme of the I.L.P. is now as follows :

" The I.L.P. is a Socialist Organisation and has for its object the establishment of the Socialist Commonwealth.

" The Socialist Commonwealth is that State of Society in which Land and Capital are communally owned, and the processes of production, distribution and exchange are social functions.

" The Independent Labour Party believes in democracy organised, both in its political and industrial aspects, for communal ends.

" The basis of political democracy must be the whole body of citizens, exercising authority through a national representative assembly, directly elected by the people, with a decentralised and extended system of local government.

" The basis of industrial democracy must be : (1) the organisation of the wage and salary earners, and (2) the organisation of consumers.

" A central body, representative of the people both as producers and consumers, must decide the amount and character of communal production and service necessary. The internal management of each industry must be in the hands of the workers, administrative, technical and manual, engaged therein, operating in conjunction with the representatives of the organised consumers. Experience will determine the methods of co-operation and the detailed form of organisation, as step by step is taken towards the attainment of the Socialist Commonwealth." (*What is Socialism?* pp. 97, 98.)

The identity between the programme of the various Socialist organisations at this date is shown by the " Joint Manifesto of British Socialist Bodies," issued in this same year of 1893, in which it is stated that :

" Our aim, one and all, is to obtain for the whole community complete ownership and control of the means of transport, the means of manufacture, the mines and the land. Thus we look to put an end for ever to the wage system, to sweep away all distinctions of class, and eventually to establish national and international communism on a sound basis." (*What is Socialism?* p. 99.)

As long ago, then, as 1893 the aim of British Socialists of all parties was admittedly *Communism*.

The particular importance of the I.L.P. consisted in the fact that, just as Engels had planned, it succeeded in penetrating the Labour movement, and this formed the first junction between the

Socialist doctrinaires and the manual workers. It was this coalition that facilitated the formation of the parliamentary group working for Socialism under the name of " Labour."

Amongst the early members of the I.L.P. were Tom Mann, formerly of the S.D.F., Bruce Glasier, J. Ramsay Macdonald, Philip Snowden, Robert Smillie, Fred Jowett, J. R. Clynes, George N. Barnes, G. H. Roberts and Robert Blatchford.

The *Labour Leader*, created by Keir Hardie as a successor to his earlier paper, *The Miner* (founded in 1887), was edited by him until 1904, when it became the official organ of the I.L.P. It is now known as the *New Leader*, appearing weekly, whilst the monthly organ of the Party is the *Socialist Review*. The offices of the I.L.P. are now at 14 Great George Street, London, S.W.1.

THE LABOUR PARTY

In 1892, the year preceding the foundation of the I.L.P., three " Labour " members were elected for the first time to Parliament. These were Keir Hardie for West Ham, John Burns for Battersea and J. H. Wilson for Middlesbrough. Ben Tillett had stood for Bradford, but failed against the Liberal candidate. On the fall of the Liberal Government in 1895, the I.L.P. took up the electoral campaign, under the leadership of Keir Hardie and Tom Mann, and put up twenty-eight candidates, all unsuccessful. The Conservatives then took office.

The Labour Representation Committee.—A further attempt was now made by the I.L.P. to capture the Trade Union movement for Socialism, and though stoutly resisted by the older trade union leaders, a resolution for co-operation between the Socialist and Labour camps was passed by 546,000 votes to 434,000 at the Trade Union Congress of 1895. The result of this decision was the formation of the Labour Representation Committee at a Conference of Labour and Socialist delegates on February 27 and 28, 1900. The Committee consisted of seven Trade Unionists, two members of the I.L.P., two members of the S.D.F., and one member of the Fabian Society; J. Ramsay Macdonald was elected secretary.

At the election of 1900 fifteen candidates were put up by the L.R.C., but only Keir Hardie and Richard Bell were successful. In 1901 the S.D.F. withdrew from the L.R.C., but individual members joined it as representatives of other organisations, trade unions, etc.

The Labour Party.—In 1906 the L.R.C. became officially known as the Labour Party.

The Party immediately became penetrated by Socialist influence. Although in its original programme it had stated that it was necessary for the trade unions of this country " to use their political power to defend their existence " and deprecated the introduction of mere party politics into the movement, at the eighth annual conference, held at Hull in 1908, an amendment was proposed by William Atkinson, S.D.F. delegate of the paper stainers, declaring that the aim of the Labour Party was:

" To organise and maintain a Parliamentary Party, with its own Whips, whose ultimate object shall be the obtaining for the workers the full results of their labour by the overthrow of the present competitive system of capitalism and the institution of a system of public ownership and control of all the means of life."

Although this purely Socialist amendment was defeated by 951,000 votes to 91,000, the same conference two days later passed a resolution no less Socialistic :

" That in the opinion of this Conference the time has arrived when the Labour Party should have as a definite object the socialisation of the means of production, distribution and exchange, to be controlled by a democratic State in the interest of the entire community ; and the complete emancipation of Labour from the domination of capitalism and landlordism, with the establishment of social and economic equality between the sexes."

By the adoption of this formula, to which it still adheres, the Labour Party proclaimed itself to be not only Socialist but Marxian Socialist. It aims, not only at the socialisation of the means of *production*, as advocated by certain peaceful groups of French Socialists and partially realised by the Co-operative movement in this country, but at the socialisation of the means of distribution, which entails the establishment of an autocratic bureaucracy. In a word, it sets out to destroy all individual enterprise and initiative.

Since 1908, therefore, the British Labour Party, controlled by the I.L.P., has ceased to represent real labour, which is in the great majority individualist, and has become simply the Party of Marxian Socialism. The offices of the Labour Party are at 33 Eccleston Square, S.W.1. Its official organ is the *Daily Herald*.

S.L.P.—The more revolutionary forms of Marxism were represented, however, at the time the Labour Party came into existence by two bodies which had split off from the S.D.F. The first of these was the Socialist Labour Party, founded in Glasgow in 1903 by Scottish Secessionists, who had fallen under the influence of Daniel de Leon and the Socialist Labour Party of America. The policy of the S.L.P. is a blend of revolutionary Marxism and Syndicalism and its principal leaders up till 1920 were Arthur MacManus, William Paul and J. T. Murphy. The S.L.P. on its foundation organised the Socialist Labour Press, and has published a great number of pamphlets on Industrial Unionism and Marxism. The headquarters of the S.L.P. are at 50 Renfrew Street, Glasgow. Its official organ is *The Socialist*.

The S.P.G.B.—The year after the formation of the S.L.P., in

August 1904, a London group of secessionists from the S.D.F. led by T. Fitzgerald, founded the Socialist Party of Great Britain on strictly Marxian lines and advocating unrelenting class warfare. A general meeting was held at the Communist Club, 107 Charlotte Street, Soho, on September 18, with J. Kent in the chair and C. Lehane as General Secretary of the new party. The lecturers for the society included F. C. Watts, I. Blaustein, H. Belsey, T. Jacobs, A. Albury, etc. In its Declaration of Principles the object of the S.P.G.B. is stated to be :

" The establishment of a system of society based upon the common ownership and democratic control of the means and instruments for producing and distributing wealth and in the interest of the whole community " (*What is Socialism ?* p. 99).

This formula seems indistinguishable from that of the Labour Party, but the S.P.G.B. goes on to declare that it " enters the field of political action determined to wage war against all other political parties, whether alleged labour or avowedly capitalist." The monthly organ of the Party, the *Socialist Standard*, has recently been loud in its denunciations of the Labour Party, largely on account of the latter's toleration of religion, which it attributes to the policy of vote-catching. In the issue for June 1925, it quotes with approval Marx's " striking phrase " : " Religion is the opium of the people " ; and Lenin's opinion given at the Congress of the Communist Internationale in 1922, that it is of paramount importance " that a magazine devoting itself to problems of militant materialism should at the same time be conducting an untiring campaign of propaganda for atheism."

In a pamphlet entitled *Socialism and Religion*, published by the S.P.G.B. in 1911, the following passages occur :

" It is therefore a profound truth that Socialism is the natural enemy of religion " (p. 27).

" A Christian Socialist is in fact an anti-Socialist " (p. 31).

" The most absurd claim of all . . . is that Christ was a Socialist. . . . Christ's denunciation of wealth is not Socialism. ' Sell that thou hast and give to the poor ' was His advice to a rich man. This is not Socialism, but anarchism and social suicide, for the wholesale distribution of alms is a ' remedy more deadly than the disease.' . . . Socialism, on the contrary, is the appreciation of the things of this world and the endeavour to make a paradise here " (pp. 36, 37).

" Christianity . . . is the very antithesis of Socialism " (p. 38).

On p. 42 Belfort Bax of the S.D.F. is quoted as saying : " It may be convenient for Socialists with a view to election expediency to seek to confine the definition of Socialism to the economic issue, abstracted from all the other issues of life and conduct " ; and the pamphlet goes on to attack the Social Democratic Party for opposing out of " election expediency " the sale of a pamphlet, *Christ the Enemy of the Human Race.*

The S.P.G.B. thus shows itself consistently Marxian. It is not, however, an important body, and its present leaders seem to be obscure individuals, who append pseudonyms to their articles in the *Socialist Standard*. The names of the members of the Executive Committee do not appear in the publications of the Society, nor in the *Labour Year Book*.

The headquarters of the S.P.G.B. are at 17 Mount Pleasant, London, W.C.1.

Socialism in Ireland

In Ireland up till 1896 the revolutionary movement had retained an almost exclusively national character. The "United Irishmen," founded in 1791 under the inspiration of the French revolutionaries and German Illuminati, the Fenians of 1858 with whom Karl Marx and the 1st Internationale entered into relation, and that most deadly of secret societies, the Irish Republican Brotherhood, resembling the Carbonari and the eleventh-century Assassins with its fearful oaths and obligations and its murder gangs, nevertheless depended for their power less on Continental aid than on Irish fanaticism. It was not until the Irish Socialist Republican Party was founded in 1896, under the leadership of the veteran agitator James Conolly, that Marxian Socialism gained a footing in the country. Marx's opinion of the man who was to represent his teaching in Ireland is interesting. On May 9, 1865, he wrote to Friedrich Engels:

"As everywhere else, there exists naturally amongst the English working men a knot of asses, fools and rogues rallying around a scoundrel. The scoundrel is in this case 'George Potter,' a rat of a man, supported by a corruptible and witty man, and as a stump orator a dangerous Irishman named Conolly . . . leader of the 'Beehive,' the official organ of the Trade Unionists" (*Briefwechsel*, III. 255).

From 1896 onwards the revolutionary movement in Ireland has been dual in character, carried out under two flags—the green flag of national and Catholic fanaticism and the red flag of International Atheist Socialism.

Socialist Party of Ireland—Irish Transport and General Workers' Union.—Theoretical Socialism has, however, never made a strong appeal to the Irish temperament, and the Marxian "Socialist Party of Ireland," founded in 1904, exercised far less influence than the "Irish Transport and General Workers' Union," inaugurated in 1909 under the leadership of James Larkin, the agitator who has played a prominent part in the troubles in Ireland and also in the Anarchist disturbances in the United States. The Irish revolutionary movement has, in fact, been largely directed from America, but by the Anarchist-Communist rather than the Socialist elements in that country; its further course must, therefore, be reserved for a later chapter.

Socialism on the Continent

On the Continent, as in Great Britain, the Marxian influence has steadily gained ground since the formation of the 1st Internationale.

Germany.—In Germany the Social Democratic Party, led during the lifetime of Marx by Wilhelm Liebknecht and August Bebel, had increased by 1903 to such proportions as to win 3,000,000 votes at the polls. Before the war the Party was divided into three groups : the Right Wing, led by Scheidemann ; the Centre by Karl Kautsky, who has since been indicted by Trotsky for his opposition to Terrorism ; and the Left Wing by Karl Liebknecht, the future Spartacist.

France.—In France it was Jules Guesde who in 1877 succeeded in capturing a large part of the Socialist movement for Marxism, in spite of the opposition of the Broussistes. A group of Independent Socialists, including Millerand, Clemenceau, Jaures and Viviani, was formed later, but moderate Marxism continued to hold its own under the leadership of Marx's grandson, Jean Longuet, until the outbreak of the Great War. The revolutionary elements in France were, however, less inclined to Socialism than to Syndicalism, with which we shall deal later.

Russia.—In Russia the revolutionary movement had been predominantly Anarchist until 1883, when the Marxists succeeded in founding a party named the " Group for the Emancipation of Labour," under the leadership of George V. Plekhanov, supported by the German-Jews, R. Axelrod and Leo Deutsch, and the Russian, Vera Zassulitch, who in 1878 had attempted to shoot Trepoff, the prefect of police in St. Petersburg.

In 1898 this Group assumed the name of the Russian Democratic Party, still led by Plekhanov, but in 1903, at a Conference held in London, split into two parties over a point of policy ; the majority, under Lenin, being known as the Bolsheviks, from the Russian word *bolshee*, signifying greater ; and the minority, under Martoff, being known as the Mensheviks, from *menshee*, signifying lesser.

Italy.—In Italy between 1880 and 1890 a Marxist group was formed under the leadership of Turati, but here, as in France and other Latin countries, the revolutionary movement was rather Syndicalist than Socialist in character.

Such was the state of Socialism in the most important countries of the world at the time of the outbreak of the Great War.

CHAPTER III
ANARCHISM AND SYNDICALISM

French Anarchists.—The origin of Anarchism and Syndicalism, as of Socialism, must be sought in France. Proudhon, known as "the Father of Anarchy," was the first to formulate the creed later to be known as Syndicalism in the phrase :

' "According to my idea, railways, a mine, a manufactory, a ship, etc., are to the workers whom they occupy what the hive is to the bees, that is, at the same time their instrument, and their dwelling, their country, their territory, their property.' Hence Proudhon opposed ' the exploitation of the railways whether by companies of Capitalists or by the State ' " (*La Révolution au XVIIIème siècle*, p. 249).

Russian Anarchists.—The German and Russian Anarchists, however, advocated no such definite scheme of industrial organisation, but concentrated solely on destruction.

Nihilists—Revolutionary Socialists.—In Russia between 1862 and 1881 the Nihilists and Revolutionary Socialists committed a series of outrages which spread to other countries and culminated in the "tragic period" inaugurated on May 1, 1891, and lasting in Paris for three years, during which Ravachol and his gang terrorised the population with bombs and dynamite. Attempts on the lives of kings and presidents continued throughout the next twenty years.

Italian Anarchists.—In Italy, where the group was led by Cafiero and Malatesta, in Spain and in Portugal, the propaganda of Anarchy found a fertile breeding-ground.

American Anarchists.—In the United States the ideas of Proudhon had gained a considerable following. His principal followers were Stephen P. Andrew, William Green and Lysander Spooner. In 1881 another Anarchist, Benjamin R. Tucker, started a periodical named *Liberty*, advocating modified Proudhonism (*Lusk Report*, p. 843).

It was in July of the same year that the Anarchists held a small International Revolutionary Congress in London, presided over by the German Anarchist Johann Most and the German-Jewish Nihilist Hartmann, who had devised the plot for blowing up the Tzar's train two years earlier. Prince Kropotkine was also present. As a result of the criminal intentions revealed at this Conference,

Johann Most was condemned to eighteen months' imprisonment, after which he left England and joined Benjamin Tucker in America. Here he continued the publication of his paper, *Freiheit*, which—owing to the recalcitrance of the printers—he had brought out with some difficulty in England. From that moment the Anarchist movement in the United States continued without a break until after the war.

English Anarchists.—In England Anarchy had been able to make little headway, either under the personal direction of Johann Most or Prince Kropotkine.

Freedom Group.—Only a small and obscure body of Kropotkine Anarchists, calling themselves the "Freedom Group," continued to carry on propaganda, and just before the war were led by S. Lindner and Rudolf Rocker, who was for a time editor of the London Yiddish revolutionary paper, *Der Arbeiter Freind*.

Communist Propaganda Groups.—In 1906 Guy Aldred seceded from the S.D.F. and entered into relations with the Freedom Group. Although an anti-Parliamentarian, Aldred remained a Marxian and did not altogether agree with pure Anarchism, so he founded the "Communist Propaganda Groups" in London in 1907. In 1910 he started *The Herald of Revolt*, and in 1912 went to Glasgow, where a number of Socialist and Anarchist groups had been established—S.L.P., I.L.P., Kropotkine Anarchists and Communist Propaganda Groups—the two latter much opposed to each other.

Glasgow Communist Group.—Aldred now founded (in 1912) the Glasgow Communist Group as an Anti-Parliamentary Communist Organisation. This became most active and succeeded in defeating the Anarchist Group, which finally collapsed. The remaining members then joined up with Aldred's Group, which, however, was from this moment until 1920 usually described as the Anarchist Group. In May 1917 it took up its present quarters at 13 Burnbank Gardens.

To the uninitiated all these differences of doctrine and nomenclature must remain incomprehensible, and we shall not attempt to explain how Aldred succeeded in combining allegiance both to Marx and Bakunin, who in their lifetimes had been bitter enemies, or why he opposed the disciples of Kropotkine, who had followed in the footsteps of Bakunin.

In Great Britain, as elsewhere, the spirit of Anarchy, like the theories of Socialism, did not become formidable until it had penetrated into the trade unions.

C.G.T.—It was when the destructive ideas of Anarchy became allied with the corporative spirit of the industrial workers under the name of Syndicalism that the revolutionary movement began to make headway. This junction was effected by the French "Confédération Générale du Travail," founded in 1895, which became divided into two camps: Reformist Syndicalists, working for industrial reorganisation on constitutional lines; and Anarcho-

Syndicalists, concentrating on the plan of the General Strike for the forcible overthrow of "Capitalism," first proposed at the Congress of the 1st Internationale in Brussels in 1868. The doctrinaires of the latter party in France were Emile Pouget, author of *Le Sabotage*, Lagardelle Griffuelhes, and especially Georges Sorel, author of *Réfléxions sur la Violence* (translated into English as *Reflections on Violence*) who succeeded in interpreting Marx's doctrines in a Syndicalist sense.

T.U.C.—At the time that Anarcho-Syndicalism was definitely formulated by the left wing of the C.G.T., Trade Unionism had not become revolutionary. The British Trade Union Congress, founded in 1868 and holding its first congress in the following year, had abjured all class warfare and concerned itself with the organisation of labour in a perfectly constitutional manner. As late as 1895 it had formally disassociated itself from "Socialist Adventurers."

American Federation of Labour.—The American Federation of Labour, founded in 1881, pursued the same moderate policy.

I.F.T.U.—In 1901 the first attempt was made to organise Trade Unionism internationally, and a Congress was held at Copenhagen. The outcome of this was the formation in 1903 of an International Secretariat, headed by Karl Legien, President of the German Federation of Trade Unions. Ten years later this developed into the International Federation of Trade Unions, with Karl Legien as President (*Labour Year Book for* 1924, p. 359).

The I.W.W.—As a counterblast to the constitutional policy of the Copenhagen Congress in 1901, an International Syndicalist Congress was held in the following year, and from this moment Syndicalism began to gain ground both in Europe and America. William D. Haywood, of the Western Federation of Miners, "the embodiment of the Sorel philosophy . . . a bundle of primitive instincts" (Ramsay Macdonald, *Syndicalism*, p. 36), took the lead in forming the "Industrial Workers of the World" in America in 1905 on Syndicalist lines, and came over to England, where he met with a warm reception. "I saw him at Copenhagen," says Ramsay Macdonald, "amidst the leaders of the working-class movements drawn up from the whole world, and there he was dumb and unnoticed; I saw him addressing a crowd in England, and there his crude appeals moved his listeners to wild applause" (*Ibid.*, p. 37).

From 1905 until the advent of the Bolsheviks to power, the I.W.W. constituted the most formidable revolutionary organisation in the United States. The American Federation of Labour, which had hitherto pursued a constitutional policy, split into two wings, both led by Jews, the right led by the sane trade union leader, Samuel Gompers, and the left by William Z. Foster of the I.W.W., who has since identified himself with every phase of revolutionary activity. The I.W.W. now became a blend of Syndicalism and revolutionary Marxism, drawing into it the Marxist leader, Daniel

ANARCHISM AND SYNDICALISM

de Leon, who in 1908 headed the Detroit branch of the new movement. From this developed in 1915 the Workers' International Industrial Union, which joined up with Daniel de Leon's "Socialist Labour Party," making the alliance between the two movements complete.

Meanwhile Syndicalism had been carried to England, where it found exponents in the S.L.P. (Socialist Labour Party) of Glasgow, which had seceded from the S.D.F. under the influence of the Socialist Labour Party of America (Beer, II. 355).

Ruskin College.—In 1899 two Americans, Walter Vrooman and Dr. Charles Beard, had gone to Oxford and founded a Labour College, named Ruskin College, with the object of teaching " men who have been merely condemning our social institutions . . . how instead to transform these institutions, so that in place of talking against the world they will begin methodically and scientifically to possess the world, to refashion it," etc. (*The Burning Question of Education*, issued by the Executive Committee of the Plebs League). The College soon won support from the trade unions, and also from prominent members of " the oppressing class "— to use the expression of a Ruskin student—such as the Dukes of Fife and Norfolk, Lords Avebury, Crewe, Rosebery, Ripon, Rothschild, etc. The University took an interest in the scheme and " many overworked tutors gave time every week which they could ill spare to small classes of Ruskin College students." But these overtures were not appreciated by the students, who strongly objected to any association with the University, which they looked upon as the enemy of the working-class and progress " (*The Burning Question of Education*, p. 3).

Plebs League.—In order, therefore, to prevent the college being dominated by University influence, the students and ex-students in October 1908 formed an organisation called the " Plebs League," with the object of bringing about a definite and more satisfactory connection between Ruskin College and the Labour movement. The Principal, Denis Hird, became editor of *Plebs*, the magazine of the League. This displeased the Executive of the College, which met and forbade Hird to have anything more to do with the Plebs movement. Hird was finally dismissed and the students went on strike. The Plebs Committee then " decided that Ruskin College as an aid to the workers was worthless " and that the trade unionists must be asked to found a college of their own.

Central Labour College.—The result was the inauguration of the Central Labour College at Oxford in September 1908, under a Provisional Committee that included Denis Hird, George Sims, S.D.P. and I.L.P., Fred Burgess, I.L.P., and Noah Ablett, I.L.P. and of the South Wales Miners' Federation. The movement had now become definitely Syndicalist.

Industrial Syndicalist League.—In the following year, 1909, the Industrial Syndicalist League, with its organ, *The Syndicalist*, was formed under the leadership of Tom Mann (who had been present at the International Conference of 1902), and in 1913 the " Miners' Reform Movement," with the Syndicalist slogan, " The Mines for the Miners," was started by Noah Ablett and A. J. Cook, the present leader of the Miners' Federation. In the pamphlet issued by this body, *The Miners' Next Step*, the Syndicalist programme was made perfectly clear.

Guild Socialism.—Meanwhile the less extreme form of Syndicalism known as " Guild Socialism " had come into the field. The leader of this movement was G. D. H. Cole of the Fabian Society and the Fabian Research Department, who at the time the latter was founded had veered from Fabianism to Revolutionary Trade Unionism. It was " as a reinforcement of Syndicalism that G. D. H. Cole wrote his *World of Labour* (1913) and as Syndicalists, Cole and Mellor (together with Mrs. Townshend, Mrs. G. R. S. Taylor, H. D. Harben and others) were compelled to take rather a different outlook from those who followed the strict letter of the Webbs." Beaten by the older Fabians—Bernard Shaw, Sidney Webb, E. R. Pease, etc.—in the Fabian Research Department, Cole and his supporters started the blend of Socialism and Syndicalism they called Guild Socialism, and which, whilst setting out to place all power in the hands of the Guilds instead of in the State, according to the system of State Socialism, does not, like Syndicalism, aim at the abolition of the State, which is to act as an umpire and " trustee for the community."

One should not, however, be misled by the name of " Guilds " into supposing that Guild Socialism visualises a return to the peaceful working guilds of the Middle Ages, no less than Syndicalism " it is to Revolutionary Trade Unionism the Guild idea looks " (*The Guild Idea*, p. 14), and Marx's doctrine of the class-war enters largely into its programme.

National Guilds League.—Guild Socialism is now practically non-existent. In April 1922 a National Guild Council had been formed representing both the producing Guilds and the National Guild League, the object being mainly propaganda. The National Guilds League has since become incorporated in the Council. In 1922 the Trade Union Congress passed a resolution welcoming and approving the activities of the Guild and the formation of the National Guild Council. The Congress decided also to associate itself actively with the work and propaganda of the Council (*Labour Year Book for* 1924). The collapse in May 1922 of the National Building Guild, instituted in 1920 under the auspices of the N.G.L., dealt a heavy blow to the Guild idea, and although the *Labour Year Book for* 1924 records that several other guilds were still working successfully at that date, its next issue of 1925, as also that of 1926, omits all reference to the movement beyond the insertion in its list of addresses of the National Guild League, 39 Cursitor Street, E.C.4.

ANARCHISM AND SYNDICALISM

Such, then, was the state of revolutionary organisation on the outbreak of war. Everywhere Marxian theory and Marxian methods had triumphed, both over the Utopian Socialism of early nineteenth-century France and over the sane Trade Unionism of England, France and America. Already the storm of social revolution was threatening when the Great War burst upon the world.

CHAPTER IV
THE WAR AND PACIFISM

THE outbreak of the War in 1914 brought another issue to the fore in the field of Socialist politics—Nationalism *versus* Internationalism. Pacifism in the sense of Internationalism was, of course, no new thing, but had existed ever since it had been denounced as a " dangerous dream " by Mirabeau in the course of the French revolution.

In this country the first pacifist groups had been formed in 1816, when (on June 14) the present " Peace Society " was founded under the name of " The Society for the Promotion of Permanent and Universal Peace," with Robert Marsden as Chairman.

But it was not until the end of the century that pacifist societies began to multiply. The following are the principal organisations formed in Great Britain before the outbreak of the Great War :

1880. *The International Arbitration and Peace Association*; Chairman : Felix Moscheles. Vice-Chairman : C. E. Maurice.
1883. *Irish Peace Society.*
1904. *British National Peace Congress.* President : Lord Courtney of Penwith (brother-in-law of Sidney Webb).
1905. *National Peace Council.* President : Hon. Lord Weardale. Secretary : Carl Heath.
1910. *Rationalist Peace Society.* President : J. M. Robertson, M.P.
1910. *Church of England Peace League.* President : Bishop of Lincoln.
1911. *School Peace League.* President : Bishop of Hereford. Chairman : C. E. Maurice.
1912. *Band of Peace Union; Comrades of Peace.* Juvenile branches of Peace Society.
1912. *Catholic Peace Society.*
1912. *Cambridge University War and Peace Society.*
1913. *The Garton Foundation.* (Allied with a number of minor Pacifist groups such as the *War and Peace Societies* of Oxford, Cambridge and London Universities, the *Norman Angell League*, etc.)
1914. *The Jewish Peace Society.* President : The Chief Rabbi, Dr. Hertz. Secretary : Miss E. Behrens.

THE WAR AND PACIFISM

Such was the network of pacifist organisation in this country on which Germany not unreasonably counted to prevent England's resistance to her scheme of world domination. On the Continent Socialist theory provided little or no obstacle to the outbreak of war, and in 1914 on both sides the national spirit triumphed over the doctrines of International Socialism. The French Socialist Party under Albert Thomas and Renaudel, the German Socialist Party under Scheidemann and Ebert, the Austrian Social Democratic Party under Renner and Pernerstorfer, the Belgian Labour Party under Vandervelde and de Brouckere, the Russian Right Wing Social Democrats—that is to say, the Nationalist Menshevik group led by Plechanov—and the Italian Socialist Union under Mussolini supported their governments in entering the War.

B.S.P.—In England only the Labour Party stood by the Government, the I.L.P., S.L.P., and S.P.G.B. all opposed the war and preached Pacifism, whilst the S.D.P., which in 1911 had become the B.S.P. (British Socialist Party)—still led by Hyndman and comprising Hunter Watts, Dan Irving, Russell Smart, Victor Fisher and Adolphe Smith—were divided on the question. At the 1916 Conference this difference of opinion led to a climax and the Party split into two. The anti-war party, comprising Albert Inkpin, E. C. Fairchild, Fineberg, Petroff and John Maclean, retaining the name of the B.S.P., whilst the party supporting the war took the name of the National Socialist Party.

New B.S.P.—The new B.S.P. was formed as follows:

General Secretary: Albert Inkpin.
Executive Committee:

F. W. Llewellyn	Fred Shaw
A. A. Watts	G. Deer
Charles Dukes	J. F. Hodgson
Albert Ward	John Maclean

Mrs. Dora B. Montefiore

Headquarters: 21A Maiden Lane, W.C.2.

The opposing faction having carried off the organ of the Party, *Justice*, the B.S.P. started a new paper, *The Call*.

The N.S.P.—The National Socialist Party, led by Hyndman, had an Executive Committee of the following:

H. M. Hyndman	G. C. Beresford
A. Burden	Councillor F. H. Gorle
F. J. Gould	Emily Hayes
Adolphe Smith	R. Travers Hyndman
(alias A. S. Headingley)	H. W. Lee
Councillor J. J. Jones	John Stokes
Councillor A. Whiting	J. Hunter Watts

J. G. Webster

Hon. Treasurer: Will Thorne.

A few members of the I.L.P. now joined the N.S.P., but the main body of the I.L.P. took up a rigidly Pacifist attitude.

I.L.P.—From the moment of the outbreak of hostilities it was the I.L.P. which took the lead in Pacifist agitation. " One of the first acts " of its National Administrative Council, which included Ramsay Macdonald, W. C. Anderson, Egerton Wake (later National Organiser of the Labour Party), Bruce Glasier, etc., " was the organisation of a campaign throughout the country against recruiting. . . . These anti-recruiting meetings of the I.L.P. formed the nucleus out of which all the Defeatist and Bolshevik movements . . . developed " (series of articles in *Morning Post*, entitled " Bolshevism in Great Britain," first week of December 1918).

U.D.C.—In September 1914 the I.L.P. was instrumental in forming the Union of Democratic Control with the following personnel :

Executive Committee :

Norman Angell (I.L.P., on Directorate of Garton Foundation)
J. A. Hobson
J. Ramsay Macdonald, M.P. (I.L.P.)
E. D. Morel (I.L.P., National Peace Council)
Arthur Ponsonby (I.L.P.)
Mrs. H. M. Swanwick
Charles Trevelyan, M.P. (I.L.P.)
Hon. Secretary : E. D. Morel.

The General Council included W. C. Anderson, H. N. Brailsford, F. Seymour Cocks, B. N. Langdon Davies, Dr. Marion Phillips, M. Philips Price, Hon. Mrs. Franklin, Arthur Henderson, G. H. Hardy, F. W. Jowett, Bertrand Russell and Israel Zangwill.

The ostensible object of the U.D.C. was :

" To aim at securing such terms that the war will not, either through the humiliation of the defeated nation, or an artificial arrangement of frontiers, merely become the starting-point for new national antagonisms and future wars."

The organ of the U.D.C., *Foreign Affairs*, was edited by E. D. Morel, really the prime mover of the organisation, who was accused in Parliament by Will Thorne of the S.D.F. on April 6, 1916, of being " a paid agent of the German Government," and in the following year (on September 4, 1917) was sentenced to six months' imprisonment for sending information out of the country.

No Conscription Fellowship.—A further outcome of the I.L.P. and U.D.C. was the " No Conscription Fellowship," formed in October 1914 with the object of opposing every effort to introduce compulsory military service. By 1916 it had succeeded in banding together in one organisation the vast majority of conscientious objectors, and in collecting a membership of 15,000 to 20,000 people, including a number of Quakers.

The Hon. Secretary was A. Fenner Brockway, the Chairman Clifford Allen, whilst among the supporters of the movement were C. H. Norman, J. H. Hudson, M.A., Lord Courtney of Penwith, Philip Snowden, Arnold Rowntree, etc.

Fellowship of Reconciliation.—Two months later, in December 1914, came the "Fellowship of Reconciliation," founded at Cambridge by a group of about 130 people professing as Christians to be "forbidden to wage war" and to be working for "the enthronement of love in personal, social, commercial and national life."

The leaders included the Rev. L. Richards (Secretary), the Rev. Dr. Orchard and Miss Maude Royden. This organisation still exists, with headquarters at 17 Red Lion Square and P. W. Bartlett as Secretary.

League of Peace and Freedom.—On July 8 and 9 the "League of Peace and Freedom" was founded, with the object of "carrying on educational propaganda for peace in the widest sense."

The Executive Committee included H. Baillie Weaver of the Theosophical Society, S. V. Bracher, A. Honora Enfield, Charles Weiss, etc. Hon. Secretary, Edward J. Smith.

The Women's International League.—In the same year the Women's International League was founded, being the British section of the "International Committee of Women for Permanent Peace," formed at the Hague Congress for Women in April 1915. An account of this will be given later in connection with the American Pacifist movement.

The British W.I.L. was formally constituted on September 30 and October 1, 1915, at a General Meeting, and the resolutions passed at the Hague Congress were accepted as a basis for defining the objects of the W.I.L. "It was agreed that the British organisation should be formed, with the object of linking together two movements felt to be vitally connected : the Women's movement and the Pacifist movement. Headquarters were established at 12 Little College Street, Westminster, with the following personnel :

Chairman : Mrs. H. M. Swanwick.
Vice-Chairmen : Miss A. Maude Royden.
Miss Margaret Ashton.
Miss K. D. Courtney.
Hon. Secretary : Mrs. Pethick Lawrence.

Other members of the Executive Committee included Lady Courtney of Penwith, Miss Margaret Bondfield, Mrs. Despard, Mrs. Philip Snowden, Mrs. Bruce Glasier, Mrs. C. P. Trevelyan, etc.

Women's Peace Crusade.—A further development of the W.I.L. was the Women's Peace Crusade, run by Mrs. Philip Snowden. Mrs. Helen Crawfurd, also of the Women's International League and now a member of the Communist Party, was the organiser of the Crusade, which began operations on the Clyde on June 10, 1917. Her speeches were described as "quite Bolshevik in tone" by the *Morning Post*, which went on to observe :

"The Women's Peace Crusade aimed at creating a panicky feeling among the women relatives of the soldiers. Mrs. Snowden was particularly anxious that conditions should arise in this country that would compel Britain and her Allies to make peace with the Central Powers before America could take a decisive part in the war. This was clearly stated at a meeting at Leicester in August of last year" (*Morning Post*, series, "Bolshevism in Great Britain," December 1918).

Workers' Peace Council.—This organisation resulted in the formation during the same year of the Workers' Peace Council in Glasgow, composed of representatives from the I.L.P., U.D.C., B.S.P., S.L.P., N.C.F., Clyde Workers' Committee, etc., which carried on continuous agitation on the Clyde.

National Council Against Conscription—National Council for Civil Liberties.—At about the same date the National Council against Conscription was organised by Adrian Stephen and Langdon-Davies—the two principal organisers in the U.D.C. office. This body, which later changed its name to the National Council for Civil Liberties, had naturally the effect of disorganising national warfare against Germany by organising anti-national warfare against Great Britain. Its activities were almost exclusively confined to munition and coal-producing (*Morning Post*, Ibid.).

The President was Robert Smillie, and Secretary B. N. Langdon-Davies, whilst the Executive Committee included Clifford Allen, C. G. Ammon, Margaret Bondfield, Alexander Gossip, George Lansbury, Robert Williams and H. W. Massingham.

1917 Club.—In 1917 a further organisation was founded called the 1917 Club, combining Pacifism with definitely revolutionary aims. The whole Executive Committee of the U.D.C., i.e. Norman Angell, J. A. Hobson, Ramsay Macdonald, E. D. Morel, Arthur Ponsonby, Mrs. H. M. Swanwick and Charles Trevelyan, became members. The prospectus of the new club, which was privately circulated, appealed to all "those who desire that the changes after the war should fundamentally alter the structure of society" (*Morniny Post*, September 12, 1917).

Amongst the signatories were the following :

W. C. Anderson
Margaret Bondfield (Trades Union Congress, Fabian Society, I.L.P.)
G. Lowes Dickinson
Alexander Gossip (N.A.F.T.A.)
J. A. Hobson (Exec. Committee, U.D.C.)
Joseph King (I.L.P.)

Henry W. Nevinson (writer)
A. Maude Royden (writer and preacher)
Evelyn Sharp (journalist, later on staff of *Daily Herald*)
Ethel Snowden (Mrs. Philip Snowden) (I.L.P.)
Josiah C. Wedgwood (I.L.P.)
L. S. Woolf (writer, T.U.C., Labour Research Department).

There is, unfortunately, not space in this book to deal with the various ramifications of Pacifism on the Continent, but a brief survey of the movement in America must be given here.

In the United States, as in England, Pacifist societies came into existence directly after the outbreak of the Great War, and there, as here, showed themselves throughout consistently Socialist and pro-German.

First Emergency Peace Federation.—As early as October 1914 the Emergency Peace Federation was organised by Louis P. Lochner, Madame Rosika Schwimmer, a Hungarian Jewess and a German agent (*Lusk Report*, p. 971), who went to America as representatives of the International Suffrage Alliance, together with Mrs. Pethick Lawrence from England.

The preliminary meeting was held in Chicago on December 5, 1914, and was presided over by Miss Jane Addams. A committee was formed to settle the War on the lines drawn up by the South German Social Democrats, the Anti-War Council of Holland, the International Peace Brethren and the U.D.C. of England. The direction of the Federation was left almost entirely to well-known Socialist leaders, including Morris Hillquit on the Executive Committee of the Socialist Party of America, whilst Lochner was an American citizen of German descent, concerned in Socialist publicity organisation.

The legislative branch of the Emergency Peace Federation was represented by the American Union Against Militarism, the American Peace Society and the Women's Peace Party.

American League to Limit Armaments.—On December 18 of the same year (1914) the "American League to Limit Armaments" was organised in New York by a committee including many of the people who were at the same time active in the Emergency Peace Federation of Chicago. These included Louis Lochner, Morris Hillquit and Jane Addams.

National Peace Federation.—In March 1915 the Emergency Peace Federation assumed the name of the National Peace Federation, and began to extend its activities to Europe.

Women's International Committee for Permanent Peace.—It was then that Jane Addams, Lochner, Rosika Schwimmer and a number of other Pacifists went to Holland and convened the Hague Congress on April 28, 1915, at which they organised the "Women's International Committee for Permanent Peace," referred to on page 35, of which the British section took the name of the Women's International League. Representatives of eighteen countries were present and the following personnel was elected:

Chairman : Jane Addams.
Vice-Chairman : Dr. Aletta Jacobs.
Secretary : Chrystal Macmillan.
Treasurer *pro tem.* and Assistant Secretary : Rosa Manus.

The Central Bureau was instituted at Keisersgracht 467, Amsterdam, and the official organ was the *International*.

American Neutral Conference.—In July 1916 the American Neutral Conference was formed, under the Chairmanship of Hamilton Holt, with Jane Addams and Dr. George Kirchwey amongst the Vice-Chairmen, and with an Executive Committee which included B. W. Huebsch, Bertha Kuntz Baker and the Rabbi Stephen Wise. The organisation was largely carried out by Miss Rebecca Shelley.

" This was short-lived ; starting in February and merging, before the middle of the summer, into the First American Conference for Democracy and Terms of Peace. But during the few months it functioned it was exceptionally active in implanting thoughts antagonistic to the United States. Amongst those prominent in this movement were Mrs. Henry Villard, Emily Green Balch, Louis Lochner— through all of the movements runs the activities of this man, now safely enthroned as a Communist publicity agent in Berlin, etc." (Fred R. Marvin, *Ye Shall Know the Truth*, 1926, p. 14).

In February 1917 the American Neutral Conference Committee in New York was transformed into a second Emergency Peace Federation, with Mrs. Henry Villard as Chairman and a number of the same Pacifists—Lochner, Rebecca Shelly, Dr. Kirchwey and Emily Green Balch—amongst the promoters.

Fellowship of Reconciliation.—A number of these, as also Jane Addams, figured again in the American branch of the " Fellowship of Reconciliation "—constituted the same year under the leadership of the Rev. Norman Thomas—and still again in the " First American Conference for Democracy and Terms of Peace," which held its first mass meeting in Madison Square on May 30, 1917, under the Chairmanship of the Rabbi Judah L. Magnes, referred to in a Report by the American miners as " head of the Jewish Kehillah in New York City " (*Attempt by Communists to seize the American Labor Movement*. Prepared by the United Mine Workers of America, Washington; Government Printing Office, January 1924).

By this time the Russian Revolution had taken place, and the programme of the Conference was therefore to "be in thorough accord with that of the Russian Council of Workmen and Soldiers," so that the people of America should "join hands with the people of Russia" in securing a peace which could only at this juncture be favourable to Germany.

From 1914 to 1917 Socialist activities were thus mainly

THE WAR AND PACIFISM

restricted to anti-war agitation redounding to the advantage of Germany, since in Germany itself the firm action of the Imperial Government and the nationalist character of the German Socialists prevented Pacifist propaganda making headway. Only the Left Wing Social Democrats, later to be known as Spartacists, led by Karl Liebknecht, refused to vote for the war credits.

Zimmerwald Congress.—In September 1915 the Socialist Pacifists of eleven countries held an International Conference at Zimmerwald in Switzerland. No English delegates were allowed by the Government to attend, but France, Germany, Italy and Russia were all represented. A Manifesto was drawn up by the Conference addressed to "The Proletariats of all Nations," accusing the capitalists of bringing on the war and calling on the workers of the world to condemn it.

Considering that the German delegates—Ledebour and Hoffman —were amongst the signatories to this Manifesto, this might appear to have been a genuine peace move, but German Imperialism had its own agent at the Conference, in the person of Nicolai Lenin, who was to be sent by the German General Staff two years later to Russia in the famous sealed train, to bring about the collapse of the Russian army and set up the Bolshevik regime. Thus the Zimmerwald Congress paved the way for the Brest-Litovsk Treaty and the establishment of the 3rd Internationale. Meanwhile revolutionary propaganda was being carried on by the agents of German Imperialism in the countries of the Allies. In England this was only partially successful, producing merely a few strikes that served to embarrass military operations—notably the railway strike of 1915 that delayed the transport of munitions to the front. Only in Russia the agents of Germany met with complete success in the autumn of 1917.

CHAPTER V
THE RUSSIAN REVOLUTION

UP to this date we have seen the World Revolutionary movement directed from several different quarters: from France during the first French Revolution and the epoch of Utopian Socialism; from the Marx-Engels faction in Switzerland in the sixties of the last century, and in London later; then Anarchy carried West from France and Russia; and finally Syndicalism arising in France, passing over to America and thence to England. But in 1917 the movement enters on a new phase, and Russia, hitherto the stronghold of autocratic monarchy, becomes the G.H.Q. of World Revolution.

The G.H.Q., but not necessarily the real centre of direction! People who are accustomed to regard the thing we call Bolshevism as a modern sporadic growth—the outcome of the world-war and of "Tzarist tyranny"—completely overlook the fact shown by the chart accompanying this book that *the whole spirit, the whole theory and plan of campaign of Bolshevism existed long before the Bolsheviks of Russia came into existence*; what the *coup d'état* of November 1917 did was to establish a visible centre of direction in Moscow which, with an army, vast wealth, a huge and fertile country at its disposal, was able to carry Marx's instructions from the domain of theory into practice. The decrees of the Soviet Government were simply the resolutions of the 1st Internationale passed into law.

The Bolsheviks, as has been shown, were in no way the outcome of the Russian Revolutionary movement. Marxism, represented by the Russian Social Democratic Party, which had developed from the little "Group for the Emancipation of Labour," had never acquired a powerful influence over the minds of the Russian "revolutionary proletariat." The indigenous revolutionary movement in Russia had always been Anarchist in character, whether of the violent order represented by Bakunin and Kropotkine, or of the visionary type represented by Tolstoi. At the same time the Social Revolutionary Party, founded on the teaching of real Russians, such as Lavroff, Ogareff and Herzen, and standing for the peasants rather than for the industrial workers, had acquired a considerable following, which in 1917 was divided into four groups—the Left Wing, led by Maria Spiridınova, the Moderate Internationalists under Tchernov, the People's Social Party under Tschaikowsky, and the

Right Wing under Kerensky. This was the Party that made the revolution of March 11-13, 1917, that overthrew the monarchy and formed the Provisional Government which ruled Russia up to the moment of the Bolshevik *coup d'état*.

The Soviet.—At the same time the Socialist and Anarchist elements of Petrograd had established a " Soviet of Soldiers', Workmen's and Sailors' Deputies," of which the first President was Tcheidze, a Menshevik, with Kerensky the Social Revolutionary as Vice-President. In May 1917 the Soviet forced the Cabinet of the Provisional Government, headed by Prince Lvoff, to resign, and Kerensky became Premier.

A month earlier Nicolai Lenin, who had been incubating Bolshevism in Switzerland with a Saxon-Jew, Fritz Platten (naturalised as German-Swiss), as his principal associate, was sent to Russia with a number of his supporters by the German Imperial Staff, acting on the advice of a member of the German Social Democratic Party—Helphand Parvus, alias Israel Lazarevitch. Lenin reached Petrograd in the famous sealed train on the night of April 16, 1917, whilst Trotsky arrived from New York at almost the same moment. On arrival, the Bolsheviks found themselves outnumbered by the rival factions; on May 18 the Soviet vote showed only seven out of forty-one to be in favour of Bolshevik theory, whilst at the first meeting of 1,000 peasants from all parts of Russia, who formed the All-Russian Congress of Peasants, it was found that hardly any held Bolshevik views, the great majority being Social Revolutionaries.

On July 17 the Bolsheviks made their first attempt to seize the reins of power by force, but were defeated, and the leaders of the rising—Lenin, Trotsky (alias Braunstein) and Zinoviev (alias Apfelbaum)—escaped to Finland.

The Provisional Government, which had established a Liberal rather than a Socialist regime, failed to follow up this victory and consolidate its position by adopting firm measures. It would not listen to General Kornilov when he urged the necessity for restoring discipline in the army, and to General Kaledine, the elected representative of the Cossacks, when he warned it that " in the bitter struggle for existence which Russia is now waging, it should utilise all the Russian people, all the vital forces of all classes in Russia."

" The Provisional Government, however, remained deaf to all appeals. It feared to be accused of being reactionary. It apparently believed that the only method to deal with the Socialist elements which were undermining its power must be to grant them greater liberties and freedom to carry on their programme of national destruction " (*Lusk Report*, I. 220).

A few months later :

" The Provisional Government was overthrown, an event which was the direct result of the oscillating, timorous and conciliatory policy which it had always maintained towards domestic enemies " (*Lusk Report*, I. 220).

It was the old story of the Girondins paving the way for the Terrorists, which was to be repeated again later in the case of Hungary, with Karolyi in the rôle of Kerensky.

Bolsheviks.—On November 7, 1917 when Lenin and Trotsky, who had returned from Finland, brought off their successful *coup d'état* which overthrew the Provisional Government, the Bolsheviks were still in the minority. Not only were they outnumbered by the Socialist Revolutionaries, but opposed by the Anarchists, and also by the Right Wing of their own Party, the Mensheviks, who had been in control of the Soviets since the March revolution. This wing was itself divided into two factions—the Nationalists, under the old Social Democratic leader, George Plechanov, and the Internationalists, under Martov.

Owing to skilful Bolshevik propaganda amongst the soldiers and lack of leadership on the part of the anti-Bolshevik majority, the Kerensky Government was forced, on this same day of November 7, to abdicate. Petrograd was captured by the Red Guards, and the Bolshevik Government was instituted, with Lenin and Trotsky at the head. All resistance was then suppressed by organised Terrorism.

The accession of the Bolsheviks to power transformed the whole Socialist movement, not only by the inauguration of a visible centre of direction, but by dividing the Marxian Socialists of every country into the same two groups which were known in Russia under the name of Bolsheviks and Mensheviks. Hitherto the Right and Left Wings of the Social Democratic Parties everywhere had worked together, but now that the principle of force had become practical politics, the Left Wings, corresponding to the Bolsheviks of Russia, definitely split off from the rest, and when the Bolshevik Party of Russia decided to call itself officially the Communist Party, the corresponding parties abroad followed suit. Thus the word Communism, which in the past had covered all forms of Collectivism, whether of the revolutionary or of the pacific and even religious variety, came to signify the policy of instituting State Socialism by means of violence and terrorism, as opposed to the institution of the same system by means of legislation. It is important to understand this point, because the perversion of the original meaning of the word Communism has created much confusion of thought. In reality all Socialists are Communists—as the Manifesto of the United Socialist bodies of Great Britain in 1893 was ready to admit —and the repudiation of the name by the Socialist opponents of force has only been necessitated by its modern identification with Bolshevism. As the late Adolphe Smith ably demonstrated, the Bolsheviks of Russia were never sincere Communists, but a gang of political adventurers sent in the first instance by Germany at the instigation of Helphand Parvus " to lay Russia low "—as Ludendorff himself expressed it (see article by Adolph Smith, " Lenin, Russian Traitor and German Agent," in the *National Review* for April 1921). Once in power, they made use only of the destructive methods of Communism as interpreted by Karl Marx—the abolition of private enterprise and of personal liberty—but never attempted to put the principles of true Communism into practice by establishing any semblance of equality. This explains why they were able later to win the support of all destructionists, not only of State Socialist variety, but of the former opponents of State Socialism— the Syndicalists.

So a strange anomaly has been created—the Bolsheviks of Russia, whilst calling themselves Communists, were never really Communists at all; on the other hand, the so-called moderate Marxian Socialists are in reality Communists because, whilst disavowing the name, they continue to preach the doctrines of Communism as formulated throughout the pre-Bolshevik era. All that the latter really mean when they say they are not Communists is that they do not wish to see the Socialist State inaugurated by means of blood and terror, but by the pacific method of winning the electorate over to their side.

It is this divergence of method which, since the rise of the Bolsheviks to power, has divided the Socialist movement into two camps, not opposed in aim, but only in method, and marching towards the same goal by different routes. These two camps are now led by the 2nd and 3rd Internationales.

The 3rd Internationale.—The idea of forming the 3rd Internationale was first made known on January 24, 1919, when a wireless message went out from Moscow to the revolutionaries of other lands. That message was the first invitation to the Inaugural Conference of the 3rd or Communist Internationale " (R. Palme Dutt, *The Two Internationals*, p. 22).

The aims and methods of the new organisation were described as follows :

" (1) The seizure of the governmental power in order to replace it by the apparatus of proletarian power ; (2) the disarming of the bourgeoisie and the general arming of the proletariat in order to make the revolution secure ; (3) the use of the dictatorship to suppress private property in the means of production and transfer it ' to the proletarian State under the Socialist administration of the working class.' The method is ' the mass-action of the proletariat as far as open conflict with arms against the governmental power of capitalism ' " (*Ibid.*, p. 24).

The 2nd Internationale.—In opposition to this programme of violence, the more moderate Socialists now made an effort to revive the 2nd Internationale, which, as has been said, went into abeyance on the outbreak of War. Its last Congress had been held at Copenhagen in 1910.

Accordingly in February 1919—the month after the message had gone out from Moscow—a Conference of Labour and Socialist bodies, both political and industrial, met at Berne. Twenty-six countries, including Great Britain, France, Germany and Italy, were represented. The Belgian Labour Party and the American Federation of Labour refused to attend, being unwilling to meet the Germans. The Swedish leader, Branting, was elected President. This was not in reality a meeting of the old 2nd Internationale, but it prepared the way for its reorganisation. At this Conference the difference of opinion on the Russian question became apparent, the majority under Branting repudiating Bolshevism, the minority under the Austrian-Jew Friedrich Adler and the French-Jew Longuet, grandson of Karl Marx, opposing the placing of any stigma on the Russian Soviet Republic (Palme Dutt, *The Two Internationals*, p. 16).

Foundation of the 3rd Internationale.—In the following month, at a Conference held in Moscow from March 2–6, 1919, the Russian Bolsheviks founded the 3rd or Communist Internationale, sometimes known as the " Komintern " from a combination of the Russian words Kommunistitcheski Internazional.

Thirty-two delegates were present representing twelve countries —Russia, Germany, Hungary, German-Austria, Sweden, Norway, Bulgaria, Roumania, Finland, Ukrainia, Esthonia and Armenia. In addition to these accredited delegates were individuals connected with the Socialist movements in other countries, some of whom took an active part in the work of the Conference; these included Rakovsky of the Balkan Socialist Federation, A. Guilbeaux and Captain Jacques Sadoul, both of the French Socialist Party, and Fritz Platten of the Swiss Socialist Party.

The Manifesto of the Conference, issued on September 8, 1919, calling upon the revolutionaries of the world, whether Socialist, Syndicalist or Anarchist, to unite as soon as possible and form a unified Communist Party, was drafted by a committee consisting of Lenin, Trotsky, Zinoviev, Rakovsky and Fritz Platten. Zinoviev, alias Radomislsky, alias Apfelbaum, alias Ovse Gershon Aronovitch, was elected President of the Executive Committee—known as the I.K.K.I. (from the initials of the Russian words Ispolnitelni Kommitet Kommunistitcheskovo Internazionala) and has occupied that position ever since. Amongst those who later formed the Executive were W. Maclaine and Tom Quelch of the B.S.P., Jack Tanner and J. T. Murphy of the Factory and Works Committee of England, Jacques Sadoul, A. Rosmer and Delignet for France, L. Fraina and A. Stoklitsky of the American Communist Party, D. Bilan of the American Communist Labour Party, the Jewish leader of the Dutch Communists, D. Wynkoop, whilst the Petrograd Committee of the Russian Communist Party was represented by N. Bukharin, V. Vorovsky (later murdered in Switzerland by Conradi), G. Klinger and Angelica Balabanova—a well-known woman revolutionary who had acted as a German agent during the War (General Spiridovitch, *L' Histoire du Bolchévisme*, Russian edition, p. 279).

A special invitation to the Conference had been sent to Sen Katayama, leader of the Socialist groups of Tokio and Yokohama, who has since played a leading part in the Japanese Communist movement and even in the World Revolution.

The foundation of the Komintern brought matters to a crisis, and the Socialist Parties of the world were called upon to decide between the principles of the two Internationales. As a result, the British, French, Belgian, Dutch and Swedish parties, the German Majority Socialists, etc., retained their allegiance to the 2nd Internationale, whilst the Norwegian Labour Party, Swedish Left Socialist Party, Hungarian Communist Party, Swiss Social Democratic Party, Italian Socialist Party, etc., declared for affiliation with the 3rd Internationale.

Amsterdam Conference—Lucerne Conference.—A further attempt was now made to revive the 2nd Internationale. A second Conference met at Amsterdam in April 1919, and a third at Lucerne in the following August, and it was then decided to call a General Congress, not a Conference, at Geneva in February 1920. This was later postponed till July 31, and then at last, in August 1920, the 2nd Internationale, contemptuously described by the Bolsheviks as the Yellow Internationale, was definitely reconstituted at Geneva.

The 2nd Internationale Reconstituted.—Many of the people who helped to organise it had, however, nothing to do with the old 2nd Internationale; as, for example, Tom Shaw, who was appointed Chairman of the Geneva Congress. Adolphe Smith, of the S.D.F., Official Anglo-French Interpreter at the Congresses of the 2nd Internationale, thus comments on the character of the revived organisation :

" One feature, and this is the worst feature, of the Second International was maintained at Geneva. The very same individuals who had pulled the strings in such a manner that the Second International had degenerated into a Pan-German Association were allowed yet again to decide what nations should be represented and how many votes they should have. It was therefore perfectly certain beforehand that the German influence would predominate at Geneva, in August 1920, as it did when the Second International last met at Copenhagen, in 1910 " (*The Times*, June 21, 1921).

This being the state of affairs, the S.D.F. " took good care not to go to Geneva," but the I.L.P. and Labour Party delegates who attended showed themselves " more pro-German than the Germans themselves " (Adolphe Smith in private correspondence).

The 2nd Internationale then decided to remove its bureau, i.e. Executive Committee, from Brussels to London, with Camille Huysmans as one of the three General Secretaries.

The 3rd Internationale Congress.—At the same moment that the "Yellow Internationale" was being reconstituted in Geneva the Red Internationale was holding its Second Congress, which on July 19, 1920, met at Petrograd, and then continued its sessions in Moscow from July 23 to August 7.

This time it was able to call itself a "World Congress," for no less than thirty-seven countries were represented. The French Socialist Party, the American Socialist Party and the German Independent Party sent delegates. The most important countries were represented as follows :

RUSSIA : N. Lenin, G. Zinoviev, N. Bukharin, L. Trotsky.
GERMANY : P. Levy, E. Meyer, J. Walcher, R. Wolfstein.
GERMAN-AUSTRIA : K. Steinhardt, K. Toman, Stromer.
FRANCE : A. Rossmer, F. Sadoul, A. Guilbeaux.
ENGLAND : T. Quelch, W. Gallagher, Sylvia Pankhurst, W. MacLaine.
AMERICA : Flynn, A. Fraina, A. Bilan, John Reed.
ITALY : D. M. Serrati, N. Bombacci, Graziadei, A. Bordiga.
NORWAY : A. Fries, Shefflo, A. Madsen.
SWEDEN : K. Dalstrom, Samuelson, Winberg.
DENMARK : O. Jorgenson, M. Nilsen.
HOLLAND : Wynkoop, Jansen, Van Leuven.
SPAIN : Pestana.
SWITZERLAND : Herzog, J. Humbert-Droz.
HUNGARY : Rakoszy, A. Rudniamsky, Varga.
POLAND : U. Marchlevsky.
INDIA : Ashtaria, Sheffik, Roy.

At this second Congress the attitude of the Komintern was made clear on two important points : Parliamentarianism and Syndicalism. With regard to the former, it was frankly stated that the aim of the Communists was to destroy parliamentarianism which " has become a ' democratic ' form of the rule of the bourgeoisie." At the same time Communists should not refrain from participating in a political campaign on the score that parliament is a bourgeois government institution. "The Communist Party enters such institutions not for the purpose of organisation work, but in order to blow up the whole bourgeois machinery and the parliament itself from within." Hence Anti-Parliamentarianism " in the sense of an absolute and categorical repudiation of participation in the elections and the parliamentary revolutionary work . . . is a naïve and childish doctrine" (*The Communist Internationale*, official organ of the Komintern, No. 13, pp. 2405–2407).

As to revolutionary Syndicalism and Industrialism, these " are a step forward only in comparison with the old, musty, counter-revolutionary ideology of the 2nd Internationale. But in comparison with the revolutionary Marxian doctrine, they were a step backwards . . . the views of Syndicalism and Industrialism

... are reactionary. The working-class cannot achieve a complete victory over the bourgeoisie by means of the General Strike alone, and by the policy of 'folded arms.' The proletariat must resort to an armed uprising " (*The Communist Internationale*, pp. 2386 and 2452). Meanwhile " iron discipline is the first commandment of the Communists " (*Ibid.*, p. 2454).

So on the one hand constitutional government and on the other revolutionary Syndicalism were to be made use of for their own destruction and the triumph of the red bureaucracy of Moscow.

The foundation of the 3rd Internationale had immensely facilitated the spread of Bolshevism by providing the Soviet Government with a camouflage for its activities. No longer could groups or individuals working in co-operation with Moscow be accused of having dealings with a foreign power, but only with an independent Socialist organisation. To correspond with Zinoviev, member of the Executive Committee of the Russian Socialist Soviet Republic, was one thing, to communicate with him as President of the I.K.K.I (Executive Committee of the Communist International) was quite another matter. So well did this ruse succeed, that for a year or two the Governments of Western Europe continued to differentiate between the Soviet Government and the Komintern, although the same men were at the head of each. The point was only cleared up when it was proved conclusively that, as shown in the diagram at the end of this book, the Political Bureau of the Russian Communist Party controlled both the TS.I.K. (Central Executive Committee) of the Russian Government and also the I.K.K.I.

West European Secretariat.—By the end of 1919 the Komintern had spread its tentacles all over Europe. In December of that year the West European Secretariat of the 3rd Internationale, a marvellous organisation controlling a network of smaller organisations, both open and secret, was established at a Conference attended by delegates from Russia, Poland, Germany, Austria, Roumania and Great Britain. At a further Conference at Amsterdam in February 1920, it was decided to mark off this Secretariat as a Central European Secretariat, with headquarters at Vienna (later known colloquially as the D.I.K.I.), and to set up a new Western Secretariat at Amsterdam. A Southern European Bureau of the 3rd Internationale and an Eastern Secretariat of Propaganda, comprising the Far East, were established later.

CHAPTER VI
WORLD BOLSHEVISM

WE shall now follow the course of the Communist movement in various countries of the world after the Bolshevik Revolution.

BOLSHEVISM IN GERMANY

The first country to follow suit was Germany, where State Socialism had always been strong, but where Bolshevism had been least able to obtain a permanent foothold. The Bolshevik regime met with instant opposition from the Right Wing of the German Social Democratic Party under Scheidemann and the Centre under Karl Kautsky, who published a denunciation of Terrorism which met with a derisive reply from Trotsky.

The German Spartacists.—The Left Wing, however, known as the Spartacists, led by Karl Liebknecht, with Franz Mehring and the two Jewesses, Rosa Luxemburg and Clara Zetkine, attempted a rising in Berlin on December 25, 1918. Street fighting continued until January 15, 1919, when the Government succeeded in suppressing the movement, and Liebknecht and Rosa Luxemburg were killed by the mob. Spartacist riots also took place in Bremen, Brunswick, Hamburg and other cities, but only met with some success in Munich, where during three weeks of March 1919 the Spartacists gained the upper hand.

In 1921 a rising was attempted under the leadership of Max Heltz, and a further one in 1923, which also proved abortive. Since the end of 1924 the influence of the Communists has decreased in favour of the Social Democrats. The membership of both parties is still large—that of the Communist Party being larger than in any other country—but although their figures may look formidable on paper, they have not prevented the rise of Field-Marshal von Hindenburg to power nor impeded the prosperity of German industry.

The principal organ of the German Socialists is still *Vorwärts,* and that of the Communists *Die Rothe Fahne.*

BOLSHEVISM IN FRANCE

In France the national spirit at first showed itself resistant to the anti-patriotic propaganda of Bolsheviks, and the Internationalist faction in the French Socialist Party remained in the minority.

Under the influence of Trotsky and other Bolsheviks, Jean Longuet, grandson of Karl Marx and leader of the Centre, associated himself with Pressemane, Frossard and others to form the moderate section of the Left Wing, of which the extreme section was led by Loriot, Rappoport, Marcel Cachin and others.

In 1918 the tide turned in favour of Internationalism, and at a National Council of the French Socialist Party held in July of that year, the former 'minoritaires' secured a clear majority. Fraternal greetings were sent both to the German Socialists—with eulogistic references to Liebknecht and Rosa Luxemburg—and also to the Russian Soviet Government. Two so-called Communist groups were now formed, but these were in the main led by Syndicalists, and it was not until two years later that the present Communist Party was formed. This was the outcome of the Congress, which took place at Tours in December 1920, when the party known as the "French Unified Socialist Party" gave their adhesion to the 3rd Internationale and became officially known as the French Communist Party.

This decisive step seems to have been largely brought about by two Jewish emissaries from Lenin, both Spartacists—Clara Zetkine and Abramovitch (alias Zalewsky, alias Albreicht) one of the most trusted councillors of Trotsky and a member of the Tcheka, who had been sent from Moscow by Lenin at the end of November to direct Bolshevist propaganda in the West of Europe. Both of them were present at the Tours Congress, where Abramovitch was referred to as "the eye of Moscow." At the end of January Abramovitch and eight of his associates were arrested by the French police, and the Bolshevist plot in France was believed to have been defeated. But the Communist Party still continues to exist in that country, with a membership of no less than 57,000, and has for its present leaders Marcel Cachin, Vaillant Couturier, Jean Doriot, André Marty, Sémard, Treint, Monmousseau, Renaud Jean, etc.

The organ of the Party is *L'Humanité*.

The French Socialist Party is led at present by Herriot, Caillaux and Léon Blum, with *La France Libre* for its organ.

Bolshevism in Italy

From the beginning of the Bolshevist regime in Russia, the Italian Socialists proclaimed their sympathy with Communism and approval of Lenin and Trotsky. These sentiments were openly expressed at the Rome Conference in October 1918. Consequently the Italian Socialist Party held aloof from the Conferences of the 2nd Internationale, and "was the first Socialist Party of power and influence to ally itself with the 3rd Internationale. This important step was taken by the National Executive Committee of the Party, which met in March 1919 at Milan" (*Lusk Report*, I. 93). At the Bologna Conference of October 1919 the Soviet faction under Serrati secured an overwhelming majority over the moderate wing under Lazzari and Turati and the anti-parliamentarian group under Bordiga. It was then decided to overthrow the monarchy and parliamentary government and replace them by the Soviet system. A complete scheme was drawn up by N. Bombacci and printed in *Avanti* for January 28, 1920.

But the tendency of the Italian revolutionary movement had always been towards Anarchism and Syndicalism, and found expression in the seizure of factories by the F.I.O.M. (Federazione italiane operai metallurgichi, or Metallurgical Workers' Federation), which met with no opposition from the timorous government. " The Government refused absolutely to intervene to protect private property. As a matter of fact, it did not dare intervene. The troops could not have been moved. The railway men would have struck. The soldiers might have refused. . . ." It was the same story as in France, Russia and Hungary before the Revolution. Only in Italy events took a different turn, and the weakness of government led to a great national movement, which crushed the revolution and established Fascismo in its place. Owing to the intensified campaign against Mussolini, the public in this country has to a great extent forgotten that Italy was passing rapidly into chaos when the former Socialist leader took over the reins of power. The factories had been seized and abandoned, the workers proving quite unable to run them, the inscription " Viva Lenin ! " was seen everywhere, peaceful citizens were threatened. Fascismo alone stemmed the tide of Bolshevism flowing westwards. It may be that Mussolini was not only the saviour of Italy but of all Europe.

BOLSHEVISM IN BELGIUM

Before the war the Labour Party was strong in Belgium, under the leadership of Vandervelde and Camille Huysmans. At the same time Brussels was the centre of International Socialism, being the headquarters of the 2nd Internationale.

After 1919 a Belgian section of the 3rd Internationale was formed under the name of the Belgian Communist Party, with a membership of 5,000 that has now risen to 35,000.

The leader is Will van Overstraeten, and the official organs of the Party are the *Drapeau Rouge* (daily) and the *Roode Vaan* (weekly). The headquarters are at 59 rue des Alexiens, Brussels.

BOLSHEVISM IN HOLLAND

Social Democratic Labour Party.—The Social Democratic Labour Party of Holland had been founded in 1894 by Troelstra and eleven others. In 1910 a more strictly Marxian group was formed, calling itself the Social Democratic Party, led by a Jew, D. Wynkoop, who, with van Ravesteyn and Ceton, formed the directorate. It was this body which sent representatives to the Zimmerwald Conference and afterwards joined the 3rd Internationale and changed its name to the Communist Party.

Communist Workers' Party.—A split took place in 1920, when the Communist Workers' Party was formed.

The leaders of the Communist Party in 1924, of which the membership was only, 1,500 were as follows :

Political Department :
D. Wynkoop, on the Executive of the 3rd Internationale.
Dr. van Ravesteyn, doctor of literature and author.
Ceton, a schoolmaster.
H. Sneevliet, a former railway employé.
Van der Glas.

Organising Department :
L. L. H. de Visser (elected chairman in 1925).
Brommert.
Sterringa.
Mrs. Stamm-Ponsen.
Bouvman.

Youth Organisation : De Zaïer
Van Lakerveld.

Amongst the intellectuals connected with the movement were Mrs. J. Roland Holst, an authoress ; Baars and Brandsteder, engineers banished from India ; and Colthoff, employed in the Colonial Office.

Recently another split has taken place, and the more extreme section has taken the name of the Bond van Kommunistische Stryd en Propaganda Clubs (B.K.S.P.).

The organs of the Communist Party of Holland are : *De Tribune* and *De Klassenstryd* (the Class Struggle), whilst the Left Wing Trade Union movement, known as the Fimmen group, publishes *Eenheit* (Unity).

Several revolutionary organisations have been formed in the Dutch East Indies (see *The Patriot* for April 23, 1925).

Bolshevism in Switzerland

The Bolshevik Revolution, as has been said, was mainly organised in Switzerland, where Lenin had for his principal associate Fritz Platten, the secretary of the Swiss Social Democratic Party. Switzerland ever since the middle of the last century has always been a centre for revolutionary plotting, and during the war it became also a centre of pan-German propaganda. But as this was conducted on the basis of a secret organisation, it does not enter into the scope of this book.

After the inauguration of the Bolshevik regime efforts were made to turn Swiss Social Democracy in the direction of Moscow, and a bureau for Bolshevist propaganda was established by a number of emissaries from Russia, headed by Jean Berzine and Lipnitski in co-operation with Platten, who was present at the 1st Congress of the Komintern in Moscow.

The allegations concerning the bribing by the Germans of the Swiss Socialist Robert Grimm, who was associated with the German agents Rakovsky and Angelica Balabanova, had the effect, however, of uniting a great majority of the Swiss Socialists against the 3rd Internationale.

Although a Communist Party now exists in Switzerland numbering 3,500 members, it presents no immediate danger.

Bolshevism in Austria

Before the War the Social Democratic Labour Party of Austria was led by Victor Adler, a Jew, father of Friedrich Adler, who during the War became the leader of the middle Left Wing of the Socialist Party. It was Friedrich who in 1916 murdered the Austrian Prime Minister, Count Sturgkh, and later became one of the two General Secretaries of the L.S.I.

At first a defender of the Soviet regime, Adler ended by strongly denouncing it.

On the advent of the Bolsheviks to power in Russia, a Communist Party was formed in Austria, and an attempt was made to bring about a revolution on November 2, 1918. This was suppressed, and the Communist Leaders, Friedländer and Steinhart, were arrested.

Further attempts were made in April 1919 and in June 1919, but both were successfully defeated by the police, though not without bloodshed on both sides.

An Austrian Communist Party still exists, however, under the leadership of Otto Bauer, the former leader of the Social Democrats.

Bolshevism in Hungary

In Hungary a Communist regime and Red Terror was inaugurated by a Directorate of Five, headed by an emissary of Moscow, Bela Kun, in March 1919, and lasted until August 1, when the Jewish camarilla were put to flight by Admiral Horthy and the troops of the Allies. Bela Kun escaped to Germany, and from thence went back to Russia to rejoin Lenin and Trotsky.

Every attempt to bring about revolution was after this checked by the band of Monarchists known as the Move or the Awakening Magyars, led by the Deputy Gömbös.

Nevertheless, a Hungarian Communist Party still exists, although declared illegal.

Bolshevism in Scandinavia

Before the War Socialism was mainly represented in Scandinavia by the Majority Socialists of Sweden, with the moderate leader Hjalmar Branting at their head. On the foundation of the 3rd

Internationale, however, the Left Wing of the Swedish Socialist Party and the Norwegian Labour Party, which was represented at the 1st Congress in Moscow, declared for affiliation. Of the two countries, Norway showed itself the more revolutionary. The leader of the Norwegian Left Wing Socialists was Martin Tranmael, who in the spring of 1918 succeeded in getting himself made secretary of the Norwegian Labour Party, whilst another Bolshevik, M. Scheflo, gained control of the official organ of the Party, the *Socialdemokrat*. Tranmael proved an apt disciple of Lenin, and openly declared his contempt for democratic government as expressed by majorities : " It is the great stupid mass that decides elections ; and we cannot tolerate that " (*Morning Post*, October 14, 1919). Accordingly Tranmael, Scheflo, a post master Eugene Nissen, and a lawyer Emil Stang, constituted themselves as the minority which should assume control over the Norwegian people. Before long they had secured a majority in the Labour Party, and throughout 1919 Norway became the scene of the wildest Bolshevist excesses, and one strike followed on another. But at the Congress of Left Wing Scandinavian Socialists, which met in Stockholm on December 8 and 10, 1919, a split took place between the Socialists and Syndicalists, and the latter won the day. By 1921 the moderate Norwegian Socialists, momentarily crushed for want of funds, succeeded in asserting themselves and started a paper, which has now resumed the old title of *Socialdemokrat*, whilst the organ of the Communists is now the *Arbeiderbladet*, with the same offices as the Labour Press Bureau and the Norwegian Labour Party in the Folkets Hus (People's House), 13 Youngstaten, Oslo. Schisms have recently taken place in the Communist Party, and opposition groups have been formed. Scheflo, P. Moe Johansen and Falk deserted from the main body, and the last named has denounced Tranmael as not sufficiently revolutionary, and has founded a paper of his own, *Mot Dag* (Towards Day). In retaliation, Einer Gerhardsen advocated the expulsion of Falk and his followers.

The principal representatives of Soviet Russia in Norway were, until recently, Alexandre Koznekow, Consul at Trömso ; Nicolaieff, chief of the Russian Trade Delegation, and Mme. Alexandre Kollontai, Minister Plenipotentiary of the Russian Republic in Norway and author of several books on Bolshevism, notably *Communism and the Family*, which advocates the emancipation of women from all domestic ties. Mme. Kollontai has just resigned her post (February 1926), owing to differences with Litvinov and Zinoviev.

BOLSHEVISM IN AMERICA

American Anarchists.—In America during the pre-war period the revolutionary movement has been, as we have seen, largely Anarchist and Syndicalist in character. During the War the Anarchists, led by Alexander Berkman and Emma Goldman, were intimately connected with the Pacifist movement. Their official organs were *Mother Earth* and *The Blast*; at the same time they distributed a large number of anonymous pamphlets. They were also the organisers of the " No Conscription League," at the offices of which, in New York City, they were arrested on June 15, 1917, and subsequently indicted for violation of the Espionage Act and imprisoned.

Their fellow Anarchists thereupon organised the League of Amnesty of Political Prisoners, with M. Eleanor Fitzgerald as secretary.

At the beginning of the Bolshevik regime the American Anarchists sent messages of congratulation to Lenin and Trotsky, although not identifying themselves with Bolshevism. One group, calling itself "The American Anarchist Federated Commune Soviets," carried on a violent campaign through an organ named the *Anarchist Soviet Bulletin*, expressing sympathy with the Soviet regime, despite the fact that in Russia their brother Anarchists were being suppressed with the utmost vigour.

Anarchist Communism.—It was no longer, however, the pure Anarchism of Proudhon or of Bakunin that these groups represented, but a kind of hybrid theory called Anarchist Communism—with Workers' Soviets as its final objective and approximating to Anarcho-Syndicalism in its advocacy of the General Strike.

Socialist Party of America.—Meanwhile the various Socialist organisations of America were taking a new form. The Socialist Labour Party had split in 1899 and the Socialist Party of America in 1912. " In 1916 a number of the extremists organised the Socialist Propaganda League at Boston and issued a newspaper known as *The New International*. In April 1917 *The Class Struggle* appeared " (*Congressional Record*, "Recognition of Russia," Part II, p. 238. 1924).

People's Council of America.—The first repercussion of the Russian Revolution in America was the formation of the "People's Council of America," founded in June 1917—that is to say, four months before the advent of the Bolsheviks to power—and modelled on the Council of Workmen's and Soldiers' Soviet of Russia. The executive secretary was Louis Lochner; Rebecca Shelly was financial secretary and Dr. David Starr Jordan was treasurer. Amongst the members of the committee were well-known Socialist leaders, such as Eugene V. Debs, Max Eastman, editor of *Masses* (New York), Morris Hillquit (alias Misca Hilkowicz), now International Secretary of the Socialist Party, James H. Maurer, the Rabbi Judah L. Magnes, and Benjamin Schlesinger, president of the International Ladies' Garment Workers' Union.

Although the plan drawn up by Lochner and Miss Shelly followed closely on Soviet lines, the Socialistic character of the People's Council was first camouflaged as a national movement. In August 1917 Roger Baldwin, an ally of Lochner's, wrote to the latter:

"Do steer away from making it look like a Socialist enterprise. Too many people have already gotten the idea that it is nine-tenths a Socialist movement. . . . Do get into the movement just as strong as possible the leaders in the labour circles. . . .

"We want also to look like patriots in everything we do. We want to get a lot of good flags, talk a good deal about the Constitution and what our forefathers wanted to make of this country, and to show that we are the folks that really stand for the spirit of our institutions."

Lochner replied:

"I agree with you that we should keep proclaiming our loyalty and patriotism, I will see to it that we have flags and similar paraphernalia." (*Lusk Report*, pp. 1057, 1058.)

All the tactics of social revolution are embodied in these lines.

Throughout the years 1917 and 1918 a Left Wing of the Socialist Party of America was developing with a more and more pronounced tendency towards Communism. A Communist propaganda league was formed in Chicago in November 1918; during the same year the Boston branch of the Socialist Party began the publication of *The Revolutionary Age*, which advocated Communist tactics and was edited by a Mexican-Jew, named Louis Friana (*Congressional Record*, "Recognition of Russia," Part II, p. 238, and *Lusk Report*, p. 684).

Left Wing of Socialist Party.—These activities led to the definite formation of a Left Wing Section of the Socialist Party at a meeting held in the Rand School of Social Science in New York on February 15, 1919. Maximilian Cohen was elected as executive secretary; L. L. Wolfe, later succeeded by Fanny Horowitz, as recording secretary, and another Jewess, Rose Pastor Stokes, as treasurer. The Executive Committee was selected, consisting of the following: Benjamin Gitlow, Nicholas I. Hourwich, George Lehman, James Larkin (the Irish agitator), L. Himmelfarb, George C. Vaughn, Benjamin Corsor, Edward I. Lindgren and Maximilian Cohen.

Foreign Language Federations.—The strikingly un-American character of the new movement may be partly accounted for by the fact that it was inspired by various foreign language federations, which formed branches of the Socialist Party, notably by the so-called "Russian Socialist Federation," led by Alexander Stoklitzky, Oscar Tywerowsky and Michael Mislig, with the *Novy Mir*, edited by Gregory Weinstein, as its official organ (*Lusk Report*, p. 676).

This committee paved the way for the Communist Party of America.

In the following month, when the 3rd Internationale was founded in Russia, S. J. Rutgers was appointed by the Left Wing Section to represent it at the Congress. The Socialist Labour Party, which had been one of the signatories to the invitation convening the Congress, was represented by Boris Reinstein.

In June a National Conference of the Left Wing Socialists met in New York to discuss the definite formation of a Communist Party, but decided that a decision should be delayed until September, in order meanwhile " to rally all the revolutionary elements." A minority, composed of Michigan delegates and those representing the Russian Socialist Federation, decided, however, on immediate action, and after withdrawing from the Conference formed a National Organisation Committee which issued in the *Novy Mir* for July 7, 1919, a " Call for a National Convention for the purpose of organising a Communist Party in America." This was signed by Dennis E. Batt, D. Elbaum, O. C. Johnson, John Keracher, S. Kopnagel, I. Stilson and Alexander Stoklitzky. On July 19 this committee published the first number of *The Communist*, as the official organ of the new party.

Communist Party of America.—It was not, however, until September 1, 1919, that the Communist Party of America was definitely founded at a Conference in Chicago. An Executive Committee was formed consisting of Charles E. Ruthenberg, Louis C. Fraina, Isaac E. Ferguson, Schwartz of the Lettish Federation of Boston, Karosses of the Lithuanian Federation of Philadelphia, Dirba, secretary of the Minnesota Socialist Party, and H. M. Wicks, a Communist from Oregon. Harry M. Winitsky was elected secretary in New York. Amongst other important leaders of the Party were those who had figured in the Left Wing Socialist Section —Isaac A. Hourwich, Alexander Stoklitzky, D. Elbaum, Bittleman, editor of the Jewish Federation paper *Der Kampf*, Jay Lovestone, Maximilian Cohen, etc.

The Constitution drawn up by the Party declared its adherence to the 3rd Internationale, and the report addressed to the I.K.K.I. prepared by Fraina ended with these words :

" The Communist Party realises the immensity of its task ; it realises that the final struggle of the Communist proletariat will be waged in the United States, our conquest of power alone assuring the World Soviet Republic. Realising all this, the Communist Party prepares for the struggle.

" Long live the Communist International ! Long live the World Revolution ! " (*Lusk Report*, p. 756.)

" After the Chicago convention the work of organising locals and branches proceeded rapidly. The local for Greater New York was organised, with Harry M. Winitsky as Executive Secretary. Its headquarters were moved from the place occupied by the old Left Wing at 43 West Twenty-ninth Street to 207 East Tenth Street, and a new weekly publication was established as the official organ of the Communist Party, Local Greater New York. This paper was called *Communist World*. Maximilian Cohen was elected editor ; Bertram D. Wolfe associate editor, and George Ashkenouzi business manager. The first issue of this periodical appeared on November 1, 1919." (*Lusk Report*, p. 758.)

The propaganda of the Party in New York City was definitely

"anti-parliamentary," and a proclamation was issued ending with the words in capitals : " BOYCOTT THE ELECTIONS ! "

But already a split had taken place in the ranks of Communism. As we have seen, the National Organisation Committee, composed of Michigan delegates and those from the language Federations that had formed the Communist Party, had at first constituted a minority at the Left Wing Conference in June. Though they later succeeded in drawing over a majority of the National Council of the Left Wing to support their call for immediate action. Certain members of the Left Wing Council, as well as a number of locals and branches which had endorsed the Left Wing movement, continued, however, to entertain the hope of capturing the Socialist Party machinery. " All through July the Federations were maligning the Left Wing Council as centrists, as a fetid swamp. Meanwhile the Council was maligning Michigan as parliamentarian and non-Bolsheviks, and both Michigan and the Federations as petty political intriguers " (*Lusk Report*, p. 800).

Communist Labour Party.—As a result of these disputes a number of Left Wing delegates presented themselves at the Socialist Party Emergency Convention on August 30, 1919, in Chicago, but were excluded, whereupon they appointed a committee of five to meet the Organisation Committee of the Communist Party formed on September 1, and later a like committee of the Communist Convention for the purpose of seeking unity. These negotiations came to nothing, so the delegates organised themselves into a separate Convention and formed the " Communist Labour Party " with a programme identical to that of the Communist Party, except in its policy of using the present political machinery for propaganda purposes. The Convention elected A. Wagenknecht executive secretary, and as members of the National Executive Committee, M. Bedacht, of California ; Alexander Bilan, Ohio ; Jack Carney, Minnesota ; L. E. Katterfeld, Kansas ; Edward Lingren, New York. Prominent in the organisation were also Charles Baker, Ohio ; James Larkin, the Irish agitator ; Benjamin Gitlow, New York ; John Reed, Ludwig Lore and Charles Krumbein. National Headquarters were opened in Cleveland, Ohio (*Lusk Report*, p. 801, and *Congressional Record*, " Recognition of Russia," Part II, p. 239). The official organ of the Party was *Communist Labor*.

The Communist Labour Party was from the first affiliated to the 3rd Internationale, and delegates were sent to the 2nd Congress in July and August 1920, where the Communist Party was also represented.

By the autumn of 1919, however, the attention of the Government had been aroused with regard to the activities of the revolutionary elements in the United States, and in June the Russian Soviet Bureau, the Rand School and the headquarters of the I.W.W. and the Left Wing Section of the Socialist Party were raided. On November 8 came the turn of the two new organisations, at whose headquarters tons of seditious and anarchist literature were seized and a number of prisoners taken. Amongst those arrested on the charge of criminal anarchy were Isaac E. Ferguson, Charles E. Ruthenberg and Harry M. Winitsky of the Communist Party and James Larkin and Benjamin Gitlow of the Communist Labour Party, who, although convicted and sentenced to long terms of imprisonment, were soon set at liberty again.

In the following month, December 1919, a number of revolutionaries were deported from America to an unknown port in Russia in the transport *Buford*, nicknamed the " Soviet Ark." Unfortunately these did not include the most active Communists, but did include the leading Anarchists, whose influence was now on the wane, Emma Goldman and Alexander Berkman, also Peter Bianki, the leader of the Anarcho-Syndicalist group, the " Union of Russian Workers." These martyrs to the cause of freedom were received in Petrograd with tremendous enthusiasm, but although they went to bless they returned to curse; and the revelations of " Red Emma," who recently visited London, have provided one of the strongest indictments of the Soviet regime.

As a result of these Government measures at the end of 1919, the Communist Party in the United States was henceforth obliged to function illegally or in an underground manner during 1920 and 1921. But neither of the two Communist Parties was destroyed, and the necessity for uniting the two was urged by the 3rd Internationale at Moscow. On January 12, 1920, Zinoviev addressed a letter to the Central Committees of the American Communist Party and the American Communist Labour Party, pointing out that the split amongst the Communists had been a heavy blow to the movement, and that in spite of differences in tactics the two should unite to seize power and to establish the dictatorship of the proletariat.

United Communist Party.—Accordingly, in obedience to the dictates of Moscow, negotiations were at once set on foot by the two Parties, with a view to achieving unity. These continued amidst mutual recriminations and denunciations throughout the summer of 1920, and finally in September a common programme was agreed upon and issued in the name of the United Communist Party. A Central Executive Committee was formed with five members from each Party.

In May 1921 a joint unity convention of the Communist Parties took place, a revised and still more extreme programme and constitution was adopted and issued by the C.E.C. This was published in the official organ of the Communist Party, *The Communist* for July.

American Labor Alliance.—The 3rd Internationale at its Third Congress of June-July 1921 now ordered the Communist Party of America to form an open political body, which could operate legally. In order to carry out this mandate, the Communist Party of America organised what was known as "The American Labor Alliance," but as this did not satisfy the 3rd International the Central Executive of the Party, on the return of its representative, Max Bedacht, from Moscow, set to work on a scheme which would serve as a cover to its activities (*Congressional Record*, "Recognition of Russia," pp. 249–54).

Workers' Party of America.—Accordingly on December 3, 1921, a call was sent out from the headquarters of the American Labor Alliance to organise "The Workers' Party of America." The first convention of the new party took place in New York on December 23, 1921. The call had been sent out from the A.L.A. and signed by that body, as also by the Workers' Council and various foreign organisations, but not by the Communist Party; but the Central Executive of the Workers' Party elected in the following August was almost exclusively composed of Communists, including a number of the same people who formed the Central Executive of the Communist Party, such as Rose Pastor Stokes, C. E. Ruthenberg, Jay Lovestone, A. Bittleman, etc. William Z. Foster, the revolutionary Syndicalist, was also made a member (*Congressional Record*, "Recognition of Russia," pp. 267, 352).

The Worker was adopted as the official organ of the Party.

In 1924 the C.E.C. of the Workers' Party was composed as follows :

Alexander Bittleman	William Z. Foster
Earl R. Browder	Benjamin Gitlow
F. Burman	Ludwig Lore
J. P. Cannon	J. Lovestone
William F. Dunne	John Pepper
J. L. Engdahl	C. E. Ruthenberg

It also has its Political Bureau :

Foster	Browder	Cannon
Pepper	Lovestone	Dunne
	Ruthenberg	

(*Reds in America*, p. 15.)

It should be noted that Pepper was the pseudonym adopted by the Hungarian-Jew, Joseph Pogany, who had been a member of Bela Kun's cabinet during the Red Terror in Hungary (*Ibid.*, p. 44).

On August 22, 1922, the whole "colossal conspiracy against the United States" was literally "unearthed" by the Michigan constabulary, who discovered two barrels of incriminating documents, buried in the ground by the leaders of a secret convention of the Communist Party in a grove near Bridgman, who, hearing that a raid was imminent, concealed their papers before taking flight. From the "names, records, checks from prominent people in the U.S.A., instructions from Moscow," etc., the "whole machinery of the underground organisation" was laid bare. The author of *Reds in America*, from which we quote, goes on to say :

"It can be stated with authority that the Workers' party of America is a branch of this organisation, placed in the field by orders direct from Moscow and supported by the illegal branches of the Communist Party. It is known that agents of the Communists are working secretly, through 'legal' bodies, in labor circles, in society, in professional groups, in the Army and Navy, in Congress, in the schools and colleges of the country, in banks and business concerns, among the farmers, in the motion picture industry—in fact, in nearly every walk of life.

"These agents are not 'lowbrows,' but are keen, clever, intelligent, educated men and women. They are experts in their several lines. Their programs, which are now known, show that their plans for inciting the negroes, the farmers, the clerks, the workmen in industry, members of Congress, employees in Government departments everywhere, to violence against the constituted authorities, have been drawn with almost uncanny appreciation of the psychology of each group, with facts and figures so manipulated as to appeal to those approached, with false premises so cleverly drawn as to fool almost anyone.

"The names of persons interested directly or indirectly in this movement are astounding. They range from bricklayers to bishops, and include many prominent official and society people. It must be understood that by far the greater number of these people do not know to what they are lending the use of their names and influence or to what they are giving their money. They have been approached to give aid to the Workers' Party, or to many of the relief organisations which have sprung up disguising Communistic activities, or to the forward-looking, "advanced" schools of political thought. They do not know that their names are on what are known in the secret circles of the Communists as 'sucker lists,' comprising the names of people who have given to one or another of the various 'causes' which are manipulated by the Communists and who can, if properly approached, be induced to give again."

In spite of this *exposé* and the wise policy adopted by the Government of the U.S.A. in refusing to recognise Soviet Russia, the Communist movement in that country, though checked, has never been entirely defeated. The Workers' Party of America still continues to exist as an open political party acting as a cover to Communist activities (*Congressional Record* for December 19, 1925, p. 3).

Friends of Soviet Russia.—Another Communist organisation formed in America on August 7, 1921, by the Central Executive Committee of the Communist Party was the "Friends of Soviet Russia," for the purpose of collecting "relief funds and supplies for direct transmission to Russian Soviet authorities," and also of presenting the real facts about Soviet Russia to the American people, with a view to the lifting of the blockade and the resumption of trade (*Reds in America*, p. 98). The organisation of this body was carried out by Caleb Harrison and Dr. Jacob W. Hartmann, and the names on the Executive and Advisory Committees included those of William Z. Foster, Rose Pastor Stokes, Jack Carney, Max Eastman and other well-known Communists. The official organ of the society was at first named *Soviet Russia*, but at the end of 1922 it was changed to the *Soviet Russia Pictorial*, which is the organ of the W.I.R. (Workers' International Relief). In fact, the "Friends of Soviet Russia" seem to be the American branch of the W.I.R. founded in the same year of 1921 in Berlin (*Congressional Record*, "Recognition of Russia," Part II, p. 391. 1924). An account of the W.I.R. will be given later.

The rest of the history of Communism in America must be reserved for the section on the Trade Union movement, with which it has now become intimately connected.

CHAPTER VII

BOLSHEVISM IN GREAT BRITAIN

Leeds Conference.—The first repercussion of the Russian Revolution in England was the Leeds Conference, which took place on June 3, 1917, mainly under the auspices of the I.L.P. and the B.S.P. with the object of stopping the War, but also, as far as a number of delegates were concerned, for the further purpose of bringing about a revolution in this country.

" This attempt to organise a revolution to end the war was supported by the U.D.C., I.L.P., B.S.P., Women's International League, Herald League (an offshoot of the *Daily Herald*), the Clyde Workers' Committee, etc. Sinn Feiners also attended the Convention. Among the supporters of the scheme were Tom Mann, Arthur MacManus, W. Gallacher (Clyde), and Noah Ablett and other Syndicalists from South Wales " (*Morning Post*, November 1918).

There were also present 371 delegates from trade union organisations, though none of the prominent trade union leaders, with the exception of Robert Smillie (president of the Miners' Federation) and Robert Williams (Transport Workers); besides these were representatives of various Pacifist bodies—the No Conscription Fellowship, Fellowship of Reconciliation, Council for Civil Liberties —and a number of aliens, Czeks and East-End Jews, as also a body calling itself the " Foreign Jews' Protection Committee."

Ramsay Macdonald moved the first resolution congratulating the people of Russia on the success of their revolution ; this was seconded by Mrs. D. B. Montefiore, of the B.S.P. and later of the Communist Party.

The second resolution, drafted and moved by Philip Snowden, pledged the Conference to work in agreement with the international democracies for peace without annexations and indemnities. But the most important resolution was the fourth, moved by W. C. Anderson, M.P., and seconded by Robert Williams, which proclaimed the setting up of Councils of Workmen's and Soldiers' Delegates in imitation of the Russian Soviet of Soldiers and Workers then existing under the Kerensky regime. Amongst the most active supporters of the movement were Ramsay Macdonald, the Snowdens and C. G. Ammon, all I.L.P.; Charles Roden Buxton, Pethick Lawrence and Bertrand Russell, U.D.C.; E. C. Fairchild and Mrs. Dora Montefiore, B.S.P.; and Sylvia Pankhurst of the Workers' Socialist Federation.

According to the *Evening Standard* the real inspirer of the Workers' and Soldiers' Council was the renegade Frenchman, E. D. Morel, formerly Edmond Morel-de-Ville, who was imprisoned a few months later for contravening the Defence of the Realm Regulations. It is amusing, in the light of the indulgence shown towards the leaders of the recent Socialist Government, to note what was once said about them when patriotism was still the fashion in this country:

" The Committee of the Workers' and Soldiers' Council is an outcome of the 'Morel' movement, which is responsible, directly or indirectly, through the parent body, the U.D.C., for the whole of the Pacifist organisations and propaganda through which 'Morel' is attempting, by a variety of insidious appeals, to weaken the war resolutions of the people and foment industrial troubles in order to cripple our military efforts. This network of organisation has been woven by the same master hand. Messrs. Philip Snowden, Ramsay Macdonald, Ponsonby, Trevelyan are, consciously or unconsciously, all creatures of 'Morel,' and quite insignificant without him. This pro-German exploits their follies and their prejudices in the same way that he uses the cowards and the shirkers and the Quakers and the Syndicalists and the elements of anarchy wherever they are to be found. He has been working cunningly and assiduously for many months to save Prussia from defeat, and he has used any instrument that came to his hand. I shall continue, therefore, to call the Workers' and Soldiers' Council a product of the 'Morel' movement, whose founder should long ago have been deprived of his naturalisation, by Act of Parliament if necessary, and expelled the country as an undesirable alien" (*Evening Standard*, July 31, 1917).

It was in May of this same year, 1917, that Ramsay Macdonald applied for a passport to go to Russia in order to consult with the Workmen's and Soldiers' Soviets, but in view of his Pacifist activities during the war the National Seamen and Firemen's Union under Havelock Wilson refused to carry him.

All this belongs, however, to the pre-Bolshevik era, since the beginning of which the Right Wing leaders of the I.L.P. referred to above have periodically professed abhorrence of the Soviet Government, though as late as October 14, 1922, Ramsay Macdonald wrote in *Forward*:

" I have been an unswerving hopeful regarding the Moscow Government. . . . We can now take the Moscow Soviet Communist Revolutionary Government under our wing, and clothe it in the furs of apology to shield it from the blasts of criticism."

" Hands off Russia " Committee.—One of the first organisations to proclaim openly its adherence to Bolshevik Russia was the "Hands off Russia" Committee, formed at the beginning of 1919 on the initiative of James Crossley, one of the founders of the B.S.P. in Manchester, with Lenin as President and Trotsky as Vice-President (evidence of W. F. Watson, member of "Hands off Russia" Committee in libel action against the Duke of Northumberland, *Daily Mail*, November 17, 1921). In all parts of the country large meetings were held under the direction of Colonel L'Estrange Malone, M.P., and Professor W. T. Goode, and on February 8, 1919, a monster demonstration took place in the Albert Hall, London. Tom Mann was in the chair, and speeches were made by Colonel Malone, Robert Williams and also by Israel Zangwill, who declared that "Bolshevism, far from being the antithesis to Christianity, was merely an applied form of it." It was also on this occasion that Zangwill observed : " The British Government is only Bolshevism in embryo and Bolshevism is only Socialism in a hurry, Socialism while you won't wait " (report of speech published by The Workers' Socialist Federation, p. 7).

On May 21, 1920, the "Hands off Russia" Committee published a big advertisement in the *Daily Herald*, advocating a twenty-four hours' General Strike to coerce the Government to let Russia alone, and not help Poland. The signatories to this appeal were as follows :

Chas. G. Ammon, L.C.C., L.P., I.L.P., 1917 Club.
John Bromley, Sec., Locomotive Engineers, L.P.
Isaac Brassington, Sec., N.U.R.
Mrs. M. Bamber, Sec., Warehouse Workers.
A. G. Cameron, Sec., Amalgamated Society Carpenters, L.P., I.L.P.
Dr. R. Dunstan, Labour candidate, I.L.P.
R. J. Davies, Union Co-operative Employees, I.L.P.
W. T. Goode, *Manchester Guardian*.
William Gallacher, Clyde worker.
Alec Gossip, Sec., Furnishing Trades.
Harold Grenfell, Naval Attaché, Russian Embassy (1912–17).
Jack Jones, M.P., S.D.F.
David Kirkwood, Clyde worker, I.L.P.
George Lansbury (*Daily Herald*), I.L.P.
Neil Maclean, M.P., I.L.P.
Tom Mann, Sec. A.E.U., I.L.P.
A. E. Mander, National Union Ex-Service Men.
Cecil L'Estrange Malone, M.P.
Tom Myers, M.P., L.P., I.L.P.
J. E. Mills, M.P., A.E.U.
George Peet, National Sec., Ship Stewards.
Robert Smillie, Pres., Miners' Federation.
Ben Spoor, M.P., L.P., U.D.C., 1917 Club.
Fred Shaw, A.S.E.
Josiah Wedgwood, M.P., I.L.P., 1917 Club.
James Winston, S. Wales Miners' Federation.

Further meetings of the "Hands off Russia" Committee were organised by John Maclean, B.S.P., who described himself as "Bolshevik Consul" in Glasgow (*The Call*, January 1919), and who had been imprisoned in May 1918 for offences under the Defence of the Realm Regulations, and W. McLaine, also B.S.P. and member of the Executive Committee of the 3rd Internationale; A MacManus, S.L.P., F. Willis, G. Ebury and others.

The H.O.R. Committee has now become the Anglo-Russian Parliamentary Committee advocating relations with Russia. The members include A. A. Purcell, J. Bromley, A. Gossip, R. Williams, W. P. Coates, etc.

At the same time that the " Hands off Russia " campaign was started in 1919, a number of Workmen's Soviet Committees were formed, with headquarters in London, under W. F. Watson of the " Hands off Russia " Committee, A. MacManus, John Maclean and Tom Anderson, I.L.P. (founder of the Glasgow Socialist Sunday Schools in 1894, and who had just started his Proletarian Sunday Schools in that city).

These operated principally on the Clyde, the centre of John Maclean's activities, where he had been indicted for saying in speeches from January to April 1918 that " a revolution should be created," that " the Clyde had helped to win the Russian Revolution," that " the present House of Commons should be superseded by a Soviet, and he did not care whether they met in the usual place or in Buckingham Palace," and that " he was prepared to run any risk if he thought he could bring about a revolution in Glasgow" (pamphlet, *Condemned from the Dock*, published by the Clyde Workers' Propaganda Defence Committee, 1918). " With a determined revolutionary minority," he declared, in 1919, " we shall be able to take control of the country and the means of production at once, and hold them tight through disciplined production under the Workshop Committees and the District and National Councils. Through the Co-operative Movement we shall be able to control the full distribution of the necessaries of life and so win the masses over to Socialism."

This was a clear intimation of the part it was intended that the Co-operatives should play in the scheme of starving the non-revolutionary portion of the community.

It is significant to notice that all the individuals and groups who at this date proclaimed themselves in sympathy with Bolshevism were those who had most strongly opposed resistance to German Imperialism during the war. In view of the fact that it was the German General Staff which, on the admission of Ludendorff and Hoffman, had sent Lenin to Russia in the sealed train, the hand of Germany, not of Socialist but Imperial Germany, is clearly seen behind the earliest Bolshevik agitation in this country. This being the case, it was natural that the B.S.P., being the section of the S.D.P. which had split off from the rest on the issue of pro-Germanism, should be the first Socialist body in this country to ally itself with Moscow. At a Conference of the Party in October 1919 it was decided by a vote of 98 branches to 4 to join up with the 3rd Internationale, and W. McLaine and Tom Quelch were then placed on the Executive Committee in Moscow.

Other British parties which by 1920 were affiliated to the Komintern were the S.L.P., the South Wales Socialist Society, the National Workers' Committee Organisation and the Workers' Socialist Federation.

Workers' Socialist Federation.—The last named had begun its career before the War, under the leadership of Sylvia Pankhurst, as the Women's Suffrage Federation; it then became the Workers' Suffrage Federation, and finally the Workers' Socialist Federation, with the *Workers' Dreadnought* as its organ.

Sylvia Pankhurst, whom Lenin at first regarded as his principal lieutenant in this country, was then ordered by him to form a Communist Party in Great Britain, as the British Section of the 3rd Internationale, and was said to have been promised £3,522 by him for the purpose. (*Morning Post*, November 3, 1920.)

First British Communist Party.—The plan was quite openly announced in the *Daily Herald* of March 20, 1920, where sympathisers with the " definite formation of a Revolutionary Communist Party, affiliated to the 3rd Internationale," were invited to communicate with an obscure individual at Ashford Junction. The proposal met with no interference from the authorities. Accordingly, on Saturday, June 19, 1920, the first British Communist Party was formed at a meeting which took place at the International Socialist Club, 28 East Road, City Road, London. This Club was a resuscitation of the old Communist Club in Charlotte Street, Soho, which had been closed at the end of 1919, and the leading spirit was described as a " Jewess of Russian extraction " whose name was not given in the press (*Evening News* for January 12, 1920).

At the Conference in question the delegates were drawn from various small Communist societies, including Sylvia Pankhurst's own Party, the Workers' Socialist Federation. The Conference then drew up the following declaration:

" We, revolutionary and Communist delegates and individuals, pledge ourselves to the Third International, the dictatorship of the proletariat, the Soviet System, non-affiliation to the Labour Party and to abstention from Parliamentary action; and decide not to take part in the August 1st unity conference or in the unity negotiations concerned with it."

The C.P.G.B.—In abjuring parliamentary action this first Communist Party had, however, failed to carry out Lenin's policy of " boring from within." Lenin, therefore, now gave his support to the other group calling itself "The Joint Provisional Committee for the Communist Party of Great Britain," led by A. MacManus, which had convoked the conference in question with a view to forming a United British Communist Party. In a letter dated July 10, 1920, Lenin wrote as follows:

" I have received the letter of the Joint Provisional Committee for the Communist Party of Britain dated June 20, and hasten to answer in reply to their request, that I entirely sympathise with the plan they have developed for the immediate organisation of a single Communist Party in England. I consider that the tactics of Comrade Sylvia Pankhurst and of the Workers' Socialist Federation are mistaken because of their refusal to join in a unification of the British Socialist Party, the Socialist Labour Party, and other organisations into one Communist Party. In particular I am personally in favour of participation in parliament and also in favour of adherence to the labor party under the condition of reserving complete freedom and independent communist action ; and I shall defend these tactics at the Second Congress of the Third International on July 15th in Moscow. I consider as most desirable the immediate organisation of one Communist Party on the basis of all these decisions of the Third International and also the bringing of that party into the closest touch with the Industrial Workers of the World and the shop stewards committee, in order to unite completely with them in the nearest future " (*Lusk Report*, II. 1605, and *Morning Post*, August 2, 1920).

The result of these instructions was the foundation of the present Communist Party of Great Britain on August 1, 1920, at a Conference held in the Cannon Street Hotel, London. About 150 delegates were present, mainly from the British Socialist Party and the Socialist Labour Party of Glasgow, others represented smaller Left Wing Socialist groups. Arthur MacManus (S.L.P.) presided and was elected chairman of the Executive Committee now formed, consisting of the following : W. Paul, Tom Bell, A. A. Watts, F. Willis, J. F. Hodgson, W. Hewlett, Fred Shaw, R. Stewart, Mrs. Dora B. Montefiore, Col. L'Estrange Malone, G. Deer, and William Mellor. A. A. Purcell, who had just returned from Russia, and Robert Williams were amongst the delegates who spoke. The general secretary of the B.S.P., Albert Inkpin, became the secretary of the C.P.G.B. (*Times* and *Daily Herald* of August 2, 1920).

Although a section of the S.L.P. now entered the C.P.G.B., the S.L.P. has continued up to the present time as a separate body, with its organ *The Socialist*. Much the same thing took place in the I.L.P., which contained a considerable Communist element. The close relations maintained between this section of the Party and the 3rd Internationale were shown in the *Report of the Second Congress of the Communist Internationale,* published in Petrograd in 1921, where an article appeared signed, " In the name of the Left Wing of the I.L.P. : Helen Crawfurd, secretary." The writer here describes the efforts of the Left Wing to swing the I.L.P. over to Communism, particularly in the North of England, Scotland and Wales—Merthyr Tydvil being indicated as the centre of the movement—and ends with the assurance that should these efforts prove unsuccessful, at any rate a section of the Party will join up with the Communists. Mrs. Crawfurd is now a member of the C.P.G.B., as are also certain other members of the I.L.P., whilst on the other hand some of the most violent Communists have remained in the I.L.P., and have not joined up with the Communist Party.

The B.S.P. became merged with the C.P.G.B. at the time of the latter's formation, and ceased to exist altogether, whilst its organ *The Call* was replaced by the organ of the new Party, *The Communist*.

Second S.D.F.—At the same time the National Socialist Party, led by Hyndman, which had formed the Right Wing of the British Socialist Party when the Left Wing split off from it in 1916, resumed the old name of the Social Democratic Federation, which it bears to-day. *Justice* continued to be its organ until 1925, when it was changed from a weekly to a monthly, with the new name *The Social Democrat*. Since the death of H. M. Hyndman in 1921 the S.D.F. has had no leader of outstanding personality. Its Executive Committee now includes the following :

Tom Kennedy, M.P. (General Secretary), H. W. Lee, Will Thorne, M.P., Jack Jones, M.P., F. Montague, M.P., W. G. Cluse, M.P. The late Dan Irving was also a member.

The offices of the S.D.F. have just been moved to the Hyndman Club and Institute, 54 Colebroke Row, Islington.

The S.D.F. has always continued to advocate Marxian Socialism as interpreted by Hyndman in the past, but it has consistently opposed Bolshevism as a violation of social democratic principles, and denounced the form of Pacifism which tends to the advantage of Germany. The late Adolphe Smith was one of its most enlightened and patriotic members, who remained to the end of his life a true friend of France and enemy of German militarism.

By the end of 1920 the Communist movement in Great Britain had passed entirely out of the hands of Sylvia Pankhurst into those of the C.P.G.B. This was owing, not only to Lenin's displeasure, but to Sylvia's arrest in October of that year by the Government of this country on the charge of publishing matter calculated to cause disaffection in the Army and Navy. At the trial she was found not only to be working directly with Lenin, Zinoviev and an East-End Jew named Rosenberg, who occupied a high position in the Foreign Office at Moscow, but also to be in touch with Louis Fraina, international secretary of the Communist Party of America, through a Russian-Jew, Jacob Nosowitsky, who acted as courier between the United States and this country, where, according to his own account given recently in the Hearst Press (*Chicago Herald*, October 11, 1925), he was also in the employment of Scotland Yard. Letters were produced addressed by Sylvia Pankhurst to Lenin and Zinoviev showing how the distress of the unemployed was being exploited by the revolutionaries and complaining of the failure of the Communist Party to " rise to the occasion." One passage ran : " The Communist Parties are not large enough or intelligent enough to make capital out of the situation. We are talking of a Communist Council of action. Colonel Malone, with whom I have just been speaking and who is a member of the Executive of the Communist Party, tells me his Executive does not wish to join with us or other parties, but to absorb us " (*Morning Post*, November 3, 1920.)

This rivalry led up finally to the excommunication of Comrade Sylvia Pankhurst by the C.P.G.B. after her release from prison, and the demand by this body that the *Workers' Dreadnought* should be handed over to them. This was not acceded to, and Sylvia retained possession of her organ. The liberty of speech enjoyed under Communism was thus described by Sylvia Pankhurst in this organ:

" Dressed in a little brief authority this Executive, which, meeting only fortnightly, is necessarily controlled by the paid officials who are always on the spot, was full of zeal to serve the Communist Party by controlling me. . . . The Comrades intended to enforce discipline in its most stultifying aspect. Comrade MacManus, as Chairman, informed me that they would not permit any member of the party to write or publish a book or pamphlet without the sanction of the Executive. Those who may differ from the Executive on any point of principle, policy or tactics, or even those whose method of dealing with agreed theory is not approved or appreciated by the Executive, are therefore to be gagged." (*Morning Post*, Sept. 19, 1921.)

Workers' Communist Movement.—Repudiated both by Lenin and the C.P.G.B., Sylvia Pankhurst now joined the 4th Internationale, started in this year, 1921, in Berlin under A. Bogdanov and claiming to be more advanced than Moscow. At the same time she continued to run her group, which in 1923 changed its name to the Workers' Communist Movement affiliated to the 4th Internationale (see account of this in *Daily Telegraph*, April 28, 1923).

Unemployed Workers' Organisation.—At about the same date she formed the " Unemployed Workers' Organisation," in which she was associated with a Miss Nora Smythe.

A.P.C.F.—These organisations have now ceased to exist and Sylvia Pankhurst has retired from the political arena, but another body, somewhat akin to hers, is still a going concern, namely, the Anti-Parliamentary Communist Federation, formed by Guy Aldred in 1921. This was the outcome of the Glasgow Anarchist Group, described in an earlier chapter of this book, which had taken over its present premises at 13 Burnbank Gardens, Glasgow, in May 1917. In May 1920 it resumed its old name of the Glasgow Communist Group, founded Bakunin House, and then, in 1921, became the A.P.C.F. divided into Federated Groups.

In view of this use of the name of Bakunin, who, at the Conference at Berne in 1869, had declared that he " abominated Communism," it is difficult to understand why Guy Aldred and his followers should call themselves Communists and not Anarchists. This may be attributed to expediency—owing to the present boom in Communism and slump in Anarchism—or perhaps to a wish to disassociate themselves from the Kropotkine Anarchists of the Freedom Group, consisting of George Barrett, Sir Walter Strickland (a Cambridge don), Will J. Owen, John Wakeman and Dr. M. Zalkind, editor of the London Yiddish paper *Der Arbeiter Freind*. For some inexplicable reason the A.P.C.F. has never been able to agree with this group.

The Communist Federation (A.P.C.F.), whilst insignificant in comparison with the Communist Party (C.P.G.B.), continues to attract a certain amount of attention—mainly amongst undesirable aliens—owing to Guy Aldred's powers of soap-box oratory.

It should be noted that although the Communist Federation supports the seditious activities of the Communist Party, the two bodies are violently opposed, indeed the *Commune*, the official paper of the former, styling itself until lately " the organ of his Majesty's Communist Opposition," and now " an Organ of the Coming Social Revolution," declares it to be the duty of every true Communist to disassociate himself from the Communist Party. This hostility apparently arises from the fact that the Communist Federation is anti-parliamentarian and disapproves of the C.P.G.B. for taking part in politics, and also for its subservience to the Bolsheviks of Russia. A number of useful truths are frequently to be found in the *Commune*, this for example in the issue of November 1925 :

" It is an admitted fact that the activities of the Communist Party are not the result of a spontaneous proletarian movement in this country, but the dictation of a select committee possessing financial power in Moscow."

And the writer (Guy Aldred himself) goes on to ask how the Communists recently arrested can complain of their treatment, whilst remaining the " bribed and hired upholders " of the Bolshevik regime, with its Red Army and Code of Criminal Laws. " How can that be wrong in London which is right in Moscow ? "

The Communist Federation has therefore never allied itself with the 3rd Internationale, and since 1920 has appeared to oppose it. In the words of Guy Aldred, it " objects to a few high priests in Moscow, mostly hypocrites, dictating to hirelings here." At the same time, the Commune has violently denounced the Anarchist Jewess, Emma Goldman, for her unfavourable report on Russia.

"Emma Goldman continues in her rôle of revolutionary scab. Her London admirers consist of Zionists who have no taste for Palestine and Jewish master tailors who prefer sweating in London to working in Moscow or Leningrad " (April 1925).

The Communist Federation is in reality a purely destructive association, to which it would be absurd to attribute any consistent policy. Guy Aldred's oratory consists mainly in a series of diatribes against the British Empire and all forms of religion. Hatred of Christianity is its most distinguishing feature.

The Hyde Park Socialist Club.—Connected with the Communist Federation is the "Hyde Park Socialist Club," established in September 1925, an association which holds meetings and gives entertainments.

Such are the Communist parties at present in this country. Of the three existing in 1923—the C.P.G.B., the A.P.C.F. and the C.W.P.—only the first two remain, and of these the C.P.G.B., being the body specially chosen and financed to carry out the dictates of Moscow, is by far the more important. Before describing its further activities it will be necessary in the next two chapters to study the development of the Trade Union movement from 1921 onwards.

Bolshevism in Ireland

It is difficult here to follow the course of Bolshevism in Ireland, owing to its connection with both secret and national movements, which do not enter into the scope of this book. Thus Sinn Fein, which in 1903 took over the work of the old Irish Nationalist movement, whilst forming an open revolutionary movement, cannot be classed as a part of the Socialist organisation, although no doubt it maintained relations with the great secret society of Ireland, the "Irish Republican Brotherhood," which in its turn co-operated with the agents of world revolution in America.

Communist Party of Ireland.—The Communist Party of Ireland, into which the former Socialist Party was transformed in 1919 after the creation of the 3rd Internationale, was a small and not very important organisation numbering only about 1,000 people. The national chairman was Roderick Conolly, son of James Conolly, founder of the Irish Socialist Republican Party, which had preceded the Socialist Party of Ireland, and the chairman of the Dublin branch, Liam O'Flaherty. Jim Larkin, after his release from imprisonment in the United States, brought into it fresh inspiration from the inner circles of the Moscow and American organisations, in both of which he played an important rôle.

The organ of the C.P.I. was *The Workers' Republic.*

Irish Workers' League—Irish Workers' Union.—In 1923 the Communist Party came to an end and the Irish Workers' League was formed by James and Peter Larkin. This in 1924 became the Irish Workers' Union.

Irish Transport Workers' Union.—Meanwhile the Irish Transport Workers' Union, under James Larkin and Conolly, took a leading part in the "red" movement.

Irish Communist Brotherhood.—The real force of the International Socialist movement, as opposed to the National Catholic movement, was supplied not so much by Russia as by the Communist Party of America, which maintained close relations with the Irish

Republican Brotherhood and the still more secret Irish Communist Brotherhood, founded in 1920 and controlled by a Supreme Council of Six. The members of these two Brotherhoods were in constant communication with both Germany and America, particularly the latter, where the Clan-na-Gael served as a cover to the I.R.B., whilst the American Association for the Recognition of the Irish Republic formed the open organisation of the Clan-na-Gael. All this being a matter of secret circles, of which the members' names cannot be given as in the case of the open organisations dealt with here, we would refer readers interested in the subject to the series of articles entitled " The Realities of Revolution," which appeared in the *Patriot* from March 15 to June 14, 1923, where the amazing plot is at least partially revealed.

CHAPTER VIII
THE CAPTURE OF TRADE UNIONISM

It will have been noticed by every attentive student of the world revolutionary movement that during 1921 and 1922 a lull occurred and for a time it seemed as if Bolshevism might be a spent force.

Communism, in the form of State Socialism administered by an autocratic bureaucracy as in Moscow, had failed to attract the working-men. Lenin's instructions concerning the "higher discipline of the toilers," the institution of " a merciless dictatorship," "the absolute submission of the masses to the single will of those who direct the labour process " (*The Soviets at Work*, pp. 25, 35, 40. English translation, published by the Socialist Information and Research Bureau) were hardly calculated to inspire enthusiasm. The slogans that have a meaning for the " revolutionary proletariat " are those that convey a concrete idea, such as physical force, material gain or destruction, which Syndicalism and its parent Anarchy have always known how to frame. " The Mines for the Miners " was naturally a more alluring cry than "the Mines for the State." Schemes of nationalisation when clearly expounded left the great majority of the workers cold.

The great triumph of the Bolsheviks lay, then, in their success in capturing the revolutionary portion of the Trade Union movement by persuading it that Syndicalism was not incompatible with Communism. Lenin's initial error had been to deny this compatibility; quite frankly he had declared that the workers could not run industry and that it was no part of the Bolshevik scheme to allow them to attempt it (see, for example, *The Chief Task of our Times*, by Lenin, p. 12.)

The I.W.W.—Zinoviev calculated more shrewdly; he knew that the only hope for Bolshevism lay in winning over the Syndicalists. His famous letter to the I.W.W. of America in January 1920 was a triumph of sophistry, and must be quoted at some length in order to show the tactics adopted by the Bolsheviks for enlisting Revolutionary Trade Unionism in their support.

Up to 1919 the Trade Union movement had shown officially little sympathy with Bolshevism. The International Federation of Trade Unions, or " Amsterdam Internationale," had for its president the wise Trade Union leader W. A. Appleton, and had not as yet developed a Left Wing.

The British Trades Union Congress had appeared to concern

itself mainly with industrial questions, and it was not until 1919 that it entered into a scheme for co-ordination with the Labour Party. A National Joint Council was finally arranged in 1921.

The Confédération Générale du Travail of France was still largely controlled by the Reformist section. In America even the revolutionary I.W.W. had held aloof from Bolshevism. Its official organ, the *One Big Union Monthly*, had asked : " Why should we follow Bolshevism ? " adding that all the Bolshevik Revolution had done was " to give the Russian people the vote."

It was in answer to this that Zinoviev, as President of the I.K.K.I., wrote his appeal. Replying to the objection here quoted, he observed :

" This is, of course, untrue. The Bolshevik Revolution has taken the factories, mills, mines, land and financial institutions out of the hands of the capitalists and transferred them to the WHOLE WORKING CLASS."

But he went on to explain that :

" The private property of the capitalist class, in order to become the SOCIAL property of the workers, cannot be turned over to individuals or groups of individuals. It must become the property of all in common, and a centralised authority is necessary to accomplish this change. The industries, too, which supply the needs of all the people, are not the concern only of the workers in each industry, but of ALL IN COMMON, and must be administered for the benefit of all."

This was of course a direct repudiation of Syndicalist theory, which advocates the control of each industry by the workers engaged therein. Moreover, what was the " centralised authority " referred to but the State which Syndicalists set out to destroy ?

Zinoviev clearly recognised these differences of opinion, and set out to explain them away one by one.

Firstly. The question of the State.

" 'Many members of the I.W.W.' . . are against 'the State in general.' They propose to overthrow the capitalist State and to establish in its place immediately the Industrial Commonwealth. . . . We, Communists, also want to abolish the State. The State can only exist so long as there is class struggle. The function of the Proletarian dictatorship is to abolish the capitalist class as a class ; in fact, to do away with all class divisions of every kind. And when this condition is reached then the PROLETARIAN DICTATORSHIP, THE STATE, AUTOMATICALLY DISAPPEARS—to make way for an industrial administrative body which will be something like the General Executive Board of the I.W.W."

We note, however, that to-day, seven years after these words were written, the State shows no signs of disappearing in Russia, but on the contrary is stronger than ever, as shown by the recent publication of its criminal code.

Secondly. Zinoviev examines the weapon of Syndicalism—the General Strike. After remarking that the Communists and the I.W.W. are in accord with regard to the necessity of attacking the Capitalist State by DIRECT ACTION he says :

" The I.W.W. proposes to attain this end by the General Strike. The Communists go further. History indicates clearly that the General Strike is not enough. The capitalists have arms. . . . Moreover, the capitalists possess stores of food, which enable them to hold out longer than the workers, always on the verge of actual want. The Communists also advocate the General Strike, but they add that it must turn into ARMED INSURRECTION. Both the General Strike and the insurrection are forms of POLITICAL ACTION."

Thirdly. Zinoviev discusses the question of parliamentarianism. " Many members of the I.W.W. are bitterly opposed to making ANY use of legislations and other Government institutions for purposes of propaganda." But he goes on to show the utility of political campaigns as providing " an opportunity for revolutionists to speak to the working-class . . . to show the futility of reforms . . . and to point out why the entire capitalist system must be overthrown."

Having thus disposed to his own satisfaction of all the differences dividing the I.W.W. from the Bolsheviks, Zinoviev concludes by appealing to it and also to the W.I.I.U. (Workers' International Industrial Union), the insurgent Unions in the A.F. of L., and the One Big Union group, to come to an agreement with the American Communists for " common revolutionary action." The letter ends with the words : " The Communist International holds out to the I.W.W. the hand of brotherhood."

The hand was grasped—by a section of the organisation. The March issue of its organ, the *One Big Union Monthly*, published an article in which the following passage appeared :

" The I.W.W. contains the identical potentialities of the Soviet. . . . The real clash of power in this country is between the I.W.W. and the A.F. of L. . . . The I.W.W. is the American Soviet."

Precisely a year before Zinoviev's letter was written, the invitation to the 1st Congress of the 3rd Internationale in March had been sent out from Moscow, and the I.W.W.s of America, Great Britain and Australia were requested to send representatives. In June the weekly organ of the I.W.W., *New Solidarity*, announced :

" The I.W.W. has recognised the Communist International by deciding to send a representative to their congress. Now Left Wingers, are you true in your preachings ? Are you Bolshevik ? . . . Do you believe in uniting all the energies of the class-conscious proletariat ? If you do there is but one course of action left. That is to join the I.W.W.

The I.W.W. in America has stood for the same principles that the Bolsheviks have—the class struggle, no compromise, the proletarian dictatorship and the final act of overthrowing capitalism. Are you consistent ? Prove it."

But the I.W.W. sympathisers with the Bolshevik regime had spoken without the assent of all their comrades. The I.W.W. as a whole declined to ally itself either with the Komintern or with the Communist Party of America, although certain leaders of factions, such as the old Syndicalist William D. Haywood, went over to the Communists. From 1919 to 1923 persistent efforts were made by the 3rd Internationale to bring the I.W.W. into line ; these efforts only met with partial success (*Congressional Record*, " Recognition of Russia," Part II, p. 422. 1924).

As a result of this refractory attitude, the Communists of America set out to undermine the I.W.W. by capturing the Trade Union movement through other bodies working in co-operation with Moscow. In this campaign a prominent part was played by William Z. Foster, I.W.W., and leader of the Left Wing of the A.F. of L., who in that organisation met with persistent opposition from the leader of the Right Wing, Samuel Gompers, a strong opponent of the Bolshevik regime.

The T.U.E.L.—Unable to swing the A.F. of L. sufficiently to the Left, William Z. Foster in April 1920 founded a new group called the Trade Union Educational League, with the object of carrying out in industrial circles the same propaganda that the Workers' Party of America was carrying out in the field of politics (*Reds in America*, p. 13). That the T.U.E.L. was actually a branch of the Communist Party was shown in a report that came to light in the Bridgman raid of 1922 (*Ibid.*, p. 131).

But, as will be shown in the following chapter, a new power had now arisen, which was to form the rallying centre for revolutionary Trade Unionism, under the banner of Moscow, and relegate the I.W.W. to the background.

Meanwhile, in England intensive propaganda was being carried on in the trade unions by the agents of Moscow, and gradually the dynamic force of the social revolution was passing from the hands of the theoretical Socialists into those of the organisers and financiers of industrial troubles. The skilful manner in which these ventriloquists projected their voices through the mouth of " Labour " was shown by Bernard Shaw of the Labour Research Department after the railway strike that took place in October 1919. On the principle of " If you don't want to be believed speak the truth," Shaw said at a Labour meeting on December 2 :

" The Labour Research Department became the Publicity Department of the railway strike, and I knew pretty well how the thing had to be carried on. Put your memory back a little. The railway strike took place on a Friday. On the Saturday the whole country was cursing the railwaymen. Your trains were all stopped. You were all convinced by your newspapers that here were the railwaymen, who had made a combination practically to extort enormous wages from the community at the expense of the general community. We set to work, and by the following Wednesday the country had become convinced that the Government had been engaged in a deliberate attempt to reduce the wages of the railwaymen." (*Morning Post,* Dec. 3,. 1919.)

Bernard Shaw's real sentiments with regard to strikes were thus callously set forth later on in the *Labour Monthly* for October 1921 :

" A Socialist State would not tolerate such an attack on the community as a strike for a moment. If a Trade Union attempted such a thing, the old capitalist law against Trade Unions as conspiracies would be re-enacted within twenty-four hours and put ruthlessly into execution. Such a monstrosity as the recent coal strike, during which the coal-miners spent all their savings in damaging their neighbours and wrecking the national industries, would be impossible under Socialism. It was miserably defeated, as it deserved to be."

The Co-operative Societies.—The railway strike of 1919 demonstrated the manner in which the advocates of the General Strike had now perfected their system. The old difficulty of how the strikers were to live during a national hold-up was believed to have been got over by a plan of joint action arranged between the Trades Union Congress Parliamentary Committee and the Central Board of the Co-operative Union. The way in which the community was to be starved out whilst the strikers thrived was thus implied by Fred Bramley, assistant secretary of the aforesaid T.U.C. Parliamentary Committee :

"We . . . set out to secure that if the railway dispute was extended (if it developed into a general strike) we should avoid, if possible, the withdrawal of men from co-operative employment in order that the co-operative movement could be used as a food-distributing agency on behalf of the workers.

"IN OTHER WORDS, WE WERE NOT GOING TO CUT OFF OUR OWN SUPPLIES." (*Evening Standard,* Oct. 17, 1919.)

Thus the co-operative societies, the sanest and most progressive movement that " Labour " had produced in this country, had now become an important part of the revolutionary machine. No wonder that Lenin, desiring above all the downfall of Great Britain, boasted that 1920 would realise his hopes.

Council of Action.—On August 9 of that year the Executive of the Labour Party, the Parliamentary Committee of the T.U.C. and the Parliamentary Labour Party met in an emergency conference at the House of Commons on the pretext that the Government was contemplating taking up arms against Soviet Russia for the defence of Poland. It was then decided to form a " Council of

Action" for the purpose of organising the workers to "down tools" in such an eventuality. This Council was formed of members of the three bodies participating, as follows :

P.L.P. :
W. Adamson, M.P. (elected Chairman)
J. R. Clynes, M.P.
Harry Gosling
A. Swales
Colonel Wedgwood, M.P., T.U.C.

A. A. Purcell
R. B. Walker
Margaret Bondfield

Executive of L.P. :
A. G. Cameron
C. T. Cramp
Frank Hodges

Robert Williams
J. Bromley

Local Councils of Action were set up all over the country.

As in 1848 in France Poland, then the martyr country of the revolutionary Socialists but now the object of their anathemas, served merely as a pretext for rallying the forces of revolution, and it was obvious that " the machinery thus erected would be available for a general strike, with other objects in view " (*Morning Post*, September 21, 1920). As shown by a document published in this issue of the *Morning Post*, an essential point in the programme was again : " The capture by Labour of the local Co-operative Society so as to ensure the distribution of food to the strikers and their families." To this plan of campaign the so-called moderate Labour leaders on the Council lent their support.

What was not generally known at the time was that the real inspirer of the Council of Action was Kamenev, alias Rosenfeld, who had come over to London with Krassin in the Trade Delegation in the spring of 1920. Such was one of the first acts of a delegate from what the British Government chose to regard as a friendly power. At a Congress of Bolshevist Directors of Propaganda in Foreign Countries, held at Bremen in December of the same year, it was stated that the expenses incurred by the Trade Delegation to London (Kamenev and Krassin) in the organisation of centres of agitation in Great Britain amounted to £23,750 per month (*Times*, February 1, 1921).

The Triple Alliance.—Constitutional trade union leaders had, however, become aware of the danger of permeation by Bolshevism. In 1920 W. A. Appleton had resigned his presidency of the Amsterdam Internationale (I.F.T.U.) because it was becoming too revolutionary, and his place had been taken by J. H. Thomas. The Triple Alliance—that is to say, the leaders of miners, railwaymen and transport workers—then arranged for the General Strike to take place on April 15, 1921. The defeat of this plan was a terrible set-back for the revolutionary movement. England having been the main objective of the world revolutionaries from Marx to Lenin, the failure to reduce her to chaos meant, momentarily at least, the failure of world revolution. For this failure there were several causes. The Prime Minister (Lloyd George), who had not yet discovered the nationalisation of the land to be the solution of all our troubles, uttered a warning to the nation on the "Great Peril," the rise of a party to power which "calls itself Labour, but is really Socialist," which wants "to plant the wild and poisonous berries of Karl Marxism in this country." There were some people who thought Socialism was "merely a bogey," but he knew it was "a terrible machine" that would "tear society to pieces" (*Morning Post*, March 24, 1921). At the same time he mobilised his forces precisely as the present Government did in May 1926. A further obstacle was provided by the railwaymen, who, it was found at the last moment, were unwilling to come out.

The result of the railwaymen's attitude was the decision to call off the strike on what is known in revolutionary circles as "black Friday" (April 15), and so to defeat the alien plot against England. It is impossible to attribute this to the restraining influence on the part of the trade union leaders. At the most critical moment of the crisis, on April 11, a Manifesto was published by the Triple Alliance calculated to inflame passions to the highest degree. The Government was accused of standing in with the mineowners in an attack on "Labour," and of having adopted provocative measures by organising a defence force in view of the anarchy to which, as the railwaymen clearly saw, the strike would inevitably lead :

"The present government," said this manifesto, "is not an impartial arbitrator in industrial negotiations, but an active, if secret partisan, and while it speaks of peace it behaves in a manner calculated to encourage war. . . . In addition to calling up the Reserves, it has adopted the new and odious expedient of forming a volunteer force as an instrument to be used against organised labour. In so doing it has lightly assumed the grave responsibility of provoking bloodshed and civil war.

"Therefore, in view of . . . the obvious, calculated and persistent hostility of the Government to the working classes, the Triple Alliance has decided to throw its full weight on the side of the miners."

This document bore the names of Herbert Smith and Frank Hodges on behalf of the Miners' Federation, of J. H. Thomas, C. T. Cramp and W. T. Abraham on behalf of the N.U.R., and of R. Gosling and Robert Williams on behalf of the Transport Workers' Federation. (*Evening Standard*, April 12, 1921).

The I.F.T.U.—A fortnight later, after the collapse of the strike, the Amsterdam Internationale (I.F.T.U.) published a further call to class warfare in celebration of May 1, which since 1889 has been known as "Labour Day."

"This year," declared the Amsterdam Manifesto, "the demonstration of Labour must be mightier than ever. Reaction has raised up its head more audaciously in all countries ; ever greater is the resistance of the bourgeoisie to the just demands of the workers ; ever rigorous are the persecutions to which class-conscious organised workers are subjected by Governments. . . . We need only recall the horrors perpetrated against our fellow-workers in Hungary, Finland, Spain, etc. . . . We need only point out the recalcitrance of leaders of the League of Nations in dealing effectively with the economic restoration of Europe by solution of the problem of exchange or by improvement in the distribution of raw material. What care these gentlemen if their negligence will contribute everywhere to an increase of unemployment, and, consequently, of destitution among the working-classes."

This was signed by :

    J. H. Thomas, Acting President.
    L. Jouhaux, 1st Vice-President.
    C. Mertens, 2nd Vice-President.
    Edo Fimmen } Secretaries.
    J. Oudegeest }

One might have supposed from this that the I.F.T.U. had gone red enough to satisfy even the most thorough-going of revolutionaries, but it will be noticed their particular degree of redness has never been the criterion by which the Bolsheviks of Russia have judged groups or individuals. This is why the term "Extremist," applied to their supporters in this country, is entirely misleading. One may go to the most extreme limit of revolutionary violence without satisfying the present rulers of Russia—as was shown by their abandonment of Sylvia Pankhurst. The real desideratum is absolute subservience to the dictatorship of Moscow. This was the rock on which the Amsterdammers and the Muscovites split : the former, whilst comprising a number of extreme revolutionaries, were not, as a whole, prepared to renounce all independence of action ; further, they committed the unpardonable sin of demanding that Germany should be made responsible for the damage she had done during the war in the devastated regions of France and Belgium. Consequently it was decided to destroy Amsterdam and set up an opposition Trade Union Internationale.

Of course, Trade Unionism in Russia could only be a farce, since, as Robespierre perceived, under the dictatorship of the proletariat corporations of workers could not logically exist. As Trotsky himself stated : " In all Communist States officials are appointed by the State, and trade unions must only defend the interests of the workers by helping to raise production, and not by various exaggerated demands and threats of strikes" (*Pravda*, December 1920).

Hence in Soviet Russia the trade unions, all of quite recent birth, are not trade unions in our sense of the word at all, but simply regiments of workers controlled by leaders who are at the same time members of the Government. This was shown very clearly in the chart published by the United States Congress in 1924, when the same names were found in the list of trade union leaders and the Central Executive of the Government of Russia.

In order to bring the workers under the heel of Moscow it was necessary, however, to set up a pretence of trade union organisation in Russia. Accordingly, the " All Russian Congress of Trade Unions " was formed in 1918 ; from this arose the " All Russian Central Council of Trade Unions " under Tomski (alias Joseph Isbitsky). At a conference of the Central Executive of the Russian trade unions held in Moscow on June 15, 1920, at which Robert Williams and A. A. Purcell were present, the plan of uniting all the left elements in the trade unions outside Russia was discussed, and these parleys continued until July 15, when an agreement was reached between the Russian trade unions, the Italian Federation of Labour, the Spanish, Jugo-Slav and Bulgarian trade unions to fight the Amsterdam Internationale, and set up a new Trade Union International in its place. The propaganda centre thus created was given the name of " The International Council of Trade and Industrial Unions."

This was the embryo of the R.I.L.U. or " Red Internationale of Labour Unions," known also as the " Profintern "—from the Russian words Professionalye Internazional—which held its first Congress from July 3-19 in the following year, 1921. This time England was represented by Tom Mann, Nat Watkins, J. T. Murphy and Ellen Wilkinson, and the following International Executive Committee was formed :

Gen. Sec. : A. Losovsky (*alias* Solomon Dridzo).
England : Tom Mann.
Germany : Anton Mayer.
Russia : Nogin.
Spain : Orlandez.
United States : George Andreychine.

In the subsidiary propaganda organisations of the R.I.L.U., the English representatives included J. T. Murphy (Metal Workers), Nat Watkins (Miners) and Ellen Wilkinson (Workers' Union) (Krassnee Internazional Profsoyusov, *Bulletin Ispolneetelnovo Buro*, No. I).

The foundation of the Red Internationale of Labour Unions was a triumph of Bolshevik strategy. What the Komintern with its bureaucratic Communist propaganda had been unable to accomplish the R.I.L.U. was to succeed in carrying out by appealing to the corporative spirit of the workers. It was probably this stroke of diplomacy that turned the whole course of events, that averted the collapse of Bolshevism in 1921 and brought about the recrudescence of the revolutionary movement which has led to the crisis of to-day.

Just as the 3rd or Communist Internationale was intended to defeat the 2nd or Socialist Internationale of Brussels in the political field, the R.I.L.U. was instituted to defeat the I.F.T.U. or Amsterdam Internationale in the industrial field. From this moment the word "Yellow" applied to the 2nd (Socialist) Internationale was always applied to the Amsterdam Trade Union Internationale, whilst the word "Red" was officially assumed by the Moscow Trade Union Internationale, of which the propaganda consisted largely of imprecations against the hated "Amsterdammers."

The R.I.L.U. was from the beginning avowedly "Anarcho-Syndicalist." In the resolutions of its 2nd Congress it is stated that : " The Congress approves of the attempts of the Executive Bureau to draw all the anarcho-syndicalist organisations into the R.I.L.U. for the joint struggle against the bourgeoisie and against reformism." The adherents of the R.I.L.U. in England, America, Holland and France were specially charged with the task of rallying the workers to the banner of the new Red Internationale. One of the first bodies to join up with it was the Anarcho-Syndicalist wing of the French C.G.T. (Confédération Générale du Travail), which on February 16, 1922, constituted itself as the C.G.T.U. (Confédération Générale du Travail Unitaire) and soon after decided to affiliate with the R.I.L.U. The leader of this party was Dondicol.

In the United States the T.U.E.L. (Trade Union Educational League), founded by William Z. Foster, was specially indicated as the body to be entrusted with the work of the R.I.L.U., whilst a Council was recommended for co-ordinating the work of the minorities in the A.F. of L., the I.W.W. and the independent unions. The most active of the latter were :

(1) The Amalgamated Clothing Workers' Union, a split from the "United Garment Workers of America," dated from 1914, and working particularly for the idea of the "One Big Union." The President was Joseph Hillman and the leading members were :

Joseph Schlossberg	August Bellanca
Hyman Lumberg	Alex Kohen
Samuel Levin	Lazarus Mariovitz
A. D. Marimmpetri	Frank Rosenblum

(2) The International Ladies' Garment Workers' Union, started in connection with the Rand School in 1914 ; the President was Benjamin Schlesinger, Fania M. Cohn Vice-President, and the official organ *Justice*, with S. Wyonopsky as editor and E. Liebermann as business manager. This was affiliated with the "Workers' Defence Union," of which Benjamin Schlesinger was also the President and Elizabeth Gurley Flynn the principal leader.

(3) The "Amalgamated Textile Workers," started in 1919 with A. J. Muste as General Secretary.

In a report discovered at the Bridgman raid of 1922 it was stated :

"At best the prospects of our influencing the labour movement are mainly in the predominantly Jewish organisations like the Inter-

THE CAPTURE OF TRADE UNIONISM 83

national Ladies' Garment Workers, Amalgamated Clothing Workers, Hat, Cap and Millinery Workers, etc. Our activities in the I.W.W. have led to their liquidation in a number of Eastern cities."

The R.I.L.U. now formed the rallying point for all these revolutionary groups, and found in William Z. Foster its most valuable agent. At the Bridgman Convention he pointed out that the failure of the Socialist Party had been not to understand the importance of industrial work :

"The Communist Party is not going to make the same mistake. This laying so much stress on the importance of the trade union work is one of the most helpful features of the movement. When we lay stress on the importance of this work, we realise that we must capture the trade unions if we want to get anywhere. Different Communists differ as to the importance of capturing the unions in the revolutionary struggle. Some say that the trade union does not amount to anything ; that it is just a neutral organisation and will never become a revolutionary unit. Others say that it is one of the really revolutionary instruments of the workers and will function as such in the revolutionary struggle. Syndicalists take the position that trade union work is the only thing. Although we may differ as to the positive value of the trade union work, we must agree with the negative, namely, that it is absolutely impossible to have a revolution in the country unless we will control the mass trade unions. This fact alone should justify the policy that the Communist Party of the United States is working out. If we wish a revolution, we must have their support. After our delegation came back from Moscow last year, it brought with us a program which we thought was a good practical program for this country, and we want to tell you this—a lot of people say that those in Moscow do not understand the situation. I want to dispute that. I found in the Red Trades Union International and in the Communist International and generally in Moscow, a keen understanding of the fundamentals of our situation in this country. I can say that I found a better understanding of the general fundamental situation in America than we can boast of here. It was a peculiar thing to find men like Radek and Lenin telling American revolutionary organisations that their industrial policy was wrong" (*The Reds in America*, p. 29).

So were "free-born Americans" to be taught to manage their own affairs by middle-class doctrinaires in the East of Europe with no history of trade union organisation behind them.

CHAPTER IX

THE BOLSHEVISATION OF BRITISH TRADE UNIONISM

British Bureau of R.I.L.U.—In England the R.I.L.U. of Moscow found allies ready to hand. In December 1920 J. T. Murphy came back from Russia with plans for the organisation of the movement, and in this same month the " British Bureau " of the " Provisional International Council of Trade and Industrial Unions " was established in Manchester, with George Peet (of Manchester) corresponding secretary and E. Lismer (of Sheffield) as organising secretary.

An inaugural meeting was held on January 23, 1921, with the following as members of the Bureau :

Chairman : Tom Mann, A.E.U., formerly Gen. Secretary I.L.P. and leader of the Industrial Syndicalist League, " Hands Off Russia " Committee.
J. T. Murphy, A.E.U., formerly on Executive Committee S.L.P., C.P.G.B., British representative on I.K.K.I.
Robert Williams, Secretary National Transport Workers' Federation, I.L.P., " Hands Off Russia " Committee, director of *Daily Herald*, Council of Action (1920).
A. A. Purcell, N.A.F.T.A., C.P.G.B., now M.P.
Emile Burns, N.U.C.
G. Kay.
V. Williams, Yorkshire Miners' Association.
T. Bell, Scottish Iron Moulders.

Amongst those who later joined the movement were :

Mrs. M. Bamber, National Union of Distributive and Allied Workers.
Ellen Wilkinson, now M.P. (N.U.D.A.W.), C.P.G.B., and British delegate to Moscow R.I.L.U.
Robert Page Arnot, N.U.C., C.P.G.B.
A. J. Cook, Executive Committee M.F.G.B., I.L.P.
Noah Ablett, Executive Committee M.F.G.B.
Richard Coppock, General Secretary National Federation Building Trade Operatives.
Harry Pollitt, boiler-maker, C.P.G.B.
Jack Tanner (A.E.U.), formerly Syndicalist and I.W.W.
George Hardy, formerly I.W.W.

In September 1921 the British Bureau of the R.I.L.U. was

THE BOLSHEVISATION OF BRITISH TRADE UNIONISM

transferred from Manchester to London, with offices at 3 Wellington Street, Strand.

The Constitution of the Bureau stated that it should be independent of the Communist Party of Great Britain but should work in co-operation with it, thus making it clear that the British Bureau was not the outcome of the British Communists, but was directly under the control of the Executive of the Profintern in Moscow, just as the British Communist Party was under the control of the Executive of the Komintern.

A further clause in the Constitution declared that:

"The Bureau and its Committees shall conduct a vigorous campaign within the trade unions on behalf of the R.I. of L.U., prepare the programmes of action for adoption by the unions as alternatives to the compromising programmes of the yellow leaders of Amsterdam, and do all in its power to revolutionise the practice of the unions and draw them into the Red International of Labour Unions."

The two organs of the British Bureau were *All Power* (monthly), edited by H. Pollitt, and *The Worker* (weekly), published in Glasgow and previously the organ of the National Workers' Committee.

The British Bureau of the R.I.L.U. thus formed the first junction between the Syndicalist and Communist movements in this country. With Tom Mann, the old Syndicalist leader, at its head and Noah Ablett, who had figured in the "Mines for the Miners Movement" in 1913, supported by A. A. Purcell, one of the prime movers of the C.P.G.B., the two camps hitherto hostile had now established a point of contact which was to develop three years later into a larger organisation.

National Minority Movement.—This was the National Minority Movement, which began as the National Miners' Minority Movement, and was inaugurated at an R.I.L.U. conference of miners in London on January 26, 1924. Nat Watkins of the Moscow organisation was appointed organising secretary.

Minority groups were then formed in other important industries, so that the movement now consists of the following six groups:

> Miners' Minority Movement.
> Transport Workers' Minority Movement.
> Metal Workers' Minority Movement.
> Building Workers' Minority Movement.
> General Workers' Minority Movement.
> Printers' Section.

The Executive of the combined movement was formed as follows:

> Hon. Chairman : Tom Mann.
> Gen. Secretary : H. Pollitt.
> Organising Secretary : George Hardy.

After Pollitt's imprisonment in November 1925, George Hardy became Acting-General Secretary and his place as Organising Secretary was taken by Nat Watkins, now on the Presidium of the Executive Committee of the R.I.L.U. in Moscow.

Other leading members of the movement are Wal Hannington, Tom Quelch, Lœber, Horner, Sam Elsbury, Thom, Booth, etc.

The offices of the National Minority Movement are at 38 Great Ormonde Street, London, and its official organs are *The Worker* and *The Mine Worker*.

It is usual to describe the National Minority Movement as the outcome of the British Communist Party. This is incorrect. The Minority Movement developed historically from Syndicalism, beginning with the Industrial Syndicalist Educational League of 1910, under Tom Mann, through the Miners' Reform Movement and the British Bureau of the R.I.L.U., at which point the alliance with Communism was made. This was directly carried out under the orders of the "Profintern." In the Foreword written by Tom Quelch to the English translation of the *Resolutions and Decisions of the Third World Congress of the R.I.L.U.*, the Minority Movement of Great Britain is referred to as having been initiated and inspired by the R.I.L.U. Amongst the resolutions passed at this Congress, which took place in Moscow in July 1924, we read the following :

"It is a question of conquering the minds of the masses, of winning them for the idea of Communism. No matter how obnoxious the Labour bureaucracy, and it is becoming more obnoxious every day, the revolutionary work within the Labour organisations should be continued steadily and systematically. . . . Sensing the approaching danger, the Labour bureaucracy sweeps away the remnants of democracy in the trade unions ; everything is decided by the officialdom. It is necessary to strengthen the struggle against the union officialdom, etc." (*The Tasks of the International Trade Union Movement*, p. 9. Published by the National Minority Movement, 38 Great Ormonde Street, W.C.1).

Further on the mandarins of Moscow observe :

"**NOT ONE MASS ACTION OF THE BRITISH PROLETARIAT MUST TAKE PLACE WITHOUT OUR PARTICIPATION**" (*Ibid.*, p. 77).

So the British workers were not only to be turned against their employers, but against their own trade union officials, provided these were not prepared to take their orders from Moscow—the tyranny of native leaders was to be replaced by the tyranny of a foreign power. This was the real meaning of the "One Big Union" idea, borrowed from the American I.W.W.—no longer a union among the workers of the world, but the uniting of the workers of the world under the yoke of the Moscow bureaucracy. These British trade union leaders who joined the Minority Movement thus proclaimed themselves traitors to Trade Unionism and the agents of a foreign power.

It was at this same conference in Moscow that the promoters of the National Minority Movement in England received their orders and the inaugural conference was announced to take place in London in the following month of August 1924.

It will be seen, then, that the Minority Movement did not develop out of the Communist Party of Great Britain, but out of the Syndicalist movement after its capture by the Red Trade Union International of Moscow. The C.P.G.B., however, is now definitely linked up with the Minority Movement, and at the 1925 Congress of the Party two leaders of the Minority Movement—George Hardy and Nat Watkins—were present as " fraternal delegates."

By means of this intensive propaganda carried on by Communist agents amongst the industrial workers, the British Trade Union movement had veered steadily more and more towards Moscow. An obstacle was, however, presented by the International Federation of Trade Unions, or Amsterdam International, which still refused to affiliate with the R.I.L.U. In 1924 the personnel of the I.F.T.U. was as follows :

President : J. H. Thomas, M.P. (Great Britain).
Vice-President : L. Jouhaux (France).
C. Mertens (Belgium).
Th. Leipart (Germany).
Secretaries : J. Oudegeest (Holland), J. Sassenbach (Germany), J. W. Brown (Great Britain).

These were leaders denounced by Moscow as "yellow " or " reformist"; nevertheless, the I.F.T.U. had its Left or " Red " Wing, which included such men as A. A. Purcell (R.I.L.U.), George Hicks and Edo Fimmen, the Dutchman. In 1925 J. H. Thomas was replaced by A. A. Purcell, the rest of the Executive remaining the same.

From the time of its formation the R.I.L.U. of Moscow had " conducted a furious campaign " against the I.F.T.U., particularly during the year 1921-22, and declared its intentions of destroying " that pestilent yellow lair." In Article II, Clause 4, of the Rules of the R.I.L.U., it was stated that :

"The object of the Red International of Labour Unions is the amalgamation of all revolutionary class elements of the International Trades Union Movement, and the waging of a definite war with the International Labour Office at the League of Nations, and with the I.F.T.U. of Amsterdam, which, as a result of its programme and general policy, constitutes a rallying point for the international bourgeoisie."

The I.F.T.U. therefore continued to refuse to negotiate with the R.I.L.U.

The T.U.C.—Meanwhile the T.U.C. (Trades Union Congress) had developed a strong Left Wing. As we have seen earlier, a National Joint Council had been arranged by the T.U.C. and Labour Party in 1921. Since then the T.U.C. had continued to move steadily to the Left, and by 1925 it had fallen completely under the control of its Left Wingers. In that year its leaders consisted of the following :

President : A. B. Swales (A.E.U.), I.L.P.
Vice-Chairman : A. A. Purcell, I.F.T.U., R.I.L.U.
Secretary : Fred Bramley (N.A.F.T.U.), I.L.P.

(All these were now made honorary members of the Moscow Soviet, see *Sunday Worker*, April 19, 1925.)

Assist. Secretary : W. M. Citrine (Electrical Trade Unions), I.L.P.

The T.U.C. being affiliated to the I.F.T.U., and the same allies of Moscow figuring in the Executive of both, it was easy to arrange a plan of combined action. An ingenious ruse was devised. Neither the I.F.T.U. as a body nor the T.U.C. were willing to join up with Losovsky and the Profintern—the open appropriation of the name " Red International " by the latter being calculated to alarm sane trade unionists—but what was there to prevent an *entente* with the trade unionists of Russia who did not designate themselves by this objectionable adjective ? The bridge leading to Losovsky and the R.I.L.U. being impassable, another bridge to Moscow must be constructed, leading to Tomski and the All Russian Central Council of Trade Unions.

That such an alliance was from the point of view of orthodox Trade Unionism as much a farce as the other would have been, is evident from the fact that the All Russian Central Council of Trade Unions, formed in 1919, was under the R.I.L.U. and therefore simply a department of the Soviet Government ; Tomski, its President, was a member of the Presidium of the TS.I.K. (Central Executive Committee of the U.S.S.R.) ; and all the following members of its Executive—Rykov, Rudzutak, Andreiev, Losovsky (of the R.I.L.U.), Schmidt, Evdokimov, Lutovinov, Melnichansky, Dogadov, Antipov, Lepse and Seniushkin—were, or had been at some time, also members of the TS.I.K., that is to say, of the Russian Government.

The overture came from Tomski himself, who appeared at the Hull Congress of the T.U.C. in 1924 to convey fraternal greetings from the All Russian Central Council of Trade Unions and appeal for " international unity." This proposal was enthusiastically received, and it was immediately decided to send a delegation to Russia to attend the Congress of the All Russian Council and report on conditions under Soviet rule (*Labour Year Book*, 1925).

The delegates, who left London on November 7, 1924, and returned on December 19, were Purcell, Herbert Smith, John

Bromley, Ben Tillett, A. A. H. Findlay, John Turner and Fred Bramley. As might be expected from the known sympathies of the majority of these delegates, they found everything delightful on arrival ; Purcell declared that "Soviet Russia was the first bright jewel in the world's working-class crown," and Tillett described it as "the hope of the world's workers " (*Daily Telegraph*, December 5, 1924). The Report, published a year later by the delegation and accepted by their British comrades, met with ridicule from Continental Socialists. Thus Friedrich Adler, ex-secretary of the L.S.I. (Labour Socialist International), wrote :

"I must openly confess that never since the excesses of the German Social-Imperialists during the war have I read a book that has so shocked me by the baseness of its outlook and the shamelessness of its assertion as this report" (*Morning Post*, June 2, 1925).

The largest group of German trade unions—the Allgemeine Deutsche Gewerkschaftbund—published the following denunciation :

"Unpleasant facts are passed over with diplomatic subtleness and the compilers are not afraid even of lies in order to put the Russian system in a better light. . . . It is shocking that seven trade unionists whose names were held in repute should go to Russia for study and circulate to the international world a wretched and clumsy piece of work in the form of a report. The Bolsheviks must be laughing up their sleeves" (*Daily Mail*, October 26, 1925).

Trade Union Unity Movement.—In the course of this visit to Russia, the British delegates arranged with the All Russian Council to set up a joint committee, and in December the plan for the "Anglo-Russian Trade Union Unity Committee" was definitely formulated by the Left Wingers of the T.U.C., with the hearty approval of *The Worker*, organ of the R.I.L.U., *The Workers' Weekly* (C.P.G.B.) and of Tom Mann, who pressed the idea at a conference of the National Trades Council in the following March, whilst Losovsky himself sent a telegram of congratulation, addressed to the *Sunday Worker*. The new movement thus had all the Communist elements at its back.

An invitation was now sent (March 1925) by the General Council of the T.U.C. to the All Russian Central Council of Trade Unions to send delegates over to England for a Conference in April. The invitation was accepted and seven representatives arrived, led by no other than Tomski himself. The conference was composed as follows :

All Russian Central Council of Trade Unions :
M. Tomski   N. P. Glebov-Avilov
V. M. Mikhailov   Olga Chernishova
G. N. Melnichansky   V. Y. Yarotsky
I. I. Lepse

General Council of British T.U.C. :

A. B. Swales	W. Thorne, M.P.
A. A. Purcell	Ben Tillett
H. Boothman	Julia Varley
J. W. Bowen	R. B. Walker
G. Hicks	Fred Bramley
E. L. Poulton	George Young

It should be noted that at any rate the first four names on the Russian delegation were those of men who were, or had been, members of the Central Executive Committee of the Russian Soviet Republics. By conferring with these people the British trade unionists were, therefore, not negotiating with fellow trade unionists, but with what corresponded to the Cabinet Ministers of a foreign government violently hostile to Great Britain. What would have been said if the British Fascists had invited a number of Signor Mussolini's ministers over to this country in order to confer with them on the project of overthrowing Parliament and replacing it by a Fascist régime ? We cannot doubt that such a proceeding would have been found contrary to the Constitution of Great Britain. But to the advent of the Bolshevik delegation no obstacle was offered. The Soviet Press itself could only account for this by the supposition that the Conservative Cabinet was now " climbing down " (*Morning Post*, March 31, 1925).

The result of admitting these delegates, described by the *Morning Post* as " all specially trained agitators and propagandists of purely ' intellectual ' origin, and in no way representative of the Russian working masses " was naturally an intensification of the revolutionary movement in the British trade unions. In this same month of April the first number of the official organ of the new movement, *Trade Union Unity*, appeared, published by the Labour Research Department at 162A Buckingham Palace Road. The editorial board was composed of Left Wingers belonging both to the T.U.C. and the I.F.T.U.—A. A. Purcell, George Hicks and also the Dutch Left Wing member of the I.F.T.U., Edo Fimmen.

Amongst contributors to *Trade Union Unity* have been A. B. Swales (Chairman of the British Trades Union Congress), Fred Bramley (Secretary of the same), Herbert Smith (President of the Miners' Federation of Great Britain), Ben Turner (General President of the National Union of Textile Workers), Ben Tillett (Transport and General Workers' Union), John Bromley, M.P. (General Secretary of Associated Society of Locomotive Engineers and Firemen), Arthur Pugh (General Secretary of the Iron and Steel Trades Federation), etc. The May number (1925) contained a message of hearty congratulation from Tomski (Joseph Isbitsky), Chairman of the All Russian Central Council of Trade Unions, together with a portrait of this personage.

The attitude of *Trade Union Unity* has throughout been

antagonistic to the I.F.T.U., to which its directors belong, and derisive towards the old I.F.T.U. leaders, such as Oudegeest, Mertens and Jouhaux—an attitude constituting treachery, not only to orthodox, that is to say non-political, Trade Unionism, but also towards Trade Unionism that works for Socialism without accepting the dictatorship of Moscow.

The further result of permitting the so-called Russian delegation—which had promised to refrain from propaganda—to land in this country and inoculate Trade Unionism still further with the Bolshevist virus was seen at the Conferences of the National Minority Movement and of the T.U.C. that followed.

At the former, which took place on August 29 and 30, 1925, with Tom Mann in the chair, the necessity of doing away with the British Empire was openly proclaimed. Saklatvala declared : " I denounce the Empire in the name of the working-classes. I am an implacable enemy of the Union Jack " (Great applause). H. Pollitt observed that : " The British Empire, as at present constituted, stands for the exploitation of the workers " (More applause). Amongst the speakers were A. Gossip and Nat Watkins. Plans were put forward for Councils of Action, for a Workers' Defence Corps, Factory Committees and for further capturing the Co-operative Movement.

" The machinery of the Co-operatives is an essential alliance in the coming struggle for the feeding of the strikers' wives and families. We must get inside the Co-ops. and link them up with the Trade Unions, ready for collective action. Every Trade Unionist should be a Co-operator and every Co-operator a Trade Unionist."

The Annual Conference of the T.U.C. took place at Scarborough in the following month of September. Tomski was once more present, together with Dogadoff, a member of the Presidium of the Profintern and formerly of the TS.I.K. The Conference then presented Tomski with a gold watch as a token of respect.

Resolutions were put forward in favour of the " One Big Union " scheme, of the destruction of (British) Capitalism and of the breakup of the British Empire, and the two latter were carried by huge majorities :

Resolution carried by 2,456,000 votes to 1,218,000 :

" This Congress declares that the Trade Union movement must organise to prepare the Trade Unions in conjunction with the party of the workers to struggle for the overthrow of Capitalism.

" At the same time Congress warns the workers against all attempts to introduce capitalist schemes of co-partnership which in the past have failed to give the workers any positive rights, but instead have usually served as fetters retarding the forward movements.

" Congress further considers that strong, well-organised Shop Committees are indispensable weapons in the struggle to force the capitalists to relinquish their grip on industry, and, therefore, pledges itself to do all in its power to develop and strengthen workshop organisation."

Resolution adopted by 3,082,000 votes to 79,000 :

"This Trades Union Congress believes that the domination of non-British peoples by the British Government is a form of capitalist exploitation having for its object the securing for British capitalists (1) of cheap sources of raw materials ; (2) the right to exploit cheap and unorganised labour and to use the competition of that labour to degrade the workers' standards in Great Britain.

"It declares its complete opposition to Imperialism, and resolves (1) to support the workers in all parts of the British Empire to organise the Trade Unions and political parties in order to further their interests, and (2) to support the right of all peoples in the British Empire to self-determination, including the right to choose complete separation from the Empire." *(Labour Year Book*, 1926.)

After the conference Citrine and George Hicks went back to Russia with Tomski and Dogadoff.

So much for the assurances given to the constitutional press in the previous month by Fred Bramley, secretary of the General Council of the T.U.C., that the revolutionaries who talked about class warfare were not likely to enlist the help of trade union leaders and did not represent trade union opinion in this country.

Much comfort was derived by the public from the fact that at the Annual Conference of the Labour Party that began at Liverpool soon after the T.U.C. Conference at Scarborough, on September 29, affiliation with the Communist Party was rejected by an overwhelming majority.

In reality the opposing decisions of the two congresses merely marked a stage in the struggle for power between rival bodies. The "moderates" of the Labour Party had realised that the centre of gravity had shifted from 33 to 32 Eccleston Square, headquarters of the T.U.C., whilst the extremists saw that 16 King Street had been superseded by 38 Great Ormonde Street. The doctrinaires of both Socialism and Communism saw that they could no longer retain their hold even on the "revolutionary proletariat." This fact became clear under the late Labour Government. In the May 1924 number of *New Standards : a Journal of Workers' Control*, edited by Mr. and Mrs. G. D. H. Cole, the apostle of Guild Socialism observed that the advent of a Labour Government had "given place to a mood of criticism and dissatisfaction." The assumption of office had brought the active men of the Labour movement "face to face with realities" ; and the questions had arisen : "Where are we going ? What are we trying to do ? "

"For years past the Labour movement has been living on its own hump. It has done no fresh thinking. It has moved forward by the momentum of ideas already old and in need of re-statement."

And G. D. H. Cole concluded with this lament :

"In plain terms, the Communist Party is a failure, the I.L.P. is played out, the S.D.F. is a mere haven of refuge for Socialists ill at

THE BOLSHEVISATION OF BRITISH TRADE UNIONISM

ease in other groups, the Fabian Society a mere table-rapping voice from the dead, and the Guild Socialist movement almost non-existent as an effective force."

In a word, "advanced thinkers" had awakened to find themselves "back numbers," Mr. Cole's pet brand of Socialism was now stigmatised as reactionary by the R.I.L.U. (see denunciation of Guild Socialism in *Report of the Third Congress of the Profintern in Moscow*, July 1924, p. 71, English trans.), and his own Labour Research Department was passing out of the hands of the Intellectuals into those of Communist trade union leaders.

Labour Research Department.—In 1925 the personnel of the L.R.D.—which must not be confused with the "Joint Research Department of the Trades Union Congress and the Labour Party"—was as follows:

George Hicks
A. L. Bacharach
G. Burgneay
Emile Burns
A. J. Cook
Maurice H. Dobb

Rajani P. Dutt
J. T. W. Newbold
Harry Pollitt
Ellen Wilkinson
R. Page Arnot

The address of the L.R.D. is now 162 Buckingham Palace Road.

The Plebs League, at the same address as the above, had in 1925 the following Executive:

Hon. Secretary: Winifred Horrabin
Office Secretary: Kathleen Starr
Executive Committee: M. H. Dobb
George Hicks
Cedar Paul
R. W. Postgate
M. Philips Price
Mark Starr
Ellen Wilkinson

The National Council of Labour Colleges, of which the *Plebs* is the official organ, had at the same date a large Executive, including the following:

Hon. President: A. A. Purcell
President: J. Hamilton
Gen. Secretary: J. P. M. Millar
Treasurer: Mark Starr
G. S. Aitken
C. Brown
W. Coxon
W. T. A. Foot
R. Coppock
A. Gossip
J. Gregory

The head office of the N.C.L.C. is at 22 Elm Row, Edinburgh. The London Labour College, founded in 1909, is at 13 Penyween Road, Earl's Court, London. Secretary : W. T. A. Foot.

In an interesting series of articles by W. Faulkner in the *Patriot* for September 24, October 1 and 8, 1925, an account was given of the dispute between the N.C.L.C and the Workers' Educational Association, founded twenty-two years ago and regarded as too moderate by the N.C.L.C., which is now in full control of the whole Labour College movement.

CHAPTER X

SUBSIDIARY COMMUNIST ORGANISATIONS

In 1925 the Central Executive of the Communist Party of Great Britain was as follows :

Chairman : A. MacManus.

H. Pollitt
J. R. Campbell
William Gallacher
T. Bell
J. T. Murphy
R. P. Arnot
A. Inkpin
R. Stewart
R. P. Dutt
W. Hannington

C. M. Roebuck
T. A. Jackson
Mrs. Helen Crawfurd
A. Horner
William Joss
A. Ferguson
Beth Turner
Nat Watkins
E. H. Brown

One of the most dangerous illusions is to suppose that the strength of Communism in this country is to be estimated by the membership of the C.P.G.B. (Communist Party of Great Britain), which the Communists themselves are anxious to assure us stands only at 5,000 and has remained throughout stationary. (Note the reiteration of this figure by one speaker after another at the last Congress of the C.P.G.B.) In reality, the number of members is probably a good deal larger, but the important point is that membership of the official Communist Party in this country is not essential to being a leading member of the Communist organisation in this country. As has been shown in the preceding chapters, some of the most ardent Communist propagandists and even the most dangerous revolutionaries in Great Britain do not figure, at any rate openly, on the lists of the British Communist Party, but belong to such bodies as the Plebs League, Labour Research Department, I.L.P., or, again, to such avowedly Communist organisations as the R.I.L.U. and Minority Movement, under the control, not of the C.P.G.B., but of Moscow itself.

But besides these larger organisations, from 1921 onwards a number of subsidiary groups have been formed by agents both of the Komintern and of the Profintern in this country. These are as follows :

The N.U.W.C.M.—Passing over the Young Communist League, which will be dealt with in the Youth Section of this book, we come to the " Unemployed Committees," which Zinoviev ordered the West European Secretariat of the I.K.K.I. to create and develop as affiliations of the International Union of Unemployed. This Union, Zinoviev in the same circular went on to observe, " may become one of the secret ramifications of our organisation in Western Europe, and serve as a base for the future work of the Secretariat. . . . By means of skilful manœuvres, the International Union of Unemployed will constitute an efficacious means for the complete overthrow of capitalism, not only in Western Europe, but throughout the entire world "   (*Sunday Pictorial*, June 21, 1925).

In conformity with this policy, the R.I.L.U. of Moscow ordered its British members to reorganise the Unemployed Committees in this country, thus bringing them under the control of Moscow (Second World Congress of the R.I.L.U. : Resolutions and Decisions published by the British Bureau of the R.I.L.U., 3 Wellington Street, Strand, W.C.2 (1922), pp. 27 and 45). Accordingly, at the end of 1921 the National Unemployed Workers' Committee Movement was formed, with offices, first at 3 Queen Square, now at 105 Hatton Garden, E.C.1.

The National Organiser of the N.U.W.C.M., which is affiliated with the C.P.G.B., was Wal Hannington, C.P.G.B. and R.I.L.U., who still retains this post. Amongst the leading members of the movement were Harry Homer, C.P.G.B. and R.I.L.U., George Cooke, Horace Newbold, George Wheeler, Holt, Haye, Jackson, Buxton, etc.

The so-called " Hunger Marches " on London that took place in November 1922 were carried out by this body. A number of the marchers, finding they had been duped by the leaders of the N.U.W.C.M. returned home in disgust, their return fares being provided through the generosity of the public. One of the marchers declared : " It is cruel that men should be deluded by being asked to march all the way from Scotland and the north of England, when nothing can be done for them by the National Unemployed Workers' Committee Movement. All that has been done for us is to feed us on a lot of Communist propaganda in which we have no interest whatever " (*Daily Mail*, December 1, 1922).

Another activity of the N.U.W.C.M. is the organisation of " Unemployment Sunday." This was celebrated last year (1925) on June 21, when meetings were arranged in co-operation with the General Council of the T.U.C., and addressed by Purcell, Swales, Robert Williams, George Hicks and Ben Tillett.

At a special conference of the I.L.P. on December 13, 1925, J. Allen Skinner moved that " the conference viewed with satisfaction the continued co-operation of the T.U.C. General Council, with the National Unemployed Workers' Committee Movement." R. G. Bowyer opposed the resolution, saying that " there was no use for the N.U.W.C.M. in the Trade Union movement as a whole. It was a subversive and disruptive movement, and it was merely used to increase the Communist representation on the Trades Councils and at the Trades Congress." Nevertheless the resolution was adopted. (*Morning Post*, December 14, 1925).

The N.U.W.C.M. has thus a double connection with Moscow —directly with the Profintern, and indirectly with the Komintern through the C.P.G.B. and through the Bolshevist sympathisers in the T.U.C. At the last Congress of the C.P.G.B. (June 1, 1925), it was officially represented by its assistant secretary, Fred Douglas. The organ of the movement is *Out of Work*.

W.I.R.—Next in order of formation was the Workers' International Relief.

The central body to which it belongs had been formed on December 4, 1921, under the inspiration of the Komintern at a Conference held in Berlin, presided over by the well-known Spartacist and "Special" member of the I.K.K.I., Clara Zetkine. The organisation took the name of "Meshrabpom," from the Russian words **Mejdu Rabochim Pomoch**, meaning, literally, Inter-Workers' Aid (*The Worker*, organ of the R.I.L.U in Glasgow. Article by Freiherr von Schoenaich, September 12, 1925). A provisional committee was formed and headquarters established at 11 Unter den Linden, Berlin, under the direction of Willi Münzenberg. The following were elected to the Presidium :

Clara Zetkine.
Krestinski, representative of the All Russian Relief Committee in Berlin.
Grassmann, General Federation of Labour, Germany.
Coates, — (Zelda Kahan ?).
Madeleine Marx, member of "Clarté."

The ostensible purpose of the W.I.R. was the relief of famine in Russia, Southern Ireland, etc., the establishment of soup kitchens in Berlin and other German towns. We note, however, that the W.I.R. has never thought of starting soup kitchens for the suffering poor of London. On the contrary, when an appeal was made for canteens for the London unemployed the *Daily Herald*, controlled by George Lansbury, one of the Vice-Presidents of the W.I.R., wrote :

"The letter is an appeal for a familiar object—soup kitchens. . . . Soup kitchen statesmanship, however well-intentioned, is but tinkering of the feeblest kind " (Date of February 23, 1923).

Yet in the *Daily Herald* of January 23, 1923, had appeared a glowing panegyric of the same idea when carried out by the W.I.R. :

"The organisation for the Russian Workers' International Relief is now working full steam here in providing hot meals and soup kitchens for unemployed and starving families in the German towns."

Apparently only German workers were to have Communist propaganda washed down with hot soup. For this was, of course, the real object of the W.I.R., as indicated in one of its official communications :

"The W.I.R. has united all sections of the workers internationally on the basis of *class-conscious impartial relief* [note the contradiction between these two adjectives !]. The W.I.R. is the first international expression of the Unity of Workers, *and has united all tendencies and sections of the Labour Movement*" (An open letter to delegates to the Minority Movement Conference, date of January 25, 1923).

That this last pretension was false is shown by the strong denunciation of the W.I.R. by Dr. Friedrich Adler (President of the Austrian Workers' Councils, and later one of the two secretaries of the L.S.I. or Second International), who was present at the inaugural conference in Berlin, and declared that he was able to see with his own eyes its purely Communist administration in every detail. (*Labour Magazine*, December 1924).

According to the detailed minutes of the W.I.R in the possession of the L.S.I., it was stated as one of the rules of the organisation that in forming National Committees "the Secretary chosen by the Committee is responsible for his activities to the Committee, and to the central office in Berlin. It is the duty of the Communist representative on this Committee to see to it that the Secretary is a Communist."

In April 1923 an appeal was sent out by the British branch of the association which was described as the W.I.R.R. (Workers' International Russian Relief), but some four months later the second R. was dropped, and the name W.I.R. was retained. Amongst the Vice-Presidents and members at this date were George Lansbury, N. Klishko of the Russian Trade Delegation in 1923, J. T. W. Newbold, C.P.G.B., the Rev. H. Dunnico, leader of the "Peace Society," A. A. Purcell, C.P.G.B., T.U.C., Edgar T. Whitehead, Philip Rabinovitch of Arcos (All Russian Co-operative Society), etc. The official organ of the movement was the *Soviet Russia Pictorial*, later known as the *Workers' International Pictorial*.

As Dr. Adler had pointed out with regard to the Berlin group : "Under the cloak of humanity they appeal to all kind-hearted people, and are always successful with this method." Yet occasionally the ruse failed, as in the case of Mrs. Katherine Bruce Glasier (I.L.P. and Fabian Society), who, having been drawn into the movement under the guise of helping starving children, denounced it in unmeasured terms as an engine of class warfare—an accusation which met with no official repudiation (see her letter and reply by the W.I.R. reproduced in the *Patriot* for April 23, 1923).

In 1925 the leading members of the W.I.R. were given officially as follows :

SUBSIDIARY COMMUNIST ORGANISATIONS

International Centre in Berlin.
Germany: Münzenberg, Ledebour, Clara Zetkine.
France: Reynaud, Toller, Henri Barbusse (founder of "Clarté," a secret society under the direction of the Grand Orient, see later, p. 103).
Russia: Gasparowa, Kameneva.
Ireland: Mrs. Despard, Larkin, McBride, Daly, Lawlor.
Australia: Pickard.
Italy: Misiano.

The British organisation was as follows:

Headquarters: 26 Bedford Row, London, W.C.1.
Vice-Presidents:

Alfred Barnes, M.P.	G. Lansbury
J. Bromley	J. T. W. Newbold
Alexander Gossip	J. O'Grady, M.P.
David Kirkwood	W. Straker
N. Klishko	A. A. Purcell, M.P.

Executive Committee:
Chairman: H. J. May (Sec., International Co-operative Alliance)

Mrs. Helen Crawfurd	Mrs. Winifred Horrabin
Rev. H. Dunnico, M.P.	(Hon. Sec., Plebs League)
Miss A. Honora Enfield	George Lansbury, M.P.
(Sec., Women's Co-op. Guild)	Miss Nellie Lansbury
W. N. Ewer	Mrs. Montefiore, C.P.G.B.
Mrs. Ewer	Mrs. Marjorie Newbold
Walter Holmes	Mrs. Hilda Saxe-Meynell
Miss Ella Klein	S. Saklatvala, C.P.G.B.
Neil McLean, M.P.	Miss Evelyn Sharp
W. McLaine, C.P.G.B.	Mrs. Mark Starr
Dr. V. N. Polovtsev	Robert Stewart, C.P.G.B.
Philip Rabinovitch	Miss Ellen Wilkinson
Miss Rose Cohen, C.P.G.B.	Dr. Robert Dunstan, I.L.P.
Dr. Margaret Dunstan	

Secretary: Mrs. Helen Crawfurd, C.P.G.B.

The headquarters of the Irish Committee are at 47 Parnell Square, Dublin. Hon. Secretary, R. Stewart.

The I.C.W.P.A.—In 1925 the International Class-War Prisoners' Aid was started, a branch of another Russian organisation formed in 1922 by the Komintern, under the leadership of Zinoviev and known as the M.O.P.R., from the initials of the Russian words Mejdunarodnoe Obshtchestvo Pomochi Rabochim, meaning literally International Society for Help of Workers, but since in Russian the words for workmen and for revolutionaries begin with the same letter R—signifying to the initiated for the Help of Revolutionaries. In fact, in the West of Europe no secret is made of this double interpretation, and the M.O.P.R. is officially known as the Secours Rouge International, and in England sometimes as the International Red Aid. Here, however, it was judged prudent to follow the precedent of Moscow by painting the words "International Workers' Aid " on the office door of the I.C.W.P.A.

The inauguration of the British branch is thus described in the *Daily Herald* of January 8, 1925 :

" A British branch of the ' International Class-War Prisoners' Aid ' has been started at 10 Fetter-lane, London, E.C.4.

" The secretary, W. Hannington, in announcing the formation, says :

" ' It is the British section of the International Class-War Prisoners' Aid that was started in 1922, arising out of the wholesale and terrible persecution of the active fighters of the working class in Germany, Poland, Bulgaria, Italy, Rumania, Hungary and Esthonia, and many of the British Colonies.' "

On the following day Wal Hannington, who, it will be remembered, was also the leader of the N.U.W.C.M., gave the same account in the *Workers' Weekly* and went on to say :

" ' We have now established in Great Britain the British section of the I.R.A., which we shall call in this country the ' International Class-War Prisoners' Aid.'

" The following will be the nature of its work :

" (1) To spread amongst the British workers information concerning the capitalist persecution and tyranny against the workers in all parts of the world.

" (2) The propaganda to carry emphasis of the increasing need for international working-class solidarity.

" (3) To raise money to provide legal defence and financial assistance to all class-war prisoners and their dependents.

" (4) To organise campaigns for bringing pressure to bear upon the Governments to release all those lying in jail because of their working-class activities."

By October 1925 the members of the Committee of the I.C.W.P.A. included the following :

Secretary : Wal Hannington.
Mrs. Helen Crawfurd
Tom Mann
A. Gossip
Chaman Lal
Emile Burns
Lajpat Rai

Harry Pollitt
S. Saklatvala
J. D. Thom
R. Stoker
Bob Lovell

The last named has acted as secretary since the imprisonment of Hannington in November 1925.

The press in this country constantly confuse the I.C.W.P.A. and the W.I.R. *It should, therefore, be carefully noted that the I.C.W.P.A. is the British branch of the M.O.P.R., founded in Moscow in 1922, and the W.I.R. is the British branch of the Meshrabpom. founded in Berlin in 1921.* The two organisations are, therefore, quite distinct, although both are directed by the Komintern. In

SUBSIDIARY COMMUNIST ORGANISATIONS 101

Russian, as we have shown, their names are almost identical. These resemblances are probably intentional, being designed to create confusion and lead the " Capitalist press " into committing blunders.

The S.C.R.—A more intellectual group, organised for the purpose of co-operation with Moscow, is the " Society for Cultural Relations Between the Peoples of the British Commonwealth and the Union of Socialist Soviet Republics," founded in May 1924, and run by Miss Llewelyn Davies of the Women's Co-operative Guild and Mrs. Catherine Rabinovitch, wife of Philip Rabinovitch of Arcos.

Amongst the principal supporters were the following :

H. Baillie-Weaver (Theosophical Society)
H. N. Brailsford
Fred Bramley
C. Roden Buxton
G. D. H. Cole
Dr. Robert Dunstan, I.L.P.
J. L. Garvin, editor of *Observer*
J. M. Keynes
Joseph King, I.L.P., 1917 Club
H. J. May
Bertrand Russell
G. Bernard Shaw
R. H. Tawney, Fabian Society
Miss Sybil Thorndike
Mrs. Sidney Webb
H. G. Wells
E. F. Wise
Mrs. Wise
Leonard Woolf
Michael S. Farbman

The offices of this society are at 23 Tavistock Square, and its ostensible mission is to supply information about conditions of life in Russia. Usefulness to Moscow is indicated by the following description : " The Communist International favours it (the S.C.R.) as a fertile ground for Communist propaganda of the intellectual variety."

The first three of the above organisations are absolutely Communist in aim, not under the direction of the British Communist Party, but of Moscow. It will, therefore, be seen that in arresting the leaders of the C.P.G.B. the Government was only interfering with one section of the Communist organisation in this country. These arrests were made as the result of a raid on the headquarters of the C.P.G.B. in King Street in October 1925, and twelve members of the Party—MacManus, Pollitt, Gallacher, Inkpin, Hannington, Cant, Rust, Campbell, Wintringham, J. T. Murphy, T. Bell and Page Arnot—were sentenced to short terms of imprisonment. These men were not perhaps the most dangerous revolutionaries in this country, who, though not—at any rate avowedly—members of the C.P.G.B., belong either to the R.I.L.U., Minority Movement, Trade Union Unity Movement or one of the organisations which have been described.

It cannot be too strongly emphasised that a close connection exists between all these, and at the same time between each and Moscow, hence their activities are skilfully co-ordinated under a central command. In this way joint demonstrations are frequently organised by members of the different groups. Thus on March 29 of this year a meeting ending in disorderly scenes was organised in Hyde Park by Bob Lovell of the I.C.W.P.A. and M. Prooth of the N.U.W.C.M. Again we find agitation for the release of political prisoners, carried out jointly by the I.C.W.P.A. and W.I.R. In April speakers on Clapham Common at a demonstration for this object included MacManus, C.P.G.B., Robert Stewart, C.P.G.B. and W.I.R., Nat Watkins, R.I.L.U., George Hardy, Minority Movement, H. N. Brailsford, I.L.P., whilst members of the S.C.R. contributed to the funds of the I.C.W.P.A. for the release of men imprisoned during the General Strike under the Emergency Powers Act. The signatories to the appeal sent out for this purpose by the I.C.W.P.A. included William Paul, Rutland Boughton, A. J. Cook, Dr. Marion Phillips, Dr. Dunstan, George Lansbury and other members of Parliament.

Left Wing Movements.—Another method adopted by the Communists for camouflaging their activities is to form so-called " Left Wing Movements " in the Labour Party, I.L.P. or trade union groups. These have been organised all over the country, and serve as rallying points for Communists who, particularly since the arrests of last November, find it more politic not to describe themselves as such, so as to remain within the Labour Party, which has officially repudiated Communism. The organ of the movement is *Left Wing*. In December of last year (1925) a circular was sent out by the C.P.G.B. proposing the formation of a combined " Left Wing Group," composed of all the members of the Labour Party who had voted against the decision of the Liverpool Conference of the Labour Party, to exclude the Communists. The moving spirit behind this movement is said to be W. Paul, a member of the C.P.G.B. Executive, whilst the secretary of the Greater London group known as the " Left Wing Provisional Committee " is W. T. Colyer, arrested in America in 1920 as a member of the American Communist Party, who at the Liverpool Conference seconded the resolution that " the British Empire must be entirely smashed if the workers of this country were to improve their conditions " (*Daily Herald*, October 1, 1925).

It is, therefore, easy to see how, by the simple device of not registering as a member of the group in King Street, a man may proclaim himself not to be a Communist whilst working as an active agent of Communism under the direct control of Moscow.

CHAPTER XI
POST-WAR PACIFISM

In Chapter IV a survey was made of the Pacifist activities of Socialists in England and America during the War. From an examination of the points there given, two important facts emerge : namely, (1) That the same people who distinguished themselves in the peace-at-any-price movement when this country was threatened by a foreign foe were equally prominent in the war-at-any-price movement directed against British industry and the prosperity of the Empire after the international conflict had ended; (2) That the concern displayed by our Pacifists for the interests of the foreigner applied only to our enemies and never to our allies. The same people who wept over the starving children of Germany or Russia remained dry-eyed over the sufferings of the French and Belgian children during the war and amidst their professions of love for humanity were capable of giving vent to vitriolic sentiments with regard to France. The intimate connection between pro-Germanism and Bolshevism will thus be shown by incontrovertible evidence.

We shall now follow this double rôle of Pacifism since the War ended.

Amongst the organisations active between 1914 and 1918, the " No Conscription Fellowship " has ceased to exist ; the rest have continued their campaign, which since it is no longer a matter of ensuring a triumph for German arms, has been waged for the purpose of enabling Germany to evade the payment of reparations, of breaking our Entente with France, and of helping the restoration of German industry by spreading discontent amongst our own industrial workers.

The U.D.C.—Since the ending of the War, the subversive rôle of the Union of Democratic Control has been made still more apparent by its avowed connection with " Clarté," the International of Socialist Intellectuals, founded in Paris in 1919, with headquarters at 49 Rue de Bretagne, offices at 12 Rue Feydeau and a lodge at 279 Rue des Pyrénées under the jurisdiction of the Grand Orient of France. The leader of this society was Henri Barbusse, author of the defeatest novel *Le Feu*, and amongst prominent members were Anatole France, Professor Aulard of the Sorbonne, Georges Brandes, Madeleine Marx, Victor Cyril, Vaillant Couturier and a number of prominent British Pacifists and Socialist writers. " Clarté," being a secret society, does not enter into the scope of this book, except in its relation to the U.D.C., which the latter has now admitted, though without revealing the names of those British members who are known from other sources of information to have belonged to it.

Mrs. Philip Snowden, herself a leading member of the U.D.C., stated in reference to the " Clarté " group that " their policy is very much the same as that of the Union of Democratic Control in England " (*A Political Pilgrim in Europe*, p. 129). This admission throws a significant light on the character of the U.D.C., in view of the fact that " Clarté " ended by definitely joining up with the French Communist Party (Mrs. H. M. Swanwick, *Builders of Peace*, p. 130). Since 1924, however, " Clarté " appears to have ceased to exist, though more probably it has only gone further underground and continues to work under another name.

The U.D.C., however, is still going strong. In 1923 it published a Manifesto on " The State of Europe," declaring that the Versailles Treaty had " created an impossible situation in Europe," and that the nation should " insist upon dropping once and for all the demand for Reparations." This Manifesto was signed on behalf of the Executive of the U.D.C. by Major C. R. Attlee, Mary Hamilton, J. A. Hobson, E. D. Morel, Arthur Ponsonby, F. J. Shaw, (Mrs.) H. M. Swanwick, H. B. Lees-Smith, Charles Trevelyan and Hamilton Fyfe, the present editor of the *Daily Herald*, which has always shown itself consistently pro-German. E. D. Morel, as editor of the U.D.C. organ *Foreign Affairs*, until his death in 1924 continued his work for Germany even to the point of denouncing the Socialist Government of luke-warmness in the matter of letting Germany off reparations (see article by W. Faulkner, " Morel & Co. Again " in *Patriot* for July 31 and August 7, 1924).

The W.I.L.—The Women's International League for Peace and Freedom is still active. Its headquarters are now at Maison Internationale, 12 Rue de Vieux Collège, Geneva, with Jane Addams still as President and Miss Madeleine Doty as secretary.

The offices of the British section are at International House, 55 Gower Street, W.C.1, with, in 1925, an Executive Committee that included the following:

President : Mrs. H. M. Swanwick.
Chairman : Miss K. D. Courtney.
Hon. National Secretary : Miss Mary Chick.
Hon. Foreign Relations Secretary : Dr. Hilda Clark.
Hon. Treasurer : The Lady Courtney of Penwith.
Hon. Assistant Treasurer : Mrs. Laurence Binyon.
Miss Margaret Ashton   Lady Parmoor
Miss Adela Coit   Dr. Ethel Williams
Miss Emily Leaf

The N.M.W.M.—Another Pacifist organisation that has been active since 1919 is the No More War Movement (known until recently as the No More War Committee), an offshot of the now defunct No Conscription Fellowship, which joined up with the "War Resisters' International," formed by various Resisters' groups in France, Holland, Germany, America, Austria, Scandinavia, Bulgaria, Czecho-Slovakia, Switzerland, Australia, New Zealand, etc.

The Constitution of the N.M.W.M. is officially given as follows :

"The Movement shall be known as the No More War Movement, being the British Section of the War Resisters' International.

"The object of the Movement shall be to make the idea of personal resistance to War, by refusal to assist in any way in armed conflict, the backbone of every movement towards World Peace and Universal Brotherhood. Together with this purpose, the Movement seeks to assist in removing the causes of War and in building a new social order based on National and International co-operation for the common good.

"Membership shall be open to all who sign the Declaration.

"THE DECLARATION

"Believing that all war is wrong, and that the arming of nations, whether by sea, land, or air, is treason to the spiritual unity and intelligence of mankind, I declare it to be my intention never to take part in war, offensive or defensive, international or civil, whether by bearing arms, making or handling munitions, voluntarily subscribing to war loans, or using my labour for the purpose of setting others free for war service. Further, I declare my intention to strive for the removal of all causes of war and to work for the establishment of a new social order based on co-operation for the common good."

In 1925 the personnel of the N.M.W.M. was composed of the following :

    Chairman : George Lansbury, M.P.
    Treasurer : Harold J. Morland.
    Financial Secretary : Ida J. Tinkler.
    Press Sec. and Editor : *No More War*, W. J. Chamberlain.
    Secretary : Beatrice C. M. Brown.
    Organising Secretary : Lucy A. Cox.

Executive Committee

Bertram Appleby	Margaret Newboult
Walter Ayles	Helen Peile
Harold F. Bing	A. Noel Simpson
A. Fenner Brockway	E. V. Watering
H. Runham Brown	Wilfred Wellcock
J. Theodore Harris	Theodora Wilson Wilson
Marguerite Louis	

The offices of the N.M.W.M., which were at 304 High Holborn, have recently been changed to 11 Doughty Street, W.C.1.

There is also a Youth Section, of which the secretary is Phyllis Bing, 6 Alton Road, Croydon. The organ of the Movement *No More War* appears monthly.

Fellowship of Reconciliation.—The No More War demonstrations that take place from time to time all over the country appear not to be organised directly by the N.M.W.M., but by the Fellowship of Reconciliation working in collaboration with the N.M.W.M. The origins of the F.O.R. have been given earlier (see p. 35), but since the War it has been organised on a larger scale, and now calls itself in England the "International Fellowship of Reconciliation"; in France, "La Réconciliation," and in Germany the "Versöhnungsbund," with the further title of a "Movement Towards a Christian International."

The International Secretariat is at 16 Red Lion Square, London, W.C.1. The General Secretary is the Rev. Oliver Dryer and the Assistant Secretary Miss M. L. Moll.

At a Conference held in Holland in 1920 the so-called "Christian International" thus formulated its declaration of faith:

"We believe that it is our Father's will that the present social order should cease, and be replaced by a new order wherein the means of production will be used to supply the simple needs of all mankind. Under a system of private capitalism this seems to us impossible."

The International Peace Society.—Another international Pacifist organisation is the Peace Society, dating from 1816, of which the origins were given in Chapter IV of this book (see p. 32), and which is now described as the International Peace Society, with Continental headquarters at 38 Avenue Marceau, Courbevoie, Paris.

The objects of the Society are stated to be:

"To diffuse information tending to show that war is inconsistent with the spirit of Christianity and the true interests of mankind; and to point out the means best calculated to maintain permanent and universal Peace, upon the basis of Christian principles."

The British headquarters are at King's Buildings, Dean Stanley Street, Westminster, S.W.1., and its personnel is as follows:

President: E. T. John.

Vice-Presidents

The Bishop of Ripon.
The Bishop of Truro.
The Suffragan Bishop of Plymouth.
Lord Ashton.
Lord Shaw.
Lord H. Cavendish-Bentinck.
Barrow Cadbury.
Sir W. H. Dickinson.
T. R. Ferens.
Lord Emmott.
Rev. Robert F. Horton, M.A., D.D.
Rev. John Hutton, D.D.
Sir Donald Maclean.
T. P. O'Connor, M.P.
Miss P. H. Peckover.
Rev. Thomas Phillips, B.A.
Sir John Simon, M.P.
Philip Snowden, M.P.
The Chief Rabbi.
The Canon of Westminster Abbey.

Treasurer: Jonathan Edward Hodgkin.
Director and Secretary: Rev. Herbert Dunnico, J.P., M.P., C.C.

Executive Committee

A. Kemp Brown, M.A.	Rev. W. Long.
Rev. Humphrey Chalmers, M.A.	The Hon. Mrs. J. Doyle Penrose.
Miss M. Evans.	Rev. T. Phillips, B.A.
Hubert A. Gill, M.A.	T. Richardson.
Thos. Groves, M.P.	R. Simpson.
J. J. Hayward, M.A.	Ben Spoor, M.P.
David Hunter, O.B.E.	Walter Windsor, M.P.
Morgan Jones, M.P.	W. Wright, M.P.

The organ of the Peace Society is *The Herald of Peace*.
Two offshoots of the Peace Society are :

The United Peace Fellowship—Peace Scouts.—The United Peace Fellowship of the Churches, also under the Rev. H. Dunnico, with headquarters at 47 New Broad Street, E.C.2, and the International Peace Scouts, formed in February 1923, as an amalgamation of the " Band of Peace Union," the " Crusaders of Peace " and the London section of the " British Boys' and Girls' Peace Scouts." The President is again the Rev. H. Dunnico and the Vice-Presidents :

A. Barnes, M.P.	Alderman Ben Turner, M.P.
Thomas Groves, M.P.	W. Windsor, M.P.
George Lansbury, M.P.	W. Wright, M.P.

The National Council for the Prevention of War.—The National Council for the Prevention of War was formerly the National Peace Council referred to in Chapter IV (see p. 32) and changed its name in 1925. It is described as " a federation of organisations working against war."
The official declaration of principles is as follows :

" The Council does not seek to take over the work of any existing organisation working against war, but desires to strengthen the work of each organisation by the co-ordination of all.

" GENERAL OBJECTS

" (a) To promote, organise, co-ordinate and make effective public opinion in favour of, and efforts for, the prevention of war and the development of international goodwill and co-operation ;

" (b) To co-operate with other organisations or bodies in the international peace movement ;

" (c) To secure in the schools and colleges an education for international friendship and understanding ;

" (d) To take all such steps as may, in the opinion of the Council, be necessary or desirable to give effect to the above purposes.

" IMMEDIATE AIMS

" (a) Progressive revision of the Peace Treaties ;

" (b) Immediate and progressive Reduction of Armaments by International Agreement ;

" (c) Support and extension of the work of the League of Nations."

108   THE SOCIALIST NETWORK

The Executive is composed of the following :

    President : Earl Beauchamp, K.G.
    Ex-President : The Lady Parmoor.
    Chairman : Mr. Oswald Mosley, L.P.
    Treasurers : Mrs. George Cadbury, M.A., C.B.E.
              Mr. F. C. Linfield.
    Directing Secretary : Mr. J. H. Hudson, M.A., M.P.
    Publication Secretary : Mr. Norman Angell.

The offices of the Council are at Millbank House, 2 Wood Street, S.W.1.

Some of the principal people who have associated themselves with the work of the National Council are : Major C. R. Attlee, M.P., the Bishop of Birmingham, J. R. Clynes, M.P., the Rev. H. Dunnico, M.P. (director of the Peace Society), Sir William Goode, Arthur Henderson, M.P., J. A. Hobson, M.A. (U.D.C.), E. T. John (President of the Peace Society), George Lansbury, M.P. (Chairman of the No More War Movement), the Bishop of Manchester, Professor Gilbert Murray, L.N.U., the Rev. Thomas Nightingale, Lord and Lady Parmoor, Philip Snowden, M.P. (U.D.C.), Mrs. Philip Snowden (U.D.C.), Mrs. H. M. Swanwick, M.S. (President of the W.I.L.), Charles Trevelyan, M.P. (U.D.C.), and the late H. Baillie Weaver.

Thirty or forty organisations are now affiliated to the Council. The chief are :

    The National Free Church Council.
    The National Brotherhood Council.
    The Co-operative Union (with 4,000,000 members).
    The Women's International League.
    The Women's Co-operative Guild.
    The Iron and Steel Trades' Confederation.
    The National Reform Union.
    Co-operative Holidays' Association.
    The Cobden Club.
    The No More War Movement.
    The Friends' Peace Committee.
    The Union of Democratic Control.
    The Church of England Peace League.
    The National Association of Schoolmasters.

The National Council for the Prevention of War has a working agreement with the League of Nations Union by which Professor Gilbert Murray, Chairman of the L.N.U., sat on the Executive Committee of the Council, and Baillie Weaver, member of the Council, sat on the Executive Committee of the Union.

The L.N.U.—The League of Nations Union, founded on October

13, 1918, comprises a strange assortment of people, ranging from orthodox Conservatives to revolutionary Socialists, united by the aim " to secure the whole-hearted acceptance by the British people of the League of Nations." The agreement to sink party differences in this common cause seems, however, to work out in a somewhat one-sided manner, as described in a communication to the *Patriot* :

"There are speakers of all shades of this political belief on their lists. But there is the difference in their attitude that Conservatives who speak on behalf of that body drop their party creed and stake their all on the League. The Socialist Wing, however, do not drop their own pet theories ; they find themselves in their element prating about Internationalism and World Brotherhood, and making gibes at patriotism" (*Patriot*, February 21, 1924).

The writer goes on to quote the instance of an L.N.U. speaker in Glasgow, who proclaimed himself a strong adherent of the Labour Party, attacked France and urged the restoration of Germany's possessions in East Africa. There seems, therefore, some ground for the opinion held in certain quarters that the L.N.U. " is rapidly degenerating into a pro-German society " (*Daily Mail*, March 13, 1926).

Such are the principal Peace Societies, which have been active in this country since the War ; besides those described above may be mentioned the Women's Union for Peace, the Arbitrate First Bureau, the Friends' Council for International Service (Secretary, Carl Heath of the National Peace Council), the Society of Friends' Peace Committee, the Jewish Peace Society, the League to Abolish War, etc.

It is now time to turn to America, and follow the connection between the Pacifist groups described in Chapter IV and the Bolshevist movement.

People's Council of America.—At the point where this account broke off, the " First American Conference of Democracy and Terms of Peace " had declared itself in sympathy with the " Russian Council of Workmen and Soldiers," formed under Kerensky (see p. 38) and on p. 54 another group was mentioned, the " People's Council of America," formed in June 1917 after the Russian model. Amongst the members of the latter organisation were again the leading Pacifists—Emily Green Balch, Morris Hillquit, the Rabbi Magnes, Louis Lochner, Rebecca Shelly, Joseph Schlossberg, etc.

People's Freedom Union.—This was absorbed after the signing of the Armistice by the " People's Freedom Union," under Charles Recht, a lawyer, later on legal adviser to Ludwig Martens, a German subject, who was afterwards appointed by the Bolsheviks the representative of Russia in the United States (*Lusk Report*, p. 641), but finally deported.

Women's International League for Peace and Freedom.—The

Pacifists now set about organising a further peace demonstration, and in May 1919 the Women's International Committee for Permanent Peace held an International Conference at Zurich, when the name of the organisation was changed to the Women's International League for Peace and Freedom. Jane Addams, who had again come over from the United States, was elected International President, with Emily Green Balch as secretary.

An interesting light is thrown on the leadership of the W.I.L. in America, in the report presented to the United States Congress on the subversive activities of the American Civil Liberties Union in 1925 :

" On the A.C.L.U. committee we also find the three chief leaders of the Women's International League for Peace and Freedom, which is endeavouring to prepare the way for the communist uprising by bringing about complete disarmament of the country. They are Sophonisba P. Breckenridge ; Agnes Brown Leach, wife of Henry Goddard Leach, of the pink Forum ; and Jane Addams. Miss Addams, with anarchist Berkman's friend, Frank P. Walsh, was in February, 1920, one of the Vice-Presidents of the Public Ownership League, in association with Glenn E. Plumb, Frederic C. Howe, J. L. Engdahl, etc. She was listed as a stockbroker in the Russian-American Industrial Corporation, with Lenin, Debs, and others. She is a member of the Fellowship of Reconciliation. At a dinner given by the Fellowship of Reconciliation on June 9 in California specimen guests were representatives of the Communist Federated Press, members of the Industrial Workers of the World and communist workers, a leader of the Young Communist Internationale, a director of the local American Civil Liberties Union branch, and an attorney for communists and Industrial Workers of the World. At another meeting a member, after praising Miss Addams, announced that she would never be patriotic until she gained the communist ends she strove for."

American Civil Liberties Union.—The most important Bolshevist-Pacifist organisation in the United States, since the rise of the Soviet regime, is the " American Civil Liberties Union," a reorganisation of the National Civil Liberties Bureau, into which were merged a number of the preceding Pacifist bodies—the American League to Limit Armaments, the American Union Against Militarism, the People's Freedom Union, the Emergency Peace Federation, etc. This new body came into existence on January 12, 1920, with Roger Baldwin, a notorious Pacifist and " an old hanger-on of the Berkman Anarchist gang," as its director (*Congressional Record* for December 19, 1925, p. 3).

On its Committee were found, besides the leaders of the Pacifist societies mentioned above—Jane Addams, Rabbi Magnes, Sophonisba P. Breckenridge, Agnes Brown Leach, Morris Hillquit, representative of the Soviet Bureau, etc., Elizabeth Gurley Flynn, an I.W.W. agitator—avowed revolutionaries such as William Z. Foster (of the T.U.E.L.), James H. Maurer, friend, aider and abettor of Anarchists and Communists, and Norman Hapgood of the Hearst Press.

At a Congress of the United States Senate last December (1925), the poisonous activities of this organisation were fully revealed in the course of a communication from Francis Ralston Welsh, in which it was stated that the A.C.L.U.—which should have been called the Unamerican Criminal Licence Union, had consistently supported Communists, murderers, dynamiters and other criminals.

National Council for the Prevention of War.—The American organisation, known as the National Council for the Prevention of War, was formed in about 1921, some years before the National Peace Council in England adopted this name. It is not clear if there is any connection between the two societies. The American one, which was formerly the National Council for the Reduction of Armaments, was reorganised by Frederick J. Libby, a notorious Pacifist, who, on the call to arms when America joined the war, hastily became a Quaker, and secured safe employment in administering relief (Marvin, *op. cit.*, p. 59). By means of this organisation, which has been described as " virtually a Communist affair " (*Congressional Record*, " Recognition of Russia," 1924, p. 5), affiliation and co-operation were brought about with a large number of societies and individuals, the openly acknowledged purpose of which is to undermine the loyalty of American citizens (Marvin, *op. cit.*, p. 59). A Woman's Joint Congressional Committee was formed to bring in women's movements, such as the National League of Women Voters, the Women's Committee for World Disarmament and the Women's International League for Peace and Freedom, of which the National Chairman in America was Mrs. George T. Odell.

The societies that have now been enumerated are only a few, but the most important, of the countless Pacifist groups working in this country and America—the list could be enormously extended. In reviewing this vast network of Pacifist organisation, in which one finds the same people figuring again and again, one is inevitably brought to inquire why all these separate societies apparently working for the same end continue to exist. Whence comes the money to finance these innumerable offices, secretaries and publications ? The answer is surely that since, in the words of Mr. Fred A. Marvin, " Pacifism is but a name given to one form of action to create world Communism and Socialism " (*Ye Shall Know the Truth*, p. 50), the organisation of both is carried out on the same principle—that of forming a ramification of groups which by their number elude observation and by the slightly differing shades of redness appeal to people of all kinds, ranging from mild visionaries to the advocates of forcible revolution. The great fault we have to find with our Socialist-Pacifists is that they are not really out for peace at all. From Marx's " iron battalions of the proletariat " to the words of the " Red Flag," the language particularly affected by the Socialists who vaunt the blessings of peace has always held a strong military flavour. Not only do these opponents of war between nations and professed advocates of arbitration demand that there should be no "truce with Capitalism" and no arbitration between employers and employed, but even the ordinary machinery of war inspires them with no indignation, provided it is manipulated by the two most military nations of the world to-day. Neither the ruthless legions of Imperial Germany nor the red troops of Soviet Russia, but only the simple and kindly soldiery of Britain, France, Belgium and America have been the objects of their denunciations. Indeed, our Socialists, on their visits to Bolshevia, have been known to address hearty congratulations to the troops, whilst George Lansbury, Chairman of the "No More War Movement," has declared : " The war-cry of the Red Army is ' Freedom for All ! ' We in England must take our stand with them ! "

It is this obvious inconsistency which distinguishes the anti-patriots we know as Pacifists from the sincere seekers after world peace.

CHAPTER XII
YOUTH MOVEMENTS

THE earliest attempt made by Socialists to gain influence over the minds of the youth of this country was the Socialist Sunday School Movement, started by members of the S.D.F. In *Justice* of May 16, 1891, A. A. Watts wrote a letter to the Editor saying : " I throw out as a suggestion for our members and our Executive the formation of Socialist Sunday Schools."

The idea was carried out in the following year, and in November 1892 the first Sunday School was started in Battersea, with two scholars ; these increased to eighty-six in the course of the next two years.

In the issue of *Justice* for February 10, 1894, a letter appeared under the heading of " Save the Children," signed by Charles R. Vincent (Canning Town), Mary Grey (Battersea) and T. Partridge (Walworth), saying : " We have agreed to the following resolution as the best means to save the children from the prevailing ignorance and superstition :

" ' That we endeavour during 1894 to establish a Sunday School Union in connection with the S.D.F.' "

In the same month J. Watts, Treasurer and Hon. Secretary of the British Socialist Sunday School Committee, wrote that a Committee had been appointed by the Bristol Socialist Sunday Society for the purpose of forming a Sunday School in that city.

The Battersea Sunday School seems to have proved highly successful, for in the issue of *Justice* for September 8, 1894, Mary Grey wrote to say that the children had been taken for a picnic to Kenley, and that " coming home they sang all the way, and repeatedly called : ' Three cheers for the social revolution ! ' " The movement developed largely under the influence of A. P. Hazell, of the S.D.F., and Archibald Russell, who edited the official organ, *The Young Socialist*.

In this same year of 1894 a certain Tom Anderson founded the first of the Glasgow Socialist Sunday Schools, but these were taken over in 1906 by the National Council of the British Socialist Sunday School Union, which does not inculcate the blasphemous and violent teaching of Tom Anderson, continued later in his Proletarian schools. The attitude of the Socialist Sunday Schools towards religion—in contradistinction to that of the Proletarian and also the Communist Schools, which will be dealt with later—was described in 1923 by Stanley Mayne, formerly General Secretary to the National Council, in the words : " Within the Socialist Sunday School Movement we have opinion ranging from atheist and agnostic over the whole gamut of the Christian Church." Owing to the disinclination of the S.S.S. and the Communist Party—with which Mayne appears to have sympathised—to unite, he resigned his post a few months later. The question of religion was perhaps more concisely put last year at a Conference of the S.S.S. in London, by Councillor R. Chandler, of West Ham, who was reported as saying :

" The Socialist Sunday School movement is not opposed to religion, neither are we supporting it ; we are merely cutting it out. Our Socialist movement is greater than any religion, its ideals are greater than Christ or greater even than God, and we want to bring about a universal brotherhood " (*Patriot* for February 26, 1925).

Precisely by their appearance of moderation and professions of idealism—derided by the Bolsheviks—the Socialist Sunday Schools are more insidious than the openly revolutionary and atheistic variety. They have always borne a noticeably German character ; the hymn-books used contain a number of German names over the words or tunes. The air of the " Red Flag " is, of course, that of the old folk-song, " O ! Tannenbaum, o, Tannenbaum, wie schön sind deine Blätter." The same German inspiration may be observed throughout the Continental Youth Movement, of which it is now necessary to trace the origins.

In 1900 a Congress of the 2nd Internationale, which, as we have seen, had passed completely under the control of the German Social Democrats, took place in Paris, and the plan of organising a more systematic Socialist Youth movement was put forward but not immediately organised on an international basis. Isolated groups were soon formed, however : the first in Holland by some members of the Social Democratic Labour Party (S.D.A.P.) and named " De Zaaïer " (the Sowers) ; others followed in Sweden (1903), in Denmark, Finland and Spain (1906), in Norway and Italy (1907) (*Armia Kommunistitcheskovo Internazionala*, published by the 3rd Internationale in 1921, pp. 91–6).

International of Socialist Youth.—In this same year of 1907 the movement was at last internationally organised in Germany, and the " International Relations Committee of the Socialist Youth Organisations," briefly known as the " Internationale of Socialist Youth," at first completely revolutionary in character, was founded during the International Socialist Congress in Stuttgart. The leaders were Karl Liebknecht, Rolland Holst and Alber. In 1910 the more moderate Socialists succeeded in obtaining an influence, but in 1915 further attempts were made to turn the movement in a revolutionary direction. Its organ, *The International of Youth*, continued publication throughout the War.

Young Communist International.—After the War and the Russian Revolution, on November 20–29, 1919, the Left elements of this organisation held an International Conference in Berlin, and took the name of the "Communist Youth International" or "Young Communist International," which proceeded to affiliate itself with the 3rd Internationale (*Labour Year Book*, 1924, pp. 381, 388).

It was from the headquarters of the Communist Youth International at 63 Feurigstrasse, Berlin, that the publications of the Communist Youth movement continued to be sent out in different languages. These included the following, the first of which, it will be noted, retained the old name of the Socialist Youth organ :

Jugend-Internationale (monthly), translated into English as *The Young International*, later as *The International Youth*.
Internationale Jugendkorrespondenz (every ten days).

For children :

Der junge Genosse (The Young Comrade).
Das Proletarische Kind (The Proletarian Child).

The English translation of the last named (printed in Berlin) was sold in Glasgow under the title of *An International Magazine for Proletarian Children*. Amongst the contributors were the editor, E. Hörnle, and such names as Max Barthel, Morris Rosenfeld, Leo Andreas, Hella Rosenblum, etc.

Besides this literature printed in Berlin, each country had its own organs printed and published at home under the inspiration of Berlin and Moscow. Some of these were as follows :

ENGLAND : *The Young Worker* (weekly).
The Red Dawn (monthly).
FRANCE : *L' Avant Garde Communiste et Ouvrière*.
HOLLAND : *Der jonge Communist*.
SWITZERLAND : *Die Neue Jugend*.
ITALY : *Avanguardia*.
UNITED STATES : *The Young Communist* (illegal).
RUSSIA : *Youni Kommunist*.
Youni Proletar.
NORWAY : *Klassekampen*.
AUSTRIA : *Die Kommunistische Jugend*, etc.

Young Communist League.—The result of the first (Berlin) Congress of the Communist Youth International was to create Communist Leagues of Youth in a number of different countries, and when the second Congress met in Moscow from July 9 to 20, 1920, the representatives of these leagues from no less than forty countries were present (*Internazionale Molodyeji*, No. 12, 1921, p. 6). An important centre of direction was now created in Moscow by the Russian section of the movement, under the control of the Komintern, which came to be called the " Komsomol " from the Russian words **Kom**munistitcheski **So**yuz **Mo**lodyeji, meaning Communist League of Youth. The members of the Central Committee in Moscow included Lazar Shatzkin (on the Berlin Executive Committee), Ignat, Plasunov, Smarodin and Feïgin. A later development of the Komsomol was the " Young Pioneers."

The Young Communist Leagues now formed in the different countries were thus not branches of the Komsomol of Moscow but of the Young Communist International of Berlin—known in Russia as the **Kim** (Kommunistitcheski Internazional Molodyeje)— affiliated to the Komintern of Moscow. At the same time, all these Young Communist Leagues, being directed by the Communist Parties in the countries to which they belonged, and the Communist Party of each country being affiliated with the Komintern, they were also connected with the latter, and were, therefore, under the double control of Berlin and Moscow.

Before the foundation of the British Y.C.L. in 1921 the Communist Youth movement in this country was represented by three bodies. These were : (1) The **Young Socialist League,** which joined up with the Young Communist International after the Berlin Congress in 1919 (*Communist International*, No. 13, p. 2617). The organ of the Y.S.L. was the *Red Flag*, edited by Nathan B. Whycer, a teacher in the Central London Socialist Sunday School, and a frequenter of the " Brotherhood Church " in North London which was started before the War, and where the speakers have included Saklatvala, Sylvia Pankhurst, and P. H. Lewis, the Communist who is frequently heard in Hyde Park. (2) The **Young Workers' League,** with its organ, *The Young Worker*; and (3) the **International Communist School Movement,** with the *Red Dawn*. In 1921 the last two were merged into the Y.C.L., and their organs combined in the *Young Communist*, with the sub-heading, " Organ of the Young Communist League : British Section of the Young Communist International." The first number, dated December 1921, states :

" With the birth of the Young Communist League, as the result of the fusion of the Young Workers' League and the International Communist School movement, and with it the first issue of *The Young Communist* (with which is incorporated *The Young Worker* and *The Red Dawn*), an epoch is marked in the history of the Young Proletarian movement in this country."

On another page the Y.C.L. of Russia is described as the " largest league within the Young Communist International," hence it is clear that the Y.C.L.s of England and Russia were both a part of the Berlin organisation, which remained in that city until 1924 (see *Labour Year Book* for 1924, p. 475), when it seems to have been moved to Moscow. The *Bulletins* of the Young Communist League, the *Young Communist Review* and *International Youth*, now appear to be out of circulation in this country.

The headquarters of the Young Communist League of Great Britain were at first the same as those of the Communist Party—16 King Street, Covent Garden—and the editor both of the *Young Communist* and another paper, the *Young Rebel*, was James Stewart, of the Y.C.L. Executive (see *Labour Who's Who* under his name). Later the headquarters were removed to 36 Lamb's Conduit Street, with S. Goldsmith as editor of the *Young Communist*, and finally to 38 Great Ormonde Street, the same address as the National Minority Movement, where they are at the present moment. About two years ago the *Young Communist* changed its name to the *Young Worker*, reverting to that of the organ of the former Young Workers' League, and now appears weekly. The Y.C.L. has also formed a children's branch, called the Young Comrades' League for boys and girls between the ages of ten and fourteen, of which the organ is the *Young Comrade* (monthly).

The National Executive Council of the Y.C.L. was not properly constituted until 1922, when the following were elected:

H. Young	McDermott
S. Goldsmith	Ballantyne
Ruskin	Ramsay
Shaw	Redfern (Secretary)

In 1925 the National Executive Committee was constituted as follows:

National Secretary: Frank D. Springhall (also leader of the Young Comrades' League).

Secretary: William Rust.

D. Wilson	H. Smith
J. Cohen	J. Robertson
W. Tapsell	J. Prothero
A. Pearce	J. Shields
E. Rothstein	H. Young
W. Duncan	C. M. Roebuck
E. Woolley	

In the following November (1925) Rust was amongst the Communists imprisoned for sedition, and in May Springhall was convicted under the Emergency Powers Act brought into force during the General Strike, and sentenced to hard labour.

The work of organising the Communist Sunday Schools, which has been going on since 1920—some of which in 1925 took over the name of Young Pioneers in imitation of Soviet Russia—has been carried on by the Y.C.L. These schools were said to have ceased to exist. This was not the case, at any rate in 1925, when forty were still in existence, mostly held in cinemas or laundries, where sex teaching of the most demoralising kind was given. The teachers were in almost all cases aliens. Admittance was very difficult to obtain, as were the *Red Catechisms* and other pamphlets provided; one of the worst of these, entitled *Communist Rules*, was published in 1921.

The Proletarian Schools, organised in 1918 by Tom Anderson (formerly of the Socialist Sunday School Movement), are confined to Glasgow and the surrounding neighbourhood (N.C.U. pamphlet, *The Truth about the Red Schools*, p. 10). Their organ is a singularly blasphemous and indecent publication named *Proletcult*: " a magazine for Girls and Boys."

The attention of the clergy has frequently been drawn to these centres for the corruption of youth with little result, and the only attempt to draw the children away from them by opposition schools has been made by the British Fascists' " Children's Clubs," providing counter-attractions in the form of wholesome amusement and simple teaching on religion and patriotism.

But the Socialist and Communist Sunday Schools are not the most important poison-centres, since parents are not obliged to send their children to them. For working-class youth the Socialist and Communist teachers in the Government schools at which attendance is compulsory are a greater danger, for in these it is the best types of working-class children they are able to pervert. But here again apparently no general action is to be taken.

The Young Socialist International.—We have seen that at the Conference of the International of Socialist Youth in Berlin in 1919 only a section of the movement constituted itself the Young Communist International, the remainder continued to disassociate themselves from the Communist movement.

The International of Working-Class Youth.—Early in 1921 the Social Democratic Young Workers' International was formed in Amsterdam by members of the parties attached to the 2nd Internationale, and at about the same time the Young Workers of Austria, the German districts of Czecho-Slovakia, etc., organised the International Union of Socialist Workers. These two Young Socialist Internationals held a number of Conferences, and finally, at Hamburg during the Session of the Labour Socialist or 2nd Internationale in 1923, a new Young Socialist International was formed, called the " Internationale of Working-Class Youth " or Sozialistische Jugend Internationale, under E. Ollenhauer, with headquarters at 3 Lindenstrasse, Berlin (*Labour Year Book* for 1924, pp. 381, 382, 475, and for 1925, p. 41). This organisation has made considerable progress, and has a membership in twenty-two different countries, by far the largest being in Germany, where it now amounts to 102,000 (*Labour Year Book* for 1926, pp. 381, 382). In Great Britain the figure of 5,000 given is drawn entirely from the I.L.P.

I.L.P. Guild of Youth.—Early in 1924 the I.L.P., true to its traditions in seeking inspiration from Germany, started to organise the " I.L.P. Guild of Youth " for bringing more young people into the Socialist and Pacifist fold. By the end of the year a large number of branches had been formed all over the country. The question of forming a " united front " with the Young Communist League has recently been discussed, but decided against by the National Committee of the Guild. A contingent of " comrades," headed by Arthur Tetley, a member of the National Committee, attended the 2nd Congress of the Socialist Youth International at Amsterdam from May 26–29, at which Eric Ollenhauer of the Berlin headquarters took the lead. The I.L.P. Guild of Youth is now affiliated to the " British League of Esperanto Socialists," in which a number of Communists are also concerned.

The official organ of the Guild is *The Flame*, edited by Clare Brockway, and published at 14 Great George Street, Westminster.

Like the Socialist Sunday Schools, the I.L.P. Guild of Youth is not avowedly revolutionary or anti-Christian, but carries on its campaign under the guise of Pacifism, brotherhood or the return to nature.

The Fellowship of Youth for Peace.—We have already referred both here and in America, to the " International Fellowship of Reconciliation " or " Versöhnungsbund," of which the International Secretariat is situated in this country, under the control of the Rev. Oliver Dryer, with offices at 16 Red Lion Square, whilst the national branch is conducted by P. W. Bartlett, with offices next door at No. 17. This organisation in America was instrumental in forming the " Fellowship of Youth for Peace " early in 1924, as part of the War Resisters' International, with which the F.O.R. is affiliated. From September 18-22, 1924, a joint conference of the F.O.R. and the F.Y. for P. was held at Seaside Park, New Jersey, and amongst members then elected to the council of the new movement were a number of members of the American Civil Liberties Union, including Roger Baldwin, A. J. Muste and John Haynes Holmes, of which the subversive aims have been described earlier, whilst several members of the W.I.L. were present as speakers. Mrs. Margaret B. L. Robinson, an ardent patriot, president of the Massachusetts Public Interests League, wrote on May 6, 1925 :

" A movement which is showing itself to be full of danger in Massachusetts is the so-called Fellowship of Youth for Peace. At a meeting held under its auspices last week in Boston, which I attended, the presiding officer was a well-known Socialist, Harry Dana, and the speaker a Belgian Socialist, Gust Muyne. Three times during the evening the audience was urged to attend a ball for the benefit of Sacco and Vanzetti " (Fred Marvin, *Ye Shall Know the Truth*, p. 66).

In the summer of 1925 William Q. Harrison and another delegate sailed for England, and a meeting was arranged for July 1 by the F.O.R. at its international headquarters, 16 Red Lion Square, at which he was to speak on " the American Youth Movement and its relation to the International Youth Movement."

Another meeting took place on the 9th of the same month at the Friends' Meeting House, 136 Bishopsgate, to welcome the two Youth Movement delegates from America. This was convened by the "Federation of British Youth Movements," of which we shall now trace the origins in Germany.

The International League of Youth.—As we have seen, the Socialist Youth Internationale existed in Germany before the War. Just after the War had ended a Pacifist Youth Internationale, named the "International League of Youth," was formed by a Dane, Hermod Lannung, and the aims of the League, drawn up at a preliminary conference in Copenhagen and confirmed in 1922 at a further conference in Hamburg, were set forth as follows:

"The aim of the International League of Youth is to awaken Youth to the inherent unity of the peoples of the world, and to make future war impossible by a fellowship based on trust and friendship.

"In the meantime, believing in the principle of compulsory arbitration, the League advocates the limitation of armaments, with a view to their ultimate abolition, and the substitution of an International Police Force for the present National Military System. It will do all in its power to further the establishment of a true League of Nations.

"To further this aim the British section has consented to act as a central International Bureau for Youth of all nations. It will collect and disseminate reports as to the activities of all Youth Movements federated to the International League of Youth, and will publish a three-monthly report in this magazine." (*Youth*, Spring 1924.)

The Central International Bureau, formed by the British Section, was located at 152 Abbey House, Westminster, under the direction of Miss Moya Jowitt; the official organ of the movement being *Youth* (quarterly), edited by Rolf Gardiner of St. John's College, Cambridge, and circulated by the headquarters in Abbey House, and also by the German agent of the League, Hans Seligo, in Leipzig.

According to the account given in *Youth* for the spring of 1924, the International League of Youth was organised in the following manner.

A number of members of the leaders' council who had been present at a great International Youth meeting at Hellerau in August 1923, afterwards met at the castle of Lauenstein and formed a circle known as the Lauensteiner Kreis, in order to engage in "a common search and discovery of new ways and means in the technique of Western politics, economics, education, art and science." For this purpose four "watch-towers" were created, from which observations could be carried out—the first at Berlin, for communication with the East and especially with Soviet Russia; the second at the Jugendheim on the Ostsee, for communication with the North—Denmark, Sweden, Norway, and Finland; the third at first stationed in Berlin and working in close connection with the Quaker offices there, but afterwards removed to 152 Abbey House, Westminster, so as to "link up Berlin and London in direct communication"; the fourth looking out on the Mediterranean, having at present no abode but in the hands of responsible members of the Union principally resident in Frankfurt-am-Main.

The chief members of the British group, besides Moya Jowitt, were John Hargrave, S. Darwin Fox, Rolf Gardiner, and Roland Berrill. These people, all of pro-German sympathies, were contributors to *Youth*, whilst in the number of that organ already referred to we note an article by Harold Bing on behalf of the Youth Section of the No More War Movement, of which Phyllis Bing was secretary. Amongst the foreign contributors we find the names of Fritz Klatt, Karl Wilker, Gustave Wyneken, Anton Mayer (the same that we encountered on the Moscow organisation of the R.I.L.U. ?) and Arnim T. Wegner. Besides publishing extraordinary blasphemies —notably in the above-mentioned number, where an article appears headed by a revolting caricature of the Crucifixion—*Youth* went in for the cult of nature.

The Nudity Movement.—In Germany before the War the so-called "physical culture movement" had become the vogue, which found expression in the cult of nudity, as practised by the sect of German Communists known as "Adamites" in the fifteenth century. "It became the *grand chic* of an advanced set (in Berlin) to give naked parties, at which the men smoked huge cigars and the women were clothed only in bracelets, anklets, tiaras and rings" (article by Austin Harrison in the *English Review*, October 1914). Since the War this movement has grown in dimensions, and owns a number of groups, institutes, libraries, holiday camps, bathing resorts, etc. A "Nudity" candidate was even put up for election to the Reichstag, and secured over 20,000 votes (article in *Sunday Express*, July 19, 1925). According to an American writer, Bruno Lasker, it has made great headway in the Youth Movement of Germany, which is described as "introducing new and stimulating elements. One of these is the cult of nakedness." Another was described as being free love. Mr. Lasker went on to describe the crusade of one of the leaders of this movement, Herr Muck-Lamberty, who "with a following of twenty-five youths and girls," walked from town to town through the forests of the mid-German hill country, leading the children in harmless games of a cheerfulness they had never known, "teaching the young men and women dances and songs drawn from the very sources . . . of the German spirit. . . . But one day it was discovered that they were living not only in economic communism, but also what seemed at first complete sexual promiscuity" (see interesting pamphlet by Mrs. Margaret L. Robinson, *The Youth Movement*, issued by the Massachusetts Public Interests League, Boston quoting article in *Survey Graphic*, December 1921).

Walter Pahl was one of the advocates of this movement, and in an article in *Youth* and the American periodical the *New Student*, which brought out a "Special Supplement published in Germany," described the religion of the movement. Before the War youth had become sceptical of Christianity; but after it the cry went up: "God is dead!" Youth became the enemy of the Church. "Naked and Free" they denied dogma and doctrine, and found a new God—the body. They were Christians no longer, so they released the body and set themselves to "the dance of the earth and the stars within us," in order to restore the great harmony and holiness into our lives. "Dancing in fact offers the greatest religious emotion to a great part of our German youth." It is here we can trace the inspiration of the eurhythmic dancing practised by the Steinerites of Germany, the Bolsheviks of Russia and certain sects in our own country, which being, however, of the secret and occult variety, do not enter into the scope of this book.

The New Gymnosophists.—One group practising the nudity cult which does not appear to be a secret society may, however, be mentioned here, that is "The New Gymnosophical Society," which was founded in 1922. The object of this group was frankly admitted to be the propagation of nude culture, because not only physical but "psychological" health is much benefited by this practice. In connection with this society, which is still in existence, or was as recently as last summer, is at least one Club, near London, where the members pass week-ends entirely without clothes. It seems that they do not always remain within bounds, since a couple were found wandering in this condition on the Sussex downs last summer (*Sunday Express*, August 20, 1925). The police appear to have taken no action in the matter.

A co-educational school is connected with this movement.

Federation of British Youth Movements—The English branch of the International League of Youth for Peace has now ceased to exist, and its work has been taken over by the "Federation of British Youth Movements," which was founded in January 1924, with headquarters at 135 Bishopsgate, under the following personnel:

Chairman : Arthur Peacock.
Secretary : Miss Margaret Porteous.
National Secretary: Theodor Besterman (of the Guild of Citizens of To-morrow, a subsidiary organisation of the Theosophical Society).
Treasurer : Miss Phyllis Bing (of the No More War Movement).

A Conference of the Federation was held on May 2 and 3, 1925, arranged by G. W. Arundale of the Theosophical Society, with which the Federation seems to be closely connected.

At a further meeting in June, held in the form of a garden-party at Kelmscott House, Hammersmith, the following Theosophical groups were represented : The Guild of Citizens of To-morrow, the Order of the Round Table, the Servers' Group of Young Theosophists, the World Federation of Young Theosophists. Besides these there were delegates from the No More War Movement, the Fellowship of Reconciliation, the Young Friends' Movement, the I.L.P. and the Order of Woodcraft Chivalry of the Kibbo Kift. The outstanding feature of this gathering of the Federation of British Youth Movements was said by an observer to be predominantly foreign, and in particular German. German songs were sung.

Kibbo Kift.—The movement known as Kibbo Kift, which also carried on the work of the International League of Youth, is generally said to have been formed in England in the spring of 1921, with branches in Germany, Russia, Holland, France, Italy and Algeria. From inside evidence it appears, however, that it was organised in this country as early as 1919—that is to say, at about the same time that the International League of Youth was formed in Copenhagen, under German auspices, so that instead of being a British movement with foreign branches, it seems not unlikely that it was all along a part of the German " Jugendbewegung," and of the International Federation of Youth. At any rate its teachings and aims are identical, whilst John Hargrave, its reputed founder, whose " anti-militarist " views had necessitated his leaving the staff of the Boy Scouts, was, as we have seen, a contributor to *Youth*, in which Kibbo Kift and its later organ the *Nomad*—the first one was called the *Mask*—were advertised. Further, the address of the Business Manager of the K.K., Kinsman G. C. Morris, was the same as the address of the British branch of the International Federation of Youth—152 Abbey House, Westminster—and Moya Jowitt, the director of this bureau, was also the organiser of the K.K. scheme, described as " world survey." The connection, if not the actual identity, between the two movements is, therefore, evident.

The K.K. is described in a leaflet by the editor of the *Nomad*, under the pseudonym of " White Fox "—presumably Hargrave himself—as being a " world peace movement," which was largely to be achieved by camping out; and its objects included the reorganisation of industry on a non-competitive basis, international disarmament, international free trade, an international currency system, and the establishment of a World Council including every civilised and primitive race or nation—formulas familiar to everyone acquainted with the literature of International Socialism or Grand Orient Masonry.

The Kibbo Kift is, in fact, a semi-secret society, and as such cannot be thoroughly gone into here. This fact is very clearly brought out in a novel, called *Young Winkle*, by John Hargrave himself, in which the references made to a mysterious, brotherhood active all over the world, to a ceremony of initiation, as also to " tribal patriotism " and the happiness of savagery, are strangely reminiscent of the German Illuminati. Leaving this occult aspect of the K.K. aside, however, no doubt can be entertained as to its anti-patriotic and subversive tendencies, the leader's sneers at the

Boy Scouts, at "militarism"—nothing, of course, about the Prussian variety—his remarks on the evil of work, his insistence on sex teaching and jeers at religion, plainly show the true character of the organisation which he controls.

The "world survey" idea of the K.K., directed by Miss Moya Jowitt, a scheme certainly more practical than occult, merits some attention. In the May 1925 number of the *Nomad*, the young "Kinsmen" are enjoined to make maps, giving the population, industries, etc. One of the directions runs :

"Visit and find out full information about, and make a list of, all the present institutions, such as hospitals, museums, schools, colleges, institutes, societies, movements, organisations, places of worship, places of amusement, theatres, etc., in your district."

Before the War German spies were known to be engaged on making maps precisely on these lines. This habit of map-making may not be all to the future advantage of Britain.

The K.K. is not confined to England; in France it acquired land at Le Talon, Chevreuse, Seine-et-Oise, where an International camp was held in August 1924. In Poland it exists as a Woodcraft League, known as the Zjednoczenie Wolnego Harcertswar; in Holland it goes under the name of "Stormvogels." The last named was at first composed of children from six to twelve years of age, who formed an avowedly Communist group led by Francine Ruygers, and in August 1924 went bodily over to the Young Communist organisation. This is illuminating, since in England the K.K. professes to have no connection with Communism, although in July 1923 it was stated that two delegates would attend the Conference of the League of Communist Youth in Dresden. In view of all this, it is interesting to read the names on the Advisory Council of the K.K. in this country, published at this date. These included Norman Angell, H. G. Wells, Rabindranath Tagore, Havelock Ellis, Stephen Graham, Professor Julian S. Huxley, Maurice Maeterlinck, Henry W. Nevinson, Maurice Hewlett, Mrs. Pethick Lawrence, Professor Patrick Geddes, and J. Howard Whitehouse. It should be noted that the last name on this list is that of the head master of a school founded at Bembridge, Isle of Wight, some six years ago, for the purpose of carrying out new methods of education, including what was termed self-government. A letter advertising the scheme appeared on its inauguration in the *Times*, and two years later a further letter was addressed to the same paper signed by the head, J. Howard Whitehouse, also by Dean Inge, Lord Henry Cavendish Bentinck, Charles F. Masterman (editor of *The Nation*), Harold Laski (London School of Economics and member of the Executive Committee of the American Civil Liberties Union), Henry W. Nevinson and Noel Buxton (Labour Party and 1917 Club). Two out of these seven supporters of the Bembridge School were, therefore, on the Council of the Kibbo Kift.

YOUTH MOVEMENTS

At the moment of this book going to press a notice appears of a meeting to be held on " The Men of the Trees," by Mr. Richard St. Barbe Baker, who, we note in the *Nomad* for December 1924, was presented by "White Fox" at Abbey House with a copper plaque, inscribed with a message of brotherhood in symbol-writing.

My object in following up all these connections is not to censure everyone who takes part in movements of this kind—e.g., it is not alleged that every supporter of the Kibbo Kift is fully cognisant or would approve of all it is and does—but to show by what an intricate system of interlockings the members of subversive organisations contrive to spread their propaganda.

The movement for the demoralisation of British youth—the undermining of patriotism and of belief in religion, and the revolt against discipline—is very skilfully organised. For the children of working-class parents there are the Socialist and Communist Sunday Schools and the teachers of the same doctrines in the Government schools; for both working-class and middle-class children the various Socialist, Communist and Pacifist leagues; for the boys and girls of the rich there is the insidious propaganda instilled by masters, mistresses, lecturers and university dons, secretly in the service of the country's enemies. And unhappily for all classes, there is the influence of those of the clergy who have sold their birthright for a mess of red pottage.

CHAPTER XIII
SOCIALISM AND CHRISTIANITY

THE Socialism professed by certain members of our clergy to-day must not be confounded with the " Christian Socialism " advocated in the middle of the last century by Kingsley and Maurice. The doctrines they taught were not at all identical with those known politically as Communism or as Socialism. If in spirit they had something in common with the Utopian Socialists of France, they held nothing of the spirit expressed in Karl Marx's *Communist Manifesto*, which appeared at the time they carried on their campaign. The formula now generally accepted as that of Socialism—" the nationalisation of all the means of production, distribution and exchange "—enters nowhere into their teaching, which was not to advocate an economic theory that had already proved a failure, but simply the reconstruction of the social order based on Christian principles. However impracticable such an idea might be in view of Christ's own statement : " My kingdom is not of this world," it was, nevertheless, sincere and free from the bitterness of modern Socialism. For, whilst denouncing social evils, nowhere did they preach class war ; on the contrary, in *Alton Locke* Charles Kingsley condemned it in unmeasured terms, whilst the anti-Christian teaching of Robert Owen in their own day and of Karl Marx—whose influence only became felt in England after their lifetimes—was the very antithesis of theirs.

Unlike Lord Shaftesbury, however, who declared Socialism to be " a plague deep-seated and rancorous," they did not realise that materialism and class hatred were almost always the accompaniments of the economic theory of Socialism ; and so, by calling themselves Socialists, they coupled together the names of two creeds which, as the German Socialist Bebel truly observed, " stand towards each other as fire and water." This was, perhaps, excusable in men who, living before the Marxian era in this country, could not see for themselves whither real Socialism must lead.

But for men who can look back on the last forty years of Socialist agitation, the position is entirely different. They know, or should know, that since the founding of the Democratic Federation in 1881, Socialism in this country has been almost entirely derived

SOCIALISM AND CHRISTIANITY

from the teaching of Marx, whose insistence on materialism, militant atheism and advocacy of the class war, has divested the word Socialism of all the idealism thrown around it by the Christian Socialists of the last century. To profess Socialism now is to range oneself, whether consciously or not, with the enemies of Christianity, as Mrs. Margaret L. Robinson has well explained in her admirable pamphlet, *Christian Socialism, a Contradiction in Terms*.

So, whilst the old Christian Socialists took the discredited word Socialism and strove to invest it with the spirit of Christianity, our so-called Christian Socialists of to-day take the pure and beautiful doctrines of Christianity and infuse into them the spirit of class hatred.

The Christian Social Union.—One of the first organisations formed to disseminate the idea of Christianity in relation to social life was the Christian Social Union, which, according to the head of the Industrial Christian Fellowship with which it joined up in 1918, originated much earlier, having been formed by Maurice and Kingsley (who died respectively in 1872 and 1875), supported by Canon Scott Holland, Bishop Gore and the Bishop of Lichfield (letter from the Rev. P. T. Kirk to the *Patriot*, November 30, 1922). The writer of this letter describes it as " most certainly not avowedly Socialistic."

Another Christian Socialist organisation was the Guild of St. Matthew, founded in 1877 by the Rev. Stuart Headlam, which also does not appear to have been revolutionary in character; but the **Church Socialist League**, formed in 1908, had for its founders two men who have taken an active part in agitation—the Rev. F. L. (now Canon) Donaldson, who describes himself as a "convinced Christian Socialist" and who led and organised a march of Unemployed from Leicester to London in 1905, and the Rev. Conrad Noel, Vicar of Thaxted, Essex, who for many years has preached the most virulent class hatred.

The Catholic Crusade.—It was not, however, until after the rise of the Bolsheviks to power that the " red clergy " openly took up their stand with the world revolutionaries. In America Bishop Montgomery Brown proclaimed himself the " Bishop of Bolsheviks and Atheists." Conrad Noel, whilst continuing to profess Christianity, started his revolutionary Catholic Crusade in 1918. The Hon. Sec. was at first the Rev. H. O. Mason, the Rectory, Elland, Yorkshire ; in 1925 Robert Woodifield; whilst supporters of the movement included the Rev. G. B. Chambers and the Rev. C. J. Bucknall, who has recently been presented with the living of Delabole, North Cornwall.

The Catholic Crusade has no official organ, but a number of pamphlets have been published by it, including *A Manifesto*, setting forth its objects, one of which is said to be " to break up the present world, and make a new in the power of the Outlaw of

Galilee : Destruction not Reconstruction "; *Creative Democracy,* which describes " Apostolic Bolshevism and Democratic Succession : the Christian Soviet and the Episcopal International "; *The Catholic Crusade,* merely incoherent and blasphemous ravings ; *The Christian Religion : Dope or Dynamite* ; *Is Jesus the Revolutionary Leader ?* etc. It is difficult to discover the doctrines of any particular brand of Socialism in these publications, which are as dull as they are revolting, and preach only a sort of aimless anarchy. There is, however, perhaps more method than might be supposed behind the madness of the Catholic Crusade, which appears to be not unconnected with a certain secret society of an occult description. To follow up this line of investigation would take us beyond the limits of this book ; it may, however, be mentioned that a certain clergyman who not long ago created a scandal by his open expression of Bolshevist views is known to the present writer by irrefutable evidence to have been a member of the society in question, whilst the bishop who supported him was head of an institution whence a number of members of the same society were drawn.

The I.C.F.—The " Industrial Christian Fellowship," which was formed out of the Navvy Mission on November 11, 1918, and afterwards amalgamated with the Christian Social Union, is a society of a very different order from the Catholic Crusade, from the leader of which it has publicly disassociated itself. Indeed, it professes not to be Socialist at all. " We stand," it declares, " for Christ and His principles, independent of party." And again, " The Fellowship is not political ; it is a spiritual effort, for we hold that Christianity must pervade every department of life."

But this does not prevent the I.C.F. in its official organ, *The Torch,* from paying tribute to such Labour members of Parliament as it may consider to be particularly fit instruments for this purpose ; as for example, J. H. Thomas, George Lansbury, C. G. Ammon, " Bob " Williams, etc. Nor did it deter one of its body of directors, the Rev. F. E. Mercer, from writing a pamphlet called *Why Churchmen should be Socialists* ; nor another from declaring at a public meeting that " the Capitalist system has broken down and will end in a rotten chaos." (*The Patriot,* August 9, 1923).

Another leading light of the I.C.F., the Rev. G. A. Studdert Kennedy, is alleged to have spoken at a Labour demonstration beside George Lansbury on October 8, 1922, and with Saklatvala at Bow Baths on February 25, 1923. It was on Armistice Day, 1921, that he levelled his famous insult against the men who had fought for England by saying that :

" He had appealed to the troops during the war, and encouraged them to fight on the ground that they were fighting for freedom and honour. He knew now it was nothing of the kind. There was no freedom and there was no end to war. We had lied as a nation and besmirched our honour. We had broken our promises and gone back on our word in half a score of cases. . . . They were mad, he said; he himself was mad; they were all mad out there. They were given decorations for what they did when they were mad" (*Morning Post*, November 12, 1921).

Remonstrances addressed to the I.C.F. with regard to such utterances have been met with the reply that the speaker was not speaking in the name of the Fellowship, but as a private individual. We have not heard of this system of dual personality leading to the appearance of a member of the I.C.F. on the platform of, say, —the British Fascists.

A dual personality appears, moreover, to be the characteristic not only of individual members of the I.C.F., but of the society itself. Thus on March 12, 1926, the present writer received a circular of the I.C.F. in which it was again stated that:

"It may not be out of place to reaffirm the fact that the I.C.F. is not pledged to any political party or to any scheme of economic reform. It stands for Christ and His principles, independent of party, and seeks for means to pursue and extend its work and to proclaim its message boldly and fearlessly as the Holy Spirit may direct."

Appended to this was a leaflet describing an I.C.F. speaker "in a poor class district" pacifying the revolutionary tendencies of the crowd.

Yet at this very moment it appears that the I.C.F. was issuing a questionnaire on the coal crisis marked "confidential," inquiring into the miners' grievances and every detail of the coal trade, and requesting that the document should be returned on March 6, just when the Report of the Coal Commission was expected (*Morning Post*, March 3, 1926). It certainly seems strange that a society, not pledged to any scheme of economic reform, and standing only for "Christ and His principles," should institute a searching inquiry into the economic aspect of the coal trade, precisely at the moment when the Government was engaged on the same task. There has been close co-operation between some of the officials and fervent Socialists who are notorious promoters of the class-war, and whose public records are no security whatever for any deep interest in the triumph of Christianity. The circulars of the I.C.F. contain many statements in exact agreement with the policy of the Socialist Party; and have been quoted in the *Patriot*, from November 9, 1922, to January 18, 1923, during its controversy with the Fellowship. In that controversy it was shown that the public literature of the I.C.F. is, in effect, a preaching that the way to the original Christian objects of the Fellowship is marked out by the Socialist Party; and is to be preceded by the destruction of the capitalist system.

130 THE SOCIALIST NETWORK

The following names, which appear on the circular of March 1926, presumably form the present personnel of the I.C.F. :

PRESIDENTS :
  The Archbishop of Canterbury.
  The Archbishop of York.
  The Archbishop of Wales.
VICE-PRESIDENT AND CHAIRMAN :
  The Bishop of Lichfield.
VICE-CHAIRMEN :
  Bishop of Woolwich.
  Major-General F. Maurice.
HON. TREASURERS :
  Everard Hesketh.
  Frank Hodges.
HON. TRUSTEE :
  Lord Henry Bentinck.
  William Cash.
  Major J. D. Birchall, M.P.
  Lord Beauchamp.
  Margaret Bigge.
  Lord Daryngton.
  Sir Lynden Macassey.
  Bishop of Manchester.
  Sir Robert Newman, M.P.
  Rev. H. R. L. Sheppard.
  Constance Smith.
  Sir Edwin Stockton.
  Rev. G. A. Studdert Kennedy.
GENERAL DIRECTOR :
  P. T. R. Kirk.

The headquarters of the I.C.F. are at Fellowship House, 4 The Sanctuary, Westminster.

The League of the Kingdom of God.—A so-called Christian society which makes no effort to conceal its Socialistic character is the " League of the Kingdom of God," the name assumed in 1923 by the Church Socialist League before mentioned. The character of the society is officially given in these words :

" The League is a band of Churchmen and Churchwomen who believe that the Catholic Faith demands a challenge to the world by the repudiation of capitalist plutocracy and the wage system ; and stands for a social order in which the means of life subserve the common weal."

The particular brand of Socialism that the League favours seems to be Guild Socialism, with which members of the Church Socialist

League, notably Maurice B. Reckitt, had been associated, when working in the Fabian Research Department with G. D. H. Cole.

The three leaders of the movement in the year that the change of name took place were Maurice B. Reckitt (Vice-Chairman of the C.S.L.), the Rev. Paul Stacy and N. E. Egerton Swann. Later the Rev. T. C. Gobat was made Chairman, H. H. Slesser (now Sir Henry Slesser) became Vice-Chairman and A. Hunter, Treasurer. George Lansbury, who is just now agitating to get the blasphemy laws revoked, and the Rev. J. Bucknall are also members.

The official organ of the League is the *Commonwealth* (monthly), edited by G. W. Wardman at Letchworth Garden City, Herts.

Society of Socialist Christians.—Another so-called Christian society that makes no secret of its political aims is the " Society of Socialist Christians," started in 1924 as an amalgamation of smaller societies. The Secretary is Charles Record, 8 Victoria Avenue, Elland, Yorkshire, and the official organ of the society is *The Crusader* (weekly), printed by G. W. Wardman (editor of the *Commonwealth*) at the Commonwealth Press, Letchworth, and published by the Crusader Committee at 1 Mitre Court, Fleet Street, E.C.4.

The aims of the Society of Socialist Christians are officially set forth as follows :

" The Society of Socialist Christians is a body of people who, acknowledging the leadership of Jesus Christ, pledge themselves to work and pray for the spiritual and economic emancipation of all people from the bondage of material things, and for the establishment of the Commonwealth of God on earth.

" Recognising that the present capitalist order of society is fundamentally anti-Christian, the Society will strive for the creation of an international Socialist order based on the communal control of the means of life and co-operation in freedom for the common weal.

" The Society will work as part of the Labour Movement. It believes that the necessary transformation of our social order requires a change of heart and mind and will, and a corresponding change of political and industrial arrangements ; substituting mutual service for exploitation, and a social democracy for the struggle of individuals and classes."

The last number of the *Crusader* (for May 28, 1926) quite frankly approved of the recent General Strike, and deplored the blindness of the *Christian World* in describing it as a failure. On another page the editor of the *Daily Herald* is referred to as " Comrade Hamilton Fyfe." Amongst contributors to the organ, and to the series of " Crusader Booklets," are Father John Corner Spokes (editor of the *Crusader*), Father Harold Buxton, the Rev. Seaward Beddow, the Rev. W. G. Peck, the Rev. W. E. Orchard, Father Gilbert Clive Binyon, Fred Hughes, B. C. Boulter, etc.

C.O.P.E.C.—In April of the same year (1924) that the Society of Socialist Christians was founded a conference took place at

Birmingham to discuss the application of Christianity to social, industrial, political and international problems, at which the following resolution was passed :

"That the Christian faith is fundamentally opposed to the spirit of Imperialism as expressed in desire of conquest, maintenance of prestige, or the pursuit, in other forms, of the selfish interests of one nation at the expense of another."

From this Conference arose the society known as C.O.P.E.C., standing for "Christian Order of Politics, Economics and Citizenship." The Conference was presided over by Lord Parmoor, then a member of the Socialist Government, who vehemently denounced war and regretted that the Churches had not been unanimously Pacifist during the Great War. Other speakers included Sir Henry Slesser, E. D. Morel, and also the Rev. Studdert Kennedy of the I.C.F., who declared that in future the Churches ought to support the right of our forces to mutiny and for our sailors to lay down their arms. It is only fair to add that in the following November Mr. Kennedy expressed what appear to be absolutely opposite views, declaring that any attempt at disarmament would be madness (*Times*, November 11, 1924). Since then, however, he seems to have reverted to anti-Imperialism. It is impossible to keep pace with the vagaries of some of these people.

A number of Pacifist and Socialist organisations, such as the U.D.C., I.L.P., Fellowship of Reconciliation, No More War Movement, League of the Kingdom of God, etc., were represented at the C.O.P.E.C. Conference. The Chairman then elected for the Committee of International Relations was E. F. Wise, who had left the Board of Trade to take employment under the Soviet Government.

The anti-patriotic and Socialist tendencies of C.O.P.E.C. have been shown up by the Rev. Prebendary Gough, in his admirable little book, *The Fight for Man*, where he wrote : "The ordinary wholesome Christian can only view all this 'Copec' parody and perversion of Christianity with disgust." Dean Inge, in a letter to the *Morning Post* on January 1, 1925, described "Copec" as "the latest and most insidious attempt to politicise the Church and capture organised Christianity for Socialism."

In these words the Dean draws attention to the greatest danger that confronts the Christian world. It is not the avowed Communists, whose very violence repels all sane and wholesome minds, who are likely to bring about the overthrow of Britain, and with her the whole of civilisation ; it is the so-called idealist and professing Christian who most effectively carries out the devil's work. Let those of the clergy, whether Church of England, Nonconformist or Roman Catholic—for renegade priests are not unknown—who are preaching Communism, anti-patriotism and class hatred under the guise of Christianity be denounced in the same unmeasured terms here as in America, where Senator Blanton, in the concluding remarks of his exposure of the Bolshevist movement in the States, declared : " If the ministers of the Gospel have sold their services to Russia, it is our duty to make it known to the public " (*Congressional Record*, December 19, 1925, p. 7).

Was it not written that in the latter days false prophets would arise and deceive the very elect ?

CHAPTER XIV
CONCLUSION

WE have now seen a fraction, but only a fraction, of the vast network of Socialism stretched over the civilised world. To pass the whole in review would be the work of years. For when we consider that in our own country alone, to which the greatest amount of space in this book has been given, only the most important societies have been mentioned, and that the list of societies, leagues, groups and " movements "—Socialist, Pacifist, pseudo-religious or frankly anti-religious—could be multiplied *ad infinitum*, what would be the result, if we were to do this in the case of every part of the world, including the Far East, on which the Bolsheviks' attention is now specially concentrated ? The network thus revealed would surely be bewildering enough to make the human brain reel. And even then the picture would be incomplete if we were still to exclude the secret societies that provide so much driving power behind the open movements. For example, in our own country one of the most influential groups working for Socialism, the inner circle of the Theosophical Society, enters into the category of secret societies, and has, therefore, necessarily been excluded.

Enough of the open network has, however, been shown to give some idea of its vastness and of its plan of construction. We have seen how the marvellous brains behind it know how to utilise everything that comes to their hand, so that they have now been able to penetrate every sphere of human endeavour—art, literature, education, women's movements, religious movements—and to gain control of all the means of publicity—the press, the theatre, the cinema, and also broadcasting, which, even under a Conservative Government, serves as a mouthpiece for Socialist propaganda.

Let us make no mistake, the disintegrating doctrines of international Socialism are spreading slowly but surely throughout our country. It is true that at the last General Election Conservatism won a sweeping victory, yet there was an increase of a million votes for the Socialist Party. It is true that the General Strike has this time been defeated, yet over three million free-born Britons came out with the docility of Russian *moujiks* at the call of their leaders in an attack on the life of the nation. In 1921 the railwaymen were clearly unwilling to join in what some of them called a Bolshevik move ; in 1926 they obeyed—not to a

CONCLUSION

man, for the few who stayed in proved the possibility of disobeying strike orders—but in a vast majority. The evil has been progressive.

Optimists have declared that the weapon of the General Strike has now been broken. It will only remain broken as long as the means for maintaining the life of the community remain in the hands of a Constitutional Government. The plan to starve the nation into submission to the dictates of the trade union leaders by means of a General Strike was the basis of the plot in 1921 and 1926. Had the offer of the T.U.C. to control the food supplies of the country been accepted, how far might this scheme not have been realised ? The present Conservative Government knew better than to accept : a Socialist Government would not dare to refuse, even if it wished to do so.

The question then arises : What are we doing to prevent the advent of a government to power which either by legislation or the General Strike will bring about the ruin of our country ? On one hand we see the vast organisation of Socialism, on the other a few patriotic societies, appealing often vainly to the public for support.

Let us examine the essential points in which Socialist organisation surpasses our own, and consider how, by taking a leaf out of the enemy's book, we might be able to put up a more effectual opposition.

I. THE SOCIALIST MOVEMENT HAS UNLIMITED FUNDS AT ITS DISPOSAL

Besides financial aid from abroad, the Socialists exact contributions from Socialist and non-Socialist workers alike. We not only tolerate this political levy being made on our own supporters, but do not counter it by subscribing generously ourselves. Conservatives who think nothing of spending a guinea for a stall at the theatre will grudge ten shillings towards anti-Socialist propaganda.

II. THE SOCIALIST MOVEMENT IS CO-ORDINATED

Although these innumerable Socialist and Pacifist groups, working in different ways for the same ends, continue to exist—since their leaders well know that amalgamation would be fatal—they are able by an ingenious system of interlocking, and by placing the same people on the councils of several different groups at a time, to co-ordinate their activities in the form of literature, meetings, demonstrations, etc.

Our societies are not only disconnected, but too often, instead of being allies, they are rivals. It is not that there are too many of them, for there would be work for all to do if only it were properly apportioned. Some plan of co-operation should be devised which would prevent them ploughing the same furrow and getting in each other's way.

III. THE SOCIALIST MOVEMENT IS INTERNATIONALLY ORGANISED

The strength of Socialism in every country depends largely on foreign support. The interchange of communications between countries not only furnishes information but brings variety and enthusiasm into the movement. International Conferences are also a great source of inspiration. In 1922 the Communist Party had no less than twenty linguists translating foreign books, papers. etc., and preparing them for publication.

The anti-Socialist societies in this country have practically no linguists, ignore much that is published abroad in the interests of the cause, and hold very little communication with kindred groups in other countries. No International Anti-Socialist Conferences have been organised that in the present writer's opinion are likely to be of any great value to the cause. What is needed is an International of Patriots, composed of the groups in every country standing for sane nationalism, private property, morality and the Christian faith.

IV. THE SOCIALIST MOVEMENT HAS INTELLIGENCE DEPARTMENTS BEHIND IT

The first thing the Bolsheviks did when they seized the reins of power was to establish a Bureau of Information. In this country the Labour Party Joint Research Department acts as a clearing-house of information for the Labour Party and the T.U.C., whilst the Labour Research Department performs the same office for associates of trade unions, local Labour parties, Socialist and Communist societies of an " extreme " kind. " The Department furnishes statistics, arguments, literature and newspaper articles to order " (*Publicity Manipulation*, pamphlet, published by the Boswell Printing and Publishing Company).

On our side neither the Conservative Party nor the independent anti-Socialist societies have any central bureau for the collection and distribution of information to which propagandists can apply with any certainty of finding the data they require. Each society collects a certain amount of information which it keeps for its own use. All this put together and collected would be of enormous value—at present each collection is necessarily incomplete.

V. THE SOCIALIST MOVEMENT WELCOMES ENTHUSIASTS

Moderate Socialists, whilst publicly professing to disapprove of " Extremists," invariably stand by them against the constitutional parties. Even when it comes to deeds of violence, the whole force of the Socialist movement—political, Pacifist and " religious "—will be put into action to save the offender from punishment.

On our side the Moderates deride enthusiasts, whom they are fond of describing as " Extremists." They fail to recognise, as do the Socialists, that the driving force of every party lies in its strongest wing. The Conservative Party must develop a Right Wing as strong as the " Labour " Party's Left Wing, if it is to hold its own.

VI. THE SOCIALIST MOVEMENT GIVES NO QUARTER TO THE ENEMY

Socialists never lose an opportunity of scoring over their opponents or fail to detect a weak spot in their armour. They believe in using every method of warfare, fair or foul.

We, on our part, from a mistaken spirit of "fair play," avoid touching our opponents on a vulnerable point and leave our strongest weapons to rust in our armoury. On the pretext of "giving the other side a hearing," the Conservative press, whilst closing its columns to " Die-hards," opens them to revolutionary Socialists. " Labour " agitators can now make large sums by writing for it. The Socialist press never makes the mistake of inviting a convincing writer to put his point of view before its readers. Socialism has it all its own way, and is able to use the organs of its opponents for its propaganda.

The above are some of the differences between Socialist and anti-Socialist organisation which, if removed, would lead to the strengthening of our cause. I do not say that we should follow the Socialists' lead on every point. For the success of Socialism is above all due to the fact that it is essentially a system of deception. It wins the uneducated classes by false promises, the semi-educated by false premises, and the unwary by camouflage. To modern Socialists, as to the Jacobins of France, " Tous les moyens sont bons."

But there is no reason why Conservatism, whilst retaining its old traditions of honour and fair play, should not free itself from the time-honoured reproach of stupidity and of inertia. Let us admit this to the credit of our opponents : they work a great deal harder than we do. The propaganda of Socialism goes on ceaselessly and with unremitting energy. Day and night it circulates in factories and mining centres, at the street corners of our great cities and in our peaceful villages. So the red tide rises steadily, and unless we work far harder than we have done before, and above all organise as we have never done, this island may be submerged as were France and Russia before us.

DIAGRAM OF THE MOSCOW ORGANISATION

THE part of the large chart accompanying this book which relates to Moscow being arranged so as to show the chronological order in which the various international departments of the Russian Communist Party came into existence, it has been thought advisable to add a diagram showing the shape the whole Moscow organisation now takes, together with its present personnel. The Bolshevist system of world government will thus be seen resting on two principal pillars : (1) the TS.I.K. (**T**sentralnii **I**spolnitelnii **K**omitet) or Central Executive Committee of the U.S.S.R. (Union of Socialist Soviet Republics), composed of Russian subjects, corresponding to our Cabinet and controlling the State Departments of the Government, and (2) the I.K.K.I. (**I**spolnitelnii **K**omitet **K**ommunisticheskovo **I**nternazionala) or Executive Committee of the Komintern (Communist Internationale), composed of representatives from all countries, directing the activities of the Communist Parties affiliated to it everywhere. Between the two comes the Profintern (**R**ed **I**nternational of **L**abour **U**nions), also international in form, exercising the same control over the Red Trade Union movement in all parts of the world.

The point this diagram is particularly intended to illustrate is that since the Polit-Bureau of the Russian Communist Party controls the TS.I.K., the I.K.K.I., the Profintern and, through this last, the All Russian Central Council of Trade Unions, and since the same men who compose it also figure in the Executives of all these bodies, therefore the Communist Parties and the Red Trade Union organisations in all countries affiliated with these are in reality controlled by the Russian Government.

It should be understood that, as the personnel of all these committees changes constantly, the lists here given only apply to the present moment.

The Sport Internationale and the Peasants' Internationale that appear both in the chart and the diagram, are not dealt with in the course of this book, as their affiliations in this country are not yet of any importance.

DIAGRAM OF THE MOSCOW ORGANISATION

POLIT-BUREAU OF THE RUSSIAN COMMUNIST PARTY,
UP TO MARCH 1926

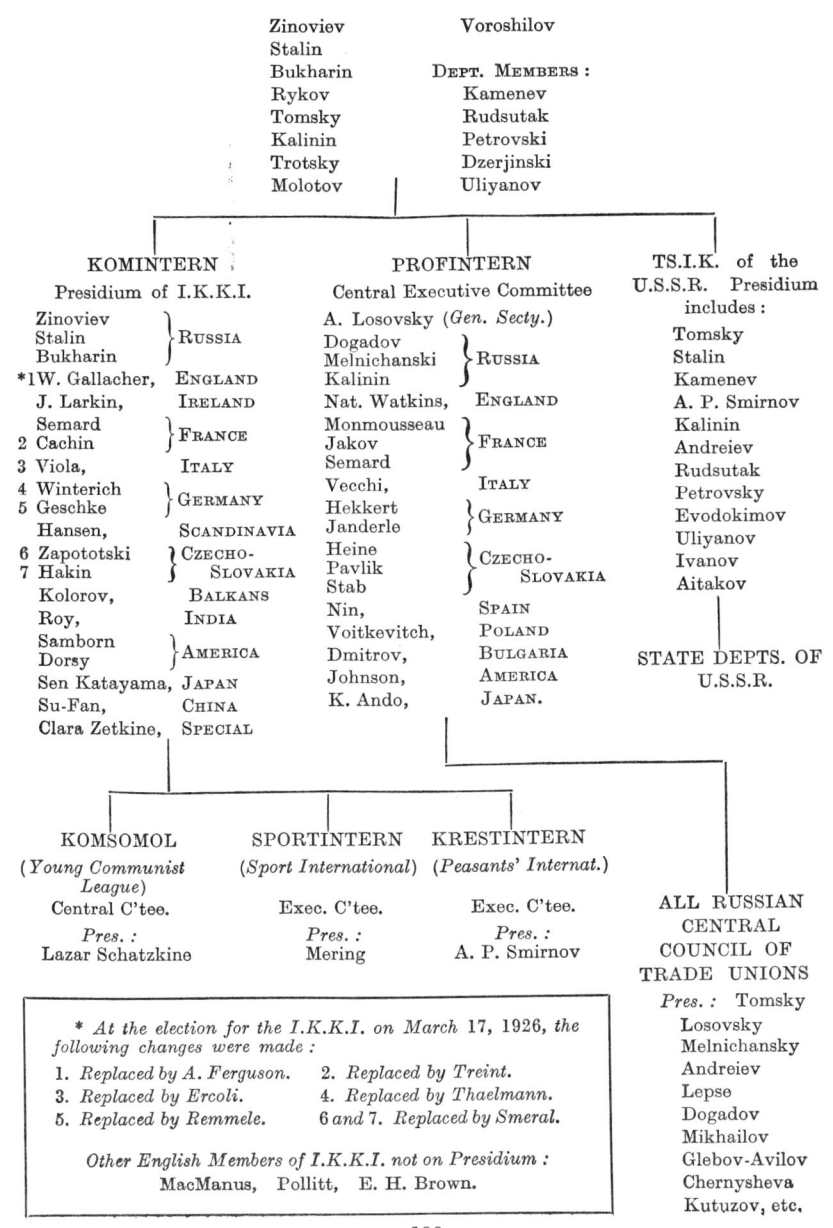

Zinoviev Voroshilov
Stalin
Bukharin DEPT. MEMBERS:
Rykov Kamenev
Tomsky Rudsutak
Kalinin Petrovski
Trotsky Dzerjinski
Molotov Uliyanov

KOMINTERN
Presidium of I.K.K.I.
Zinoviev ⎫
Stalin ⎬ RUSSIA
Bukharin ⎭
*1W. Gallacher, ENGLAND
J. Larkin, IRELAND
Semard ⎫
2 Cachin ⎬ FRANCE
3 Viola, ITALY
4 Winterich ⎫
5 Geschke ⎬ GERMANY
Hansen, SCANDINAVIA
6 Zapototski ⎫ CZECHO-
7 Hakin ⎬ SLOVAKIA
Kolorov, BALKANS
Roy, INDIA
Samborn ⎫
Dorsy ⎬ AMERICA
Sen Katayama, JAPAN
Su-Fan, CHINA
Clara Zetkine, SPECIAL

PROFINTERN
Central Executive Committee
A. Losovsky (*Gen. Secty.*)
Dogadov ⎫
Melnichanski ⎬ RUSSIA
Kalinin ⎭
Nat. Watkins, ENGLAND
Monmousseau ⎫
Jakov ⎬ FRANCE
Semard ⎭
Vecchi, ITALY
Hekkert ⎫
Janderle ⎬ GERMANY
Heine ⎫ CZECHO-
Pavlik ⎬ SLOVAKIA
Stab ⎭
Nin, SPAIN
Voitkevitch, POLAND
Dmitrov, BULGARIA
Johnson, AMERICA
K. Ando, JAPAN.

TS.I.K. of the
U.S.S.R. Presidium
includes:
Tomsky
Stalin
Kamenev
A. P. Smirnov
Kalinin
Andreiev
Rudsutak
Petrovski
Evodokimov
Uliyanov
Ivanov
Aitakov

STATE DEPTS. OF
U.S.S.R.

KOMSOMOL
(*Young Communist League*)
Central C'tee.
Pres.:
Lazar Schatzkine

SPORTINTERN
(*Sport International*)
Exec. C'tee.
Pres.:
Mering

KRESTINTERN
(*Peasants' Internat.*)
Exec. C'tee.
Pres.:
A. P. Smirnov

ALL RUSSIAN
CENTRAL
COUNCIL OF
TRADE UNIONS
Pres.: Tomsky
Losovsky
Melnichansky
Andreiev
Lepse
Dogadov
Mikhailov
Glebov-Avilov
Chernysheva
Kutuzov, etc.

* At the election for the I.K.K.I. on March 17, 1926, the following changes were made:
1. Replaced by A. Ferguson. 2. Replaced by Treint.
3. Replaced by Ercoli. 4. Replaced by Thaelmann.
5. Replaced by Remmele. 6 and 7. Replaced by Smeral.

Other English Members of I.K.K.I. not on Presidium:
MacManus, Pollitt, E. H. Brown.

ABBREVIATIONS

Note.—Where not otherwise indicated these societies belong to Great Britain.

TRADE UNIONS

A.C.W.U. (Am.)	Amalgamated Clothing Workers' Union.
A.E.U.	Amalgamated Engineering Union.
A.S.E.	Amalgamated Society of Engineers.
A.S.L.E. & F.	Associated Society of Locomotive Engineers and Firemen.
A.S.W.	Amalgamated Society of Woodworkers.
A.T.W. (Am.)	Amalgamated Textile Workers' Union.
A.U.B.T.U.	Amalgamated Union of Building Trade Unions.
I.L.G.W.U. (Am.)	International Ladies' Garment Workers' Union.
I.T.G.W.U.	Irish Transport and General Workers' Union.
N.A.F.T.A.	National Amalgamated Furnishing Trades Association.
N.F.B.T.O.	National Federation of Building Trade Operatives.
N.T.W.F.	National Transport Workers' Federation.
N.U.D.A.W.	National Union of District and Allied Workers.
N.U.G.W.	National Union of General Workers.
N.U.J.	National Union of Journalists.
N.U.R.	National Union of Railwaymen.
N.U.T.	National Union of Teachers.
S.W.M.F.	South Wales Miners' Federation.
T.W.F. (Ir.)	Transport Workers' Federation of Ireland.
U.P.W.	Union of Post Office Workers.
W.F.M. (Am.)	Western Federation of Miners.

OTHER ORGANISATIONS

A.A.	American Anarchists.
A.C.L.U.	American Civil Liberties Union.
A.F. of L.	American Federation of Labour.
A.L.L.A.	American League to Limit Armaments.
A.N.C.	American Neutral Conference.
A.P.C.F.	Anti-Parliamentary Communists' Federation.
A.R.C.C.T.U.	All Russian Central Council of Trade Unions.
A.R.C.P.	All Russian Congress of Peasants.
B.B. of R.I.L.T.U.	British Bureau of Red International of Labour Unions.
Belg. L.P.	Belgian Labour Party.
B.K.S.P.	Union of Fight-and-Propaganda Clubs (Holland).
B.N.C.P.	British National Peace Congress.
B.S.P.	British Socialist Party.
C. of A.	Council of Action.
C.A.P.	Communist Workers' Party of Holland.
C.C.	Catholic Crusade.
C.G.T. (Fr.)	Confédération Générale du Travail.
C.G.T.U.	Confédération Générale du Travail Unitaire.
C.L.C.	Central Labour College.
C.L.P. (Am.)	Communist Labour Party of America.

140

ABBREVIATIONS

C.O.	Conscientious Objector.
C.P. (Am.)	Communist Party of America.
C.P. (Aust.)	Communist Party of Austria.
C.P. (Belg.)	Communist Party of Belgium.
C.P. (Fr.)	Communist Party of France.
C.P.G.	Communist Propaganda Groups.
C.P.G.B.	Communist Party of Great Britain.
C.P. (Hol.)	Communist Party of Holland.
C.P.I.	Communist Party of Ireland.
C.S.L.	Church Socialist League.
C.S.U.	Christian Social Union.
C.W.S.D.	Councils of Workmen's and Soldiers' Delegates.
D.F.	Democratic Federation.
E.P.F. (Am.)	Emergency Peace Federation of America.
Fab.	Fabian Society
F.G.	Freedom Group.
First Am. C.D.T.P.	First American Conference for Democracy and Terms of Peace.
F.B.Y.M.	Federation of British Youth Movements.
F.I.O.M.	Federazione Italiano Operai Metallurgichi.
F.O.R.	Fellowship of Reconciliation.
F.R.D.	Fabian Research Department.
F.S.R. (Am.)	Friends of Soviet Russia.
G.C.G.	Glasgow Communist Group.
G.S.	Guild Socialism.
H.O.R.C.	Hands Off Russia Committee.
I.A.P.A.	International Arbitration and Peace Association.
I.C.F.	Industrial Christian Fellowship.
I.C.W.P.A.	International Class War Prisoners' Aid.
I.F.T.U.	International Federation of Trade Unions.
I.L.P.	Independent Labour Party.
I.L.Y.	International League of Youth.
Int. Peace Scouts	International Peace Scouts.
I.P.S.	International Peace Society.
I.S.L.	Industrial Syndicalist League.
I.S.R.B.	Irish Socialist Republican Brotherhood.
I.W.U.	Irish Workers' Union.
I.W.W.	Industrial Workers of the World.
J.P.S.	Jewish Peace Society.
K.A.	Kropotkine Anarchists.
K.K.	Kibbo Kift.
L.K.G.	League of the Kingdom of God.
L.N.U.	League of Nations Union.
L.P.	Labour Party of Great Britain
L.P. (Nor.)	Norwegian Labour Party.
L.P.F.	League of Peace and Freedom.
L.R.C.	Labour Representation Committee.
L.R.D.	Labour Research Department.
L.S.I.	Labour Socialist International = 2nd or Hamburg International.
Mensh.	Mensheviks.
M.F.G.B.	Miners' Federation of Great Britain.
M.M.M.	Miners' Minority Movement.
M.R.M.	Miners' Reform Movement.
N.C.C.	National Council Against Conscription.
N.C.C.L.	National Council for Civil Liberties.
N.C.F.	No Conscription Fellowship.
N.C.L.C.	National Council of Labour Colleges.
N.C.P.W.	National Council for the Prevention of War.
N.G.L.	National Guilds League.

ABBREVIATIONS

N.M.M.	National Minority Movement.
N.M.W.C.	National Mine Workers' Committee.
N.M.W.M.	No More War Movement.
N.P.C.	National Peace Council.
N.S.P.	National Socialist Party.
N.U.W.C.M.	National Unemployed Workers' Committee Movement.
P.C. (Am.)	People's Council of America.
P.L.	Plebs League.
P.S.S.S.M.	Proletarian Socialist Sunday School Movement.
Q.	Quaker.
R.Col.	Ruskin Labour College.
R.I.L.U.	Red International of Labour Unions.
R.P.S.	Rationalist Peace Society.
R.S.D.P.	Russian Social Democratic Party.
Russ.S.F.	Russian Socialist Federation.
S.C.R.	Society for Cultural Relations.
S.D.F.	Social Democratic Federation.
S.D.A.P. (Hol.)	Social Democratic Labour Party of Holland.
S.D.P. (Aust.)	Social Democratic Party of Austria.
S.D.P. (Ger.)	Social Democratic Party of Germany.
S.D.P. (Hol.)	Social Democratic Party of Holland.
S.D.P. (Sw.)	Social Democratic Party of Switzerland.
S.L.	Socialist League.
S.L.P.	Socialist Labour Party.
S.L.P. (Am.)	Socialist Labour Party of America.
S.P. (Am.)	Socialist Party of America.
S.P. (Fr.)	Socialist Party of France.
S.P. (Ger.)	Socialist Party of Germany.
S.P.G.B.	Socialist Party of Great Britain.
S.P. (It.)	Socialist Party of Italy.
S.P.L.	School Peace League.
S.P. (Sw.)	Socialist Party of Switzerland.
Spart.	Spartacists.
S.S.S.	Socialist Sunday Schools.
S.S.S.M.	Socialist Sunday School Movement.
T.S.	Theosophical Society.
T.U.C.	Trade Union Congress.
T.U.C. (Par. C'tee.)	Trade Union Congress Parliamentary Committee.
T.U.E.L. (Am.)	Trade Union Educational League.
T.U.U.	Trade Union Unity.
U.D.C.	Union of Democratic Control.
U.S.F.	University Socialist Federation.
W.D.U. (Am.)	Workers' Defence Union.
W.E.A.	Workers' Educational Association.
W.I.C.P.P.	Women's International Committee for Permanent Peace.
W.I.I.U. (Am.)	Workers' International Industrial Union of America.
W.I.L.	Women's International League.
W.I.L.P.F.	Women's International League for Peace and Freedom.
W.I.R.	Workers' International Relief.
W.P. of Am.	Workers' Party of America.
W.P.C.	Women's Peace Crusade.
W.S.F.	Workers' Socialist Federation.
Y.C.I.	Young Communists' Internationale.
Y.C.L.	Young Communists' League.

INDEX OF PERSONS

The initials after the names of persons denote the organisations with which each is or has been connected and of which the full title is given in the preceding list of abbreviations. In the case of trade unions, initials are enclosed in brackets. The figures following the initials indicate the page of this book on which the connection of the person with the society in question is mentioned; initials not followed by a figure indicate organisations to which the person is known from reliable sources to belong, but with which their connection may not be mentioned in the course of this book.

Ablett, Noah (M.F.G.B.), 62, 85; C.L.C. 29; M.R.M. 30; B.B. of R.I.L.U. 84
Abraham, W. (N.U.R.), 79; L.P.
Abramovitch, alias Zalewski, alias Albreicht, 49; Tcheka 49
Adamson, W. (Miners' Assoc.), C. of A. 78; M.P., L.P.
Addams, Jane, A.L.L.A. 37; W.I.C.P.P. or W.I.L.P.F. 37, 104, 109; A.N.C. 38; F.O.R. 38; A.C.L.U. 110
Adler, Friedrich, 44, 98; murderer of Count Sturgh 52; Sec. of L.S.I. 89; denounces Report of Brit. T.U. Del., 1924 89
Adler, Victor, S.D.P. (Aust.) 52
Aitken, G. S., N.C.L.C. 93
Alber, 114
Albreicht. See Abramovitch
Albury, A., 23
Aldred, Guy, S.D.F. 16; seceded from S.D.F. 27; founded Communist Propaganda Groups 27; started *Herald of Revolt* 27; founded Glasgow Communist Group 27; founded A.P.C.F. 69, 70
Allen, Clifford, N.C.F. 35; N.C.C.L. 36; Fab., I.L.P., N.G.L., 1917 Club
Ammon, C. G. (U.P.W.), 128; N.C.C.L. 36; 1917 Club 36; C.W.S.D. 62; H.O.R.C. 64; I.L.P., L.P. (Nat. Ex.)
Anderson, Tom, 113, 118; Pres. P.S.S.S.M.
Anderson, W. C., 62; I.L.P. 34; U.D.C. 34; 1917 Club 36
Andreas, Leo, 115

Andreiev, A. A., TS.I.K. (E.C.) 88; A.R.C.C.T.U. 88
Andrew, Stephen P., 26
Andreychine, George, R.I.L.U. 81
Angell, Norman, E.C. of U.D.C. 34; 1917 Club 36; N.C.P.W. 108; K.K. 124
Antipov, TS.I.K. 88; A.R.C.C.T.U. 88
Appleby, Bertram, E.C. of N.M.W.M. 105
Appleton, W. A., I.F.T.U. 73; resigns presidency of I.F.T.U. 78
Arnot, Robert Page, B.B. of R.I.L.U. 84; L.R.D. 93; C.P.G.B. 95, 101; U.S.F.
Arundale, G. W., T.S. 122
Ashtaria, 46
Ashton, Lord, Vice-Pres. of I.P.S. 106
Ashton, Margaret, E.C. of W.I.L. 35, 104
Askkenouzi, George, C.P. (Am.) 56
Attlee, Major C. R., E.C. of U.D.C. 104; N.C.P.W. 108; L.P., I.L.P., N.M.W.C.
Aulard, Professor, Clarté 103
Aveling, Dr., S.D.F. 16; S.L. 17; I.L.P. 19
Axelrod, R. 25
Ayles, Walter H., E.C. of N.M.W.M. 105; I.L.P., N.C.F., F.O.R., 1917 Club

Baars, 51; C.P. (Hol.)
Babeuf, Francis Noel, 10
Bacharach, A. L., L.R.D. 93; 1917 Club, U.S.F., C.P.G.B.
Baillie-Weaver, H., L.P.F. 35; T.S. (Gen. Sec.) 101; S.C.R. 101;

143

INDEX OF PERSONS

E.C. of L.N.U. 108; N.C.P.W. 108; I.L.P., Fab., N.P.C., 1917 Club
Baker, Bertha Kuntz, E.C. of A.N.C. 38
Baker, Charles, C.L.P. (Am.) 57
Baker, Richard St. Barbe, 125
Bakunin, Michel, 12, 40, 54
Balabanova, Angelica, 44, 52
Balch, Emily Green, First Am. C.D.T.P. 38; P.C.A. 109; Sec. W.I.L.P.F. 110
Baldwin, Roger, 54, 110, 119
Ballantyne, Y.C.L. 117
Bamber, Mrs. M., H.O.R.C. 64; B.B. of R.I.L.U. 84
Barbusse, Henri, W.I.R. 99; Clarté 103
Barnes, Alfred, Vice-Pres. W.I.R. 99; Vice-Pres. Int. Peace Scouts 107; L.P., I.L.P.
Barnes, George N., I.L.P. 21
Barrett, George, F.G. 70
Barthel, Max, 115
Bartlett, P. W., F.O.R. 35, 119
Batt, Dennis E., 56
Bauer, Otto, C.P. (Aust.) 52
Bax, Belfort, 23; S.D.F. 16; S.L. 17
Beard, Dr. Charles, R. Col. 29
Beauchamp, Earl, Pres. N.C.P.W. 108; I.C.F. 130
Bebel, August, leader of S.D.P. (Ger.) 25, 126
Bedacht, M., 59; C.L.P. (Am.) 57
Beddow, Rev. Seaward, 131
Beesley, Professor, 11, 16
Behrens, Miss E., J.P.S. 32
Bell, Richard, member of L.R.C.
Bell, Tom, E.C. of C.P.G.B. 67, 95, 101; B.B. of R.I.L.U. 84
Bellanca, August (A.C.W.U.), 82
Belsey, H., 23
Beresford, G. C., N.S.P. 33
Berrill, Roland, 121
Berkman, Alexander, A.A. 54, 58
Berzine, Jean, 52
Besant, Annie, S.D.F. 16; Fab. 18; President T.S., L.N.U.
Besterman, Theodor, F.B.Y.M. 122
Bianki, Peter, 58
Bigge, Margaret, I.C.F. 130
Bilan, Alexander, 44, 46; C.L.P. (Am.) 57
Bing, Harold F., 121; E.C. of N.M.W.M. 105
Bing, Phyllis, 121, 122; Sec. Youth Section N.M.W.M.
Binyon, Father Gilbert Clive, 131
Binyon, Mrs. Laurence, E.C. of W.I.L. 104

Birchall, Major J. D., I.C.F. 130
Birmingham, Bishop of, N.C.P.W. 108
Bittleman, Alexander, C.P. (Am.) 56; W.P.A. 59
Blanc, Louis, 10
Bland, Hubert, Fab. 18
Blanqui, 11
Blanton, Senator, 132
Blatchford, Robert, editor of the *Clarion* 20; I.L.P. 20
Blaustein, I., 23
Blizard, G. P., Hon. Sec. of F.R.D. 18; Fab., 1917 Club
Blum, Leon, S.P. (Fr.) 49
Bogdanov, A., 69
Bombacci, 46; S.P. (It.) 50
Bondfield, Margaret, E.C. of W.I.L. 35; N.C.C.L. 36; 1917 Club 36; C. of A. 78; Fab., I.L.P., L.P., T.U.C.
Booth, N.M.M. 86
Boothman, H., Gen. Council Brit. T.U.C. 90
Bordiga, A., 46; S.P. (It.) 50
Boughton, Rutland, 102
Boukharine, 10, 44, 46
Boulter, B. C., 131
Bouvman, C.P. (Hol.) 51
Bowen, J. W. (U.P.W.), Gen. Council Brit. T.U.C. 90; 1917 Club
Bowyer, R. G., 96
Bracher, S. V., L.P.F. 35; N.C.F., N.M.W.M.
Brailsford, H. N., U.D.C. 34; I.L.P. 34, 102; S.C.R. 101
Bramley, Fred (N.A.F.T.A.), Sec. T.U.C. (Parl. C'tee.), 77, 90; Sec. T.U.C. 88, 92; delegate to Russia (1924) 89; W.E.A. 94; S.C.R. 101
Brandes, Georges, Clarté 103
Brandsteder, C.P. (Hol.), 51
Branting, Hjalmar, 44, 52
Brassington, Isaac (N.U.R.), H.O.R.C. 64
Breckenridge, Sophonisba P., A.C.L.U. 110
Brockway, A. Fenner, N.C.F. 35; E.C. of N.M.W.M. 105; I.L.P., 1917 Club
Brockway, Clare, 119
Bromley, John (A.S.L.E. & F.), 90; H.O.R.C. 64; C. of A. 78; delegate to Russia, 1924 88; Vice-Pres. W.I.R. 99; T.U.C. (Gen. Counc.)
Brommert, C.P. (Hol.) 51
Browder, Earl R., W.P.A. 59
Brown, A. Kemp, E.C. of I.P.S. 107

INDEX OF PERSONS

Brown, Beatrice C. M., Sec. N.M.W.M. 105
Brown, C., N.C.L.C. 93
Brown, E. H., E.C. of C.P.G.B. 95; I.L.P.
Brown, H. Runham, E.C. of N.M.W.M. 105
Brown, J. W., I.F.T.U. 87
Buchez, 10
Bucknall, Rev. C. J., C.C. 127; L.K.G. 131
Buonarotti, 10
Burden, A., N.S.P. 33
Burgess, Fred., I.L.P. 29; C.L.C. 29
Burgess, Joseph, Labour Union of Bradford 20
Burgneay, G., L.R.D. 93
Burman, F., W.P.A. 59
Burns, Emile, B.B. of R.I.L.U. 84; L.R.D. 93; I.C.W.P.A. 100
Burns, John, S.D.F. 16; M.P. for Battersea 21
Burrows, Herbert, D.F. 16
Buxton, N.U.W.C.M. 96
Buxton, Charles Roden, S.C.R. 101; C.W.S.D., I.L.P., W.E.A.
Buxton, Harold, 131
Buxton, Noel, L.P. 124; 1917 Club 124

Cachin, Marcel, C.P. (Fr.) 49
Cadbury, Barrow, Vice-Pres. of I.P.S. 106
Cadbury, Mrs. George, Treas. of N.C.P.W. 108
Cafiero, 26
Caillaux, S.P. (Fr.) 49
Cameron, A. G. (A.S.W.), H.O.R.C. 64; C. of A. 78; L.P., I.L.P.
Campbell, John Ross, E.C. of C.P.G.B. 95, 101; R.I.L.U.
Cannon, J. P., W.P.A. 59
Cant, Ernest Walter, C.P.G.B. 101; B.S.P., C.O.
Canterbury, Archibishop of, Pres. of I.C.F. 129
Carney, Jack, C.L.P. of America 57; F.S.R. 61
Cash, William, I.C.F. 130
Cavendish-Bentinck, Lord Henry, 124; Vice-Pres. I.P.S. 106; I.C.F. 130
Ceton, S.D.P. (Hol.) 50; C.P. (Hol.) 51
Chalmers, Rev. Humphrey, E.C. of I.P.S. 107
Chaman Lal, I.C.W.P.A. 100
Chamberlain, W. J. (N.U.J.), N.M.W.M. 105; L.P., I.L.P., C.O.
Chambers, Rev. G. B., C.C. 127

Champion, H. H., D.F. 16, 127
Chandler, Councillor R., 114
Chernishova, Olga, A.R.C.C.T.U. 89
Chick, Miss Mary, Hon. Nat. Sec. W.I.L. 104
Citrine, Walter M. (Electr. T.U.), 92 T.U.C. (Assist. Sec.) 88
Clark, G. B., D.F. 16; Radical, Freethinker
Clark, Dr. Hilda, E.C. of W.I.L. 104
Clarke, William, Fab. 18
Clemenceau, 25
Cluse, W. S., S.D.F. 68
Clynes, J. R. (N.U.G.W.), I.L.P. 21; C. of A. 78; N.C.P.W. 108; L.P.
Coates, —, W.I.R. 97
Cocks, F. Seymour, U.D.C. 34
Cohen, J., Y.C.L., 117
Cohen, Maximilian, Ex. Sec. Left Wing S.P. of America 55; C.P. (Am.) 56
Cohen, Miss Rose, E.C. of W.I.R. 99; C.P.G.B.
Cohn, Fania M. (I.L.G.W.U.), 82
Coit, Miss Adela, E.C. of W.I.L. 104
Cole, G. D. H., 92, 93, 94; F.R.D. 18; Guild Socialist, 30, 92; L.R.D. 93; S.C.R. 101; 1917 Club, Fab.
Colthoff, C.P. (Hol.) 51
Colyer, W. T., C.P. (Am.), 102; Sec. Left Wing Prov. C'tee. (England) 102
Conolly, James, leader of I.S.R.B. 24, 71; Marx on, 24
Conolly, Roderick, C.P.I. 71
Conradi, 44
Cook, A. J. (M.F.G.B.), 95, 102; M.R.M. 30; B.B. of R.I.L.U. 84; E.C. of L.R.D. 93; I.L.P.
Cooke, George (A.E.U.), N.U.W.C.M. 96
Coppock, Richard (A.U.B.T.W.), B.B. of R.I.L.U. 84; N.C.L.C. 93
Corsor, Benjamin, Left Wing S.P. of America, 55
Courtney, Miss K. D., E.C. of W.I.L. 35, 104
Courtney of Penwith, Lord, B.N.P.C. 32; N.C.F. 35
Courtney of Penwith, Lady, E.C. of W.I.L. 35, 104
Couturier, Vaillant, C.P. (Fr.) 49; Clarté 103
Cowen, Joseph, D.F. 16
Cox, Lucy A., Sec. N.M.W.M. 105
Coxon, W., N.C.L.C. 93
Cramp, C. T. (N.U.R.), 79; C. of A. 78
Crawfurd, Mrs. Helen, W.P.C. 35;

INDEX OF PERSONS

E.C. of C.P.G.B. 67, 95; E.C. of W.I.R., also Secretary 99; I.C.W.P.A. 100; I.L.P.
Cremer, 11
Crossley, James, H.O.R.C. 64; B.S.P., C.P.G.B.
Cunningham Graham, Scottish Lab. Party 19
Cyril, Victor, Clarté 103

Dalstrom, K., 46
Daly, W.I.R. 99
Dana, Harry, 119
Daryngton, Lord, I.C.F. 130
Davidson, Morrison, D.F. 16
Davidson, Professor Thomas, Fab. 17
Davies, Emil, Fab. Res. Dep. 18; L.P., Fab. (E.C.), 1917 Club
Davies, Miss Llewelyn, S.C.R. 101
Davies, R. J. (N.U.D.A.W.), H.O.R.C. 64; I.L.P., L.P.
de Brouckère, L.P. (Belg.) 33
Debs, Eugene V., P.C.A. 54, 110; F.O.R. (Am.) 110
Deer, George, E.C. of B.S.P. 33; E.C. of C.P.G.B. 67
Delignet, 44
Desodoards, Fantin. 10
Despard, Mrs., W.I.L. 35; W.I.R. 99
Deutsch, Leo, 25
Dickinson, G. Lowes, 1917 Club 36
Dickinson, Sir W. H., Vice-Pres. of I.P.S. 106
Dirba, C.P. (Am.) 56
Dobb, Maurice H., E.C. of L.R.D. 93; P.L. 93
Dogadov, TS.I.K. (E.C.) 88; A.R.C.C.T.U. 88, 91
Donaldson, Canon F. L., C.S.L. 127
Dondicol, C.G.T.U. 82
Doriot, Jean, C.P. (Fr.) 49
Doty, Miss Madeleine, Sec. W.I.L.P.F. 104
Douglas, Fred, N.U.W.C.M. 97; C.P.G.B.
Dryer, the Rev. Oliver, Gen. Sec. F.O.R. 106, 119
Dukes, Charles (N.U.G.W.), E.C. of B.S.P. 33
Duncan, W., Y.C.L. 117
Dunne, William F., W.P.A. 59
Dunnico, Rev. Herbert, E.C. of W.I.R. 98, 99; Sec. of I.P.S. 106, Vice-Pres. Int. Bur. de la Paix; Pres. Int. Peace Scouts, 107; N.C.P.W. 108; L.P., I.L.P., Fab.
Dunstan, Dr. Margaret, E.C. of W.I.R. 99
Dunstan, Dr. Robert, 102; H.O.R.C.

64; E.C. of W.I.R. 99; S.C.R. 101; I.L.P.
Dutt, Rajani Palme, L.R.D. 93; E.C. of C.P.G.B. 95

Eastman, Max, P.C.A. 54; F.S.R. 61
Ebert, S.P. (Ger.) 33
Ebury, G., H.O.R.C. 65
Eccarius, 12
Elbaum, D., C.P. (Am.) 56
Ellis, Havelock, K.K. 124
Elsbury, Sam (M.F.G.B.), N.M.M. 86; L.P., I.L.P., S.D.F., S.D.P., C.P.G.B.
Emmott, Lord, Vice-Pres. of I.P.S. 106
Enfield, A. Honora, L.P.F. 35; E.C. of W.I.R. 99; N.P.C.
Engdahl, J. L., W.P.A. 59, 110
Engels, Friedrich, 11, 14, 15
Evans, Miss M., E.C. of I.P.S. 107
Evdokimov, TS.I.K. (E.C.), 88; A.R.C.C.T.U. 88
Ewer, Mrs., E.C. of W.I.R. 99
Ewer, W. N., E.C. of W.I.R., 99; Foreign editor of *Daily Herald*

Fairchild, E. C., B.S.P. 33; C.W.S.D. 63; I.L.P., S.D.F., S.D.P., L.P.
Falk, 53
Farbman, Michael, S.C.R. 101
Faulkner, W., Articles in *Patriot* 94, 104
Feïgin, Y.C.L. 116
Ferguson, A., E.C. of C.P.G.B. 95
Ferguson, Isaac E., C.P. (Am.) 56; arrest of 58
Fimmen, Edo, I.F.T.U. 80, 87, 90; W.I.R.
Findlay, A. A. H., delegate to Russia, 1924 88; G.C. of T.U.C.
Fineberg, B.S.P. 33
Fisher, Victor, B.S.P. 33
Fitzgerald, M. Eleanor, 54
Flynn, 46
Flynn, Elizabeth Gurley, W.D.U. (Am.) 82; A.C.L.U. 110; I.W.W.
Foot, W. T. A. (N.U.R.), N.C.L.C. 93
Foster, William Zebulon, 83; A.F. of L. 28; I.W.W. 28, 76; W.P.A. 59; F.S.R. 61; founded T.U.E.L. 76, 82; A.C.L.U. 110
Fourier, his phalansteries, 10
Fox, S. Darwin, 121
Fraina, Louis, 44, 46; A.C.P. 55; C.P. (Am.) 56
France, Anatole, Clarté 103
Franklin, Hon. Mrs., U.D.C. 34
Fribourg, 11
Friedländer, 52

INDEX OF PERSONS

Fries, A., 46
Frossard, 49
Frost, P. B., D.F. 16, 127
Fyfe, Hamilton (N.U.J.), 131; E.C. of U.D.C. 104; editor of *Daily Herald* 104; 1917 Club

Gallacher, W. (Lanark Miners' Union), 46, 62; H.O.R.C. 64; E.C. of C.P.G.B. 95, 101; N.M.M.
Garcia, D.F. 16
Gardiner, Rolf, 120, 121
Garvin, J. L., editor of *Observer* 101; S.C.R. 101
Gasparowa, W.I.R. 99
Geddes, Patrick, K.K. 124
Gerhardsen, Einer, 53
Gerrie, George, Scottish Lab. Party 19
Gill, Hubert A., E.C. of I.P.S. 107
Gillespie, Major H. J., F.R.D. 18
Gitlow, Benjamin, Left Wing S.P. of America, 57; C.L.P. of America, 57; arrest of 58; W.P.A. 59
Glasier, Bruce, I.L.P. 21, 34
Glasier, Mrs. Bruce, 98; E.C. of W.I.L. 35; I.L.P., T.S., Q.
Glebov-Avilov, N. P., A.R.C.C.T.U. 89; delegate to England (1925)
Gobat, Rev. T. C., Chairman L.K.G. 131
Goldman, Emma ("Red Emma"), A.A. 54, 58, 70
Goldsmith, S., Y.C.L. 117
Gömbös, 52
Gompers, Samuel, A.F.L. 28, 76
Goode, Sir William, N.C.P.W. 108
Goode, W. T., H.O.R.C., 64
Gore, Bishop, C.S.U. 127
Gorle, Councillor F. H., N.S.P. 33
Gosling, Harry (N.T.W.F.), 79; C. of A. 78; T.U.C.
Gossip, Alexander (N.A.F.T.A.), 91; 1917 Club 36; H.O.R.C. 64; N.C.C.L. 93; Vice-Pres. W.I.R. 99; I.C.W.P.A. 100; Pres. Brit. S.S.S. Union
Gough, Rev. Prebendary, on C.O.P.E.C. 132
Gould, F. J., N.S.P. 33
Grassmann, W.I.R. 97; Gen. Fed. of Lab. (Germany)
Graziadei, 46
Green, William, 26
Gregory, J., N.C.L.C. 93
Grenfell, Harold, H.O.R.C. 64
Grey, Mary, 113
Griffuelhes, 28
Grimm, Robert, 52

Groves, Thomas, E.C. of I.P.S. 107; Vice-Pres. Int. Peace Scouts, 107
Guesde, Jules, 25
Guilbeaux, A., 46; S.P. (Fr.) 44

Hamilton, J., Pres. N.C.L.C. 93; C.O.
Hamilton, Mary, E.C. of U.D.C. 104; I.L.P., 1917 Club
Hannington, Wal (A.E.U.), N.M.M. 86; E.C. of C.P.G.B. 95, 101; Nat. Organiser of N.U.W.C.M. 96; I.C.W.P.A. 100; R.I.L.U.
Hapgood, Norman, 111
Harben, H. D., G.S. 30
Hardie, Keir, 17; I.L.P. 19; Scottish Labour Party 20; editor of *Labour Leader* 21; owned *The Miner* 21; Labour member for West Ham 21; member of L.R.C.
Hardy, George, 102; U.D.C. 34; B.B. of R.I.L.U. 84; N.M.M. 85, 87; I.W.W.
Hargrave, John, 121, 122
Harris, J. Theodore, E.C. of N.M.W.M. 105
Harrison, Caleb, F.S.R. 61
Harrison, William Q., 119
Hartmann, Nihilist 26
Hartmann, Dr. Jacob W., F.S.R. 61
Haye, Percival (A.E.U.), N.U.W.C.M. 96
Hayes, Emily, N.S.P. 33
Haynes, John, 119
Hayward, J. J., E.C. of I.P.S. 107
Haywood, William D., W.F.M. 28, 76
Hazell, A. P., S.S.S.M. 113; S.D.F. 113
Headingley, A. S. See Adolphe Smith
Headlam, Rev. Stuart, 127
Heath, Carl, N.P.C. 32
Helphand. See Parvus
Heltz, Max, 48
Henderson, Arthur, U.D.C. 34; N.C.P.W. 108; L.P., T.U.C.
Hereford, Bishop of, S.P.L. 32
Herriot, S.P. (Fr.), 49
Hertz, Dr., Chief Rabbi, 32
Hertz, Moses, 12
Herzen, 40
Herzog, 46
Hesketh, Everard, I.C.F. 130
Hewlett, Maurice, K.K. 124
Hewlett, W., E.C. of C.P.G.B. 67; B.B. of R.I.L.U.
Hicks, George (N.F.B.T.O.), 92, 96; I.F.T.U. 87; Gen. Council T.U.C. 90; L.R.D. 93; P.L. 93; T.U.U.

INDEX OF PERSONS

Hilkowicz, Misca. See Morris Hillquit
Hillman, Joseph, Pres. A.C.W.U. 82
Hillquit, Morris, alias Misca Hilkowicz, 15; E.P.F. 37; A.L.L.A. 37; P.C.A. 54, 109; Int. Sec. S.P. of America, A.C.L.U.
Himmelfarb, L., Left Wing S.P. of America 55
Hindenburg, Field-Marshal von, 48
Hird, Denis, P.L. 29; C.L.C. 29
Hobson, J. A., E.C. of U.D.C. 34, 104; 1917 Club 36; N.C.P.W. 108; L.P.
Hodges, Frank (S.W.M.F.), C. of A. 78; M.F.G.B. 79; I.C.F. 130
Hodgkin, Jonathan Edward, Treas. of I.P.S. 106
Hodgson, J. F., E.C. of B.S.P. 33; E.C. of C.P.G.B. 67
Hoffman, 39, 65
Holland, Canon Scott, C.S.U. 127
Holmes, Walter, E.C. of W.I.R. 99
Holst, Roland, 114
Holst, Mrs. J. Roland, C.P. (Hol.) 51
Holt, Hamilton, A.N.C. 38; N.U.W.C.M. 96
Homer, Harry, N.U.W.C.M. 96; R.I.L.U., C.P.G.B.
Horner, A., N.M.M. 86; E.C. of C.P.G.B. 95
Hörnle, E., 115
Horowitz, Fanny, Left Wing S.P. (Am.), 55
Horrabin, Winifred, P.L. 93; E.C. of W.I.R. 99
Horthy, Admiral, 52
Horton, Rev. Robert, Vice-Pres. of I.P.S. 106
Hourwich, Nicholas I., Left Wing S.P. of America 55; C.P. of America 56
Howe, Frederick C., 110
Hudson, J. H. (N.U.T.), N.C.F. 35; Sec. of N.C.P.W. 108; I.L.P., C.O., Q.
Huebsch, B. W., E.C. of A.N.C. 38
Hughes, Fred, 131
Humbert-Droz, J., 46
Hunter, A., Treas. L.K.G. 131
Hunter, David, E.C. of I.P.S. 107
Hutchinson, W. H. (A.S.E.), E.C. of N.C.L.C., L.R.D.
Hutton, Rev. John, Vice-Pres. of I.P.S. 106
Huysmans, Camille, L.P. (Belg.) 50; 2nd Int. 45
Hyndman, H. M., 17; Leader of D.F. 16; B.S.P. 33; Leader of N.S.P. 33, 68; death of 68

Hyndman, R. Travers, N.S.P. 33

Ignat, Y.C.L. 116
Inge, Dean, 124, 132
Inkpin, Albert, Gen. Sec. B.S.P. 33; Gen. Sec. C.P.G.B. 67, 95, 101; S.D.F., Hon. Pres. Komintern at 3rd Congress in Moscow
Irving, Dan, B.S.P. 33; S.D.F. 68

Jackson, T. A., E.C. of C.P.G.B. 95; N.U.W.C.M., editor of *Communist*
Jacobs, Dr. Aletta, W.I.C.P.P. 38
Jacobs, T., 23
Jansen, 46
Jaurès, 25
Johansen, P. Moe, 53
John, E. T., Pres. N.C.P.W. 108
Johnson, O. C., 56
Johnstone, Butler, D.F. 16
Jones, Jack. See Jones, Coun. J. J.
Jones, Councillor J. J. (N.U.G.W.), N.S.P. 33; H.O.R.C. 64; S.D.F. 68
Jones, Morgan, E.C. of I.P.S. 107
Jordan, Dr. David Starr, P.C.A. 54
Jorgenson, O., 46
Joss, William, E.C. of C.P.G.B. 95
Jouhaux, L., I.F.T.U. 80, 87, 90
Jowett, Frederick W., E.C. of I.L.P. 21; U.D.C. 34
Jowitt, Miss Moya, 121; I.L.Y. 120; K.K. 123, 124
Joynes, J. L., D.F. 16, 127
Jung, Hermann, 12

Kaledine, General, 41
Kameneva, W.I.R. 99
Kamenev, alias Rosenfeld, C. of A. 78
Kautsky, Karl, S.D.P. of Germany 25, 48
Karolyi, Count, 42
Karosses, C.P. (Am.), 56
Katayama, Sen, 45
Katterfeld, L. E., C.L.P. (Am.) 57
Kay, G., B.B. of R.I.L.U. 84
Kennedy, Rev. G. A. Studdert, 132; I.C.F. 128, 130
Kennedy, Tom, Gen. Sec. S.D.F. 68
Kent, J., 23
Keracher, John, 56
Kerensky, 33, 41; government of 42
Keynes, J. M., S.C.R. 101
King, Joseph, 1917 Club 36; S.C.R. 101; L.P., I.L.P.
Kingsley, Charles, 15, 126
Kirchwey, Dr. George, A.N.C. 38
Kirk, Rev. P. T. R., 127; I.C.F. 129, 130

INDEX OF PERSONS

Kirkwood, David, H.O.R.C. 64; Vice-Pres. W.I.R. 99; I.L.P.
Kitz, Frank, 17
Klatt, Fritz, 121
Klein, Miss Ella, E.C. of W.I.R. 99
Klinger, G., 44
Klishko, N., W.I.R. 98, 99
Kohen, Alex, A.C.W.U. 82
Kollontai, Madame Alexandra, 53
Komintern, see 3rd Internationale
Kopnagel, S., 56
Kornilov, General, 41
Koznekow, Alexandre, 53
Krassin, 78
Krestinski, W.I.R. 97; Repres. All Russ. Relief Committee in Berlin
Kropotkine, Prince, 26, 27, 40; Kropotkine Anarchists, 27, 70
Krumbein, Charles, C.L.P. (Am.) 57
Kun, Bela, 52, 59

Lagardelle, 28
Langdon Davies, B. N., U.D.C. 34; N.C.C. 36; N.C.C.L. 36; I.L.P., 1917 Club
Lannung, Hermod, founder of I.L.Y. 120
Lansbury, George, 95, 102; D.F. 16; N.C.C.L. 36; H.O.R.C. 64; Vice-Pres. W.I.R. 97, 98, 99; Chairman N.M.W.M. 105; Vice-Pres. Int. Peace Scouts; and N.C.P.W. 108; and I.C.F. 128; L.K.G. 131; I.L.P., C.S.L.
Lansbury, Miss Nellie, E.C. of W.I.R. 99
Larkin, James (leader I.T.G.W.U. 24), Left Wing S.P. of America 55; C.L.P. (Am.) 57; arrest of 58; C.P.I. 71; W.I.R. 99
Larkin, Peter, I.W.U. 71
Lasker, Bruno, 121
Laski, Harold, A.C.L.U. 124
Lavroff, 40
Lawrence, Mrs. Pethick, 62; W.I.L. 35; E.P.F. 37; K.K. 124; C.W.S.D., I.L.P., 1917 Club, T.S.
Lazarevitch, Israel. See Parvus
Lazzari, It. S.P. (Soviet Faction) 50
Lawlor, W.I.R. 99
Leach, Agnes Brown, A.C.L.U. 110
Leaf, Miss Emily, E.C. of W.I.L. 104
Ledebour, 39; W.I.R. 99
Lee, H. W., N.S.P. 33; S.D.F. 68
Lees-Smith, H. B., E.C. of U.D.C. 104; L.P.
Legien, Karl, 28
Lehane, C., Gen. Sec. S.P.G.B.

Lehman, George, Left Wing S.P. of America 55
Leipart, Th., I.F.T.U. 87
Lenin, Nicolai, 39, 41, 44, 46, 49, 51, 52, 54, 66, 73, 83; H.O.R.C. 63; and S. Pankhurst, 66, 68; and A.A. 54
Leon, Daniel de, S.L.P. (America) 14; I.W.W. 29
Lessner, 12
Lepse, I. I., A.R.C.C.T.U. 88, 89; delegate to England (1925); TS.I.K. (E.C.), 88
Levin, Samuel, A.C.W.U. 82
Levy, P., 46
Lewis, P. H., 116
Libby, Frederick J., 111
Lichfield, Bishop of, C.S.U. 127; Vice-Pres. I.C.F. 130
Liebermann, E., W.D.U. (Am.) 82
Liebknecht, Karl, 49, 114; Spart. 25, 39, 48
Liebknecht, Wilhelm, leader of S.D.P. of Germany 25
Lincoln, Bishop of, C.E.P.L. 32
Lindgren, Edward I., 55; C.L.P. of America 57
Lindner, S., 27
Linfield, F. C., Treas. of N.C.P.W. 108
Lipnitski, 52
Lismer, E., 84
Litvinov, alias Finkelstein, 53
Llewellyn, F. W., E.C. of B.S.P. 33
Lochner, Louis P., E.P.F. 37; A.L.L.A. 37; W.I.C.P.P. 37; Sec. P.C.A. 109; First Am. C.D.T.P.
Lœber, N.M.M. 86
Long, Rev. W., E.C. of I.P.S. 107
Longuet, Jean, 44, 49; grandson of Marx 25
Lore, Ludwig, C.L.P. of America 57; W.P. of America 59
Loriot, 49
Losovsky, A. (Solomon Abramovitch Dridzo), 89; R.I.L.U. (Gen. Sec.) 81, 88; TS.I.K. (E.C.) 88; A.R.C.C.T.U. 88
Louis, Marguerite, E.C. of N.M.W.M. 105
Lovell, Bob, I.C.W.P.A. 100, 101
Lovestone, Jay, W.P.A. 59; C.P. of America 56
Ludendorff, General, 43, 65
Lumberg, Hyman, A.C.W.U. 82
Lutovinov, TS.I.K. (E.C.) 88; A.R.C.C.T.U. 88
Luxemburg, Rosa, 49; Spart. 48
Lvoff, Prince, 41

INDEX OF PERSONS

Macassey, Sir Lynden, I.C.F. 130
Macdonald, James, D.F. 16
Macdonald, James Ramsay, 17; I.L.P. 21, 34; Sec. L.R.C. 21; U.D.C. 34; 1917 Club 36; C.W.S.D. 62, 63
MacLaine, W. (A.E.U.), 46; E.C. of 3rd Int. 44; H.O.R.C. 64; E.C. of W.I.R. 99; B.S.P.
Maclean, Sir Donald, Vice-Pres. of I.P.S. 106
Maclean, John, 64, 65; B.S.P. 33; "Bolshevik Consul" in Glasgow 65
Maclean, Neil, H.O.R.C. 64; E.C. of W.I.R. 99; I.L.P.
MacManus, Arthur, 62; S.L.P. 22; H.O.R.C. 65; Chairman C.P.G.B. 66, 67, 69, 95, 101, 102
Macmillan, Chrystal, W.I.C.P.P. 38
Madsen, A., 46
Maeterlinck, Maurice, K.K. 124
Magnes, Rabbi Judah L., First Am. C.D.T.P. 38; P.C.A. 54, 109; A.C.L.U.
Malatesta, 26
Malon, Benoît, 12
Malone, Lieut.-Colonel Cecil John L'Estrange, H.O.R.C. 64; E.C. of C.P.G.B. 67, 69
Manchester, Bishop of, and N.C.P.W. 108; I.C.F. 130
Mander, A. E., H.O.R.C. 64
Mann, Tom, 62, 67, 86, 91; S.D.F. 16; I.L.P. 21; I.S.L. 30; H.O.R.C. 64; E.C. of R.I.L.U. in Moscow 81; B.B. of R.I.L.U. 84; Synd. 85; N.M.M. 85; I.C.W.P.A. 100
Manus, Rosa, W.I.C.P.P. 38
Marat, in Soho 16
Marchlevsky, U., 46
Marimmpetri, A. D., A.C.W.U. 82
Mariovitz, Lazarus, A.C.W.U. 82
Marsden, Robert, 32
Martens, Ludwig
Martov, 25, 42
Marty, André, F.C.P. 49
Marx, Eleanor, S.D.F. 16; S.L. 17; and I.L.P. 19
Marx, Karl, 11, 12, 14, 15, 16, 19, 25, 43; and Communist Manifesto 11, 126; and 1st Internationale 11; and Fenians 24
Marx, Madeleine, Clarté 103; W.I.R.
Mason, Rev. H. O.; Hon. Sec. C.C. 127
Massingham, H. W., N.C.C.L. 36
Masterman, Charles, 124
Maurer, James H., P.C.A. 54; A.C.L.U. 110

Maurice, C. E., I.A.P.A. 32; S.P.L. 32
Maurice, Major-Gen. F., Vice-Chairman I.C.F. 130
Maurice, Frederick, 15, 126
May, H. J., Chairman E.C. of W.I.R. 99; S.C.R. 101
Mayer, Anton, 121; R.I.L.U. 81
Mayne, Stanley, 114
Mazzini, 16
McBride, W.I.R. 99
M'Carthy, Justin, D.F. 16
McDermott, Y.C.L. 117
Mehring, Franz, Spart. 48
Mellor, William, Sec. F.R.D. 18; G.S. 30; news editor of *Daily Herald* (1924), E.C. of C.P.G.B.
Melnichansky, G. I., TS.I.K. (E.C.) 88; A.R.C.C.T.U. 88, 89; member of delegation to England (1925)
Mercer, Rev. F. E., I.C.F. 128
Mertens, C., I.F.T.U. 80, 87, 91
Meyer, E., 46
Mikhailov, A.R.C.C.T.U. 89; delegate to England (1925), TS.I.K.
Millar, J. P. M., N.C.L.C. 93; N.C.P. Plebs League
Millerand, 25
Mills, J. E. (A.E.U.), H.O.R.C. 64
Mirabeau, 32
Misiano, W.I.R. 99
Mislig, Michael, R.S.F. 55
Möll, Miss M. L., Sec. F.O.R. 106
Montague, F., E.C. of S.D.F. 68; I.L.P.
Montefiore, Mrs. Dora B., 62; E.C. of B.S.P. 33; C.W.S.D. 63; E.C. of C.P.G.B. 67; E.C. of W.I.R. 99
Morel, E. D. (Edmond Morel-de-Ville), 132; origin 63; I.L.P. 34; E.C. of U.D.C. 34, 104; editor of *Foreign Affairs*, 34, 104; 1917 Club 36; N.P.C.
Morgan, D.F. 16
Morland, Harold J., N.M.W.M. 105
Morris, G. C., K.K. 123
Morris, William, D.F. 16; S.D.F. 16; S.L. 17; editor of *Communist*; and *News from Nowhere*
Moscheles, Felix, I.A.P.A.
Mosley, Oswald, Chairman of N.C.P.W. 108; L.P.
Most, Johann, imprisoned in England 26; *Freiheit* 27
Muck-Lamberty, Herr, and Nudity Movement 121
Münzenberg, Willi, Director of W.I.R. 97, 99
Murphy, J. T. (A.E.U.), S.L.P. 22; E.C. of C.P.G.B. 67, 95, 101; E.C.

INDEX OF PERSONS

of R.I.L.U. 81 ; B.B. of R.I.L.U. 84 ; E.C. of 3rd Int.
Murray, Charles, D.F. 16
Murray, Professor Gilbert, and N.C.P.W. 108 ; Chairman of L.N.U.
Murray, James, D.F. 16
Mussolini, Benito, 50, 90 ; I.S.U. 33
Muste, A. J., 119 ; and Intercollegiate Socialist Society 15 ; Amalgamated Textile Workers 82
Muyne, Gust, 119
Myers, Tom, H.O.R.C. 64 ; L.P., I.L.P.

Nevinson, Henry W., 1917 Club 37 ; K.K. 124 ; N.L.C.
Newbold, Horace, N.U.W.C.M. 96
Newbold, J. T. Walton, L.R.D. 93 ; Vice-Pres. W.I.R. 98, 99 ; Fab., I.L.P., Plebs League, C.P.G.B.
Newbold, Mrs. Marjorie, E.C. of W.I.R. 99
Newboult, Margaret, E.C. of N.M.W.M. 105
Newman, Sir Robert, I.C.F. 130
Nicolaieff, 53
Nightingale, Rev. Thomas, and N.C.P.W. 108
Nilson, M., 46
Nissen, Eugene, 53
Noel, Rev. Conrad, vicar of Thaxted, 127 ; C.S.L. 127 ; C.C. 127
Nogin, R.I.L.U. 81
Norman, C. H., N.C.F. 32, 35 ; 1917 Club
Norman Angell League, 32
Nosowitsky, Jacob, 68

O'Connor, T. P., Vice-Pres. of I.P.S. 106
Odell, Mrs. George T., W.I.L. in America 111
Odger, 11
O'Flaherty, Liam, C.P.I. 71
O'Grady, J. (N.A.F.T.A.), Vice-Pres. W.I.R. 99 ; T.U.C.
Ogareff, 40
Olivier, Sydney, Fab. 18 ; L.P., N.L.C.
Ollenhauer, E., 118, 119
Orchard, Rev. Dr., F.O.R. 35
Orlandez, R.I.L.U. 81
Oudegeest, J., I.F.T.U. 80, 87, 91
Overstraeten, Will Van, Belg. C.P. 50
Owen, Robert, 10, 15, 126
Owen, Will J., F.G. 70

Pahl, Walter, Nudity Movement 121
Pankhurst, Sylvia, 46, 80, 116 ; C.W.S.D. 63 ; and Lenin 66 ; arrest of 68 ; and 4th Inter. 69 ; W.S.F., W.C.M.
Parmoor, Lord, 132 ; and N.C.P.W. 108
Parmoor, Lady, E.C. of W.I.L. 104 ; N.C.P.W. 108
Partridge, T., 113
Parvus (Israel Lazarevitch Helphand), 41, 43
Paul, Cedar (Mrs.), P.L. 93 ; I.L.P., C.P.G.B. ; co-editor of *Proletcult*
Paul, William, 102 ; S.L.P. 22 ; E.C. of C.P.G.B. 67 ; P.L., L.P., editor of *Socialist, Communist Review*
Peacock, Arthur, F.B.Y.M. 122
Pearce, A., Y.C.L. 117
Pease, E. R., 30 ; Hon. Sec. Fab. Soc.
Peck, W. G., 131
Peckover, Miss P. H., Vice-Pres. of I.P.S. 106
Peet, George, 84 ; H.O.R.C. 64
Peile, Helen, E.C. of N.M.W.M. 105
Penrose, the Hon. Mrs. J. Doyle, E.C. of I.P.S. 107
Pepper, John. See Pogany
Pernerstorfer, A.S.D.P. 33
Pestana, 46
Petroff, B.S.P. 33
Phillips, Dr. Marion, 102 ; U.D.C. 34 ; L.P., editor of *Labour Woman*
Phillips, Rev. Thomas, Vice-Pres. of I.P.S. 106, 107
Pickard, W.I.R. 99
Plasunov, Y.C.L. 116
Platten, Fritz, 41, 44, 52 ; Sec. S.D.P. of Switzerland 51
Plekhanov, George V., 25, 42 ; leader of Mensheviks 33
Plumb, Glenn E., A.C.L.U. 110
Plymouth, the Suffragan Bishop of, Vice-Pres. of I.P.S. 106
Pogany, Joseph, alias John Pepper, W.P.A. 59
Pollitt, Harry, boilermaker, 91 ; B.B. of R.I.L.U. 84 ; N.M.M. 85 ; L.R.D. 93 ; E.C. of C.P.G.B. 95, 101 ; I.C.W.P.A. 100 ; editor of *All Power*, L.P., T.U.C.
Polovtsev, Dr. V. N., E.C. of W.I.R. 99
Ponsonby, Arthur, 63 ; I.L.P. 34 ; E.C. of U.D.C. 34, 104 ; 1917 Club 36
Porteous, Miss Margaret, F.B.Y.M. 122
Postgate, R. W., P.L. 93 ; C.P.G.B., editor of *The Communist*

INDEX OF PERSONS

Poulton, E. L., Gen. Council Brit. T.U.C. 90
Pressemane, 49
Price, M. Philips, U.D.C. 34; P.L. 93; I.L.P., Berlin Corresp. *Daily Herald*
Prooth, M., N.U.W.C.M. 102
Prothero, J., Y.C.L. 117
Proudhon, 26, 54
Pugh, Arthur, T.U.U. 90; Pres. T.U.C. (1926); Chairman Nat. Joint Counc. T.U.C. and L.P.
Purcell, A. A. (N.A.F.T.A.), 81, 85, 96; C.P.G.B. 67; C. of A. 78; B.B. of R.I.L.U. 84; I.F.T.U. 87; delegate to Russia 1924, 88, 89; Gen. Coun. T.U.C. 88, 90; Hon. Pres. N.C.L.C. 93; Vice-Pres. W.I.R. 98, 99

Quelch, Harry, S.D.F. 16
Quelch, Tom, 44, 46, 66; N.M.M. 86

Rabbi, the Chief, Vice-Pres. of I.P.S. 106
Rabinovitch, Catherine, S.C.R. 101
Rabinovitch, Philip, E.C. of W.I.R. 98, 99
Radek, 83
Rai, Lajpat, I.C.W.P.A. 100
Rakoszy, 44, 46, 52
Ramsay, Y.C.L. 117
Rand School of Social Science, 15, 55, 57, 82
Rappoport, 49
Ravachol, 26
Recht, Charles, 109
Reckitt, Maurice B., L.K.G. 130
Record, Charles, Soc. Socialist Christians 131
Redfern, Y.C.L. 117
Reed, John, 46; C.L.P. of America 57
Reeves, Mrs. Pember, F.R.D. 18
Reinstein, Boris, 55
Renaud, Jean, C.P. (Fr.) 49
Renaudel, S.P. (Fr.) 33
Renner, A.S.D.P. 33
Reynaud, W.I.R. 99
Richards, Rev. L., F.O.R. 35
Richardson, T., E.C. of I.P.S. 107
Ripon, Bishop of, Vice-Pres. of I.P.S. 106
Roberts, G. H., I.L.P. 21
Robertson, J. M., 32; Y.C.L. 117
Robertson, Dr. Stirling, Scottish Labour Party 19
Robinson, Mrs. Margaret B. L., 121, 127; ardent patriot 119
Rocker, Rudolf, 27

Roebuck, C. M., E.C. of C.P.G.B. 95; Y.C.L. 117
Rosenberg, 68
Rosenblum, Frank, A.C.W.U. 82
Rosemblum, Hella, 115
Rosenfeld, Morris, 115
Rosenfeld. See Kamenev
Rossmer, A., 44, 46
Rothstein, E., Y.C.L. 117
Rowntree, Arnold, N.C.F. 35
Roy, 46
Royden, Maude, F.O.R. 35; W.I.L. 35; 1917 Club 37
Rudniamsky, 46
Rudzutak, J. E., TS.I.K. (E.C.) 88; A.R.C.C.T.U. 88
Ruskin, Y.C.L. 117
Russell, Archibald, S.S.S.M. 113
Russell, Bertrand, U.D.C. 34; C.W.S.D. 63
Rust, C.P.G.B. 101; Y.C.L. 117
Rutgers, S. J., 55
Ruthenberg, Charles E., C.P. of America 56; arrest of 58; W.P.A. 59
Ruygers, Francine, 124
Rykov, A., TS.I.K. (E.C.) 88; A.R.C.C.T.U. 88

Sadoul, Jacques, 44, 46; E.C. of 3rd Internt.
Saklatvala, Shapurji, 116, 128; denounces the Empire 91; E.C. of W.I.R. 99; I.C.W.P.A. 100; 1917 Club, C.P.G.B.
Samuelson, 46
Sassenbach, J., I.F.T.U. 87
Saxe-Meynell, Mrs. Hilda, E.C. of W.I.R. 99
Scheflo, M., 52
Scheidemann, 33; S.D.P. of Germany, 25, 48
Scheu, Andreas, S.D.F. 16; S.L. 17
Schlesinger, Benjamin (I.L.G.W.U.), 82; P.C.A. 54; W.D.U.
Schlossberg, Joseph (A.C.W.U.), 82; P.C.A. 109
Schmidt, V. V., TS.I.K. (E.C.) 88; A.R.C.C.T.U. 88
Schwartz, C.P. (Am.) 56
Schwimmer, Madame Rosika, E.P.F. 37; W.I.C.P.P. 37
Semard, F.C.P., 49
Seniushkin, TS.I.K. 88; A.R.C.C.T.U. 88
Serrati, D. M., 46; It. S.P. (Soviet Faction) 50
Shaftesbury, Lord, 15, 126
Sharp, Evelyn (N.U.J.), 1917 Club

INDEX OF PERSONS

37; E.C. of W.I.R. 99; W.I.L., K.K., 1917 Club
Shatzkin, Lazar, Y.C.L. 116
Shaw, Y.C.L. 117
Shaw, Fred (A.S.E.), E.C. of B.S.P. 33; H.O.R.C. 64; E.C. of C.P.G.B. 67; E.C. of U.D.C. 104
Shaw, George Bernard, 30; Fab. 18; Chairman F.R.D. 18; L.R.D. 76; S.C.R. 101
Shaw, Lord, Vice-Pres. of I.P.S. 106
Shaw, Tom, 45; Sec. 2nd Internationale
Sheffick, 46
Shefflo, 46
Shelly, Rebecca, and A.N.C. 38; P.C.A. 54, 109
Sheppard, Rev. H. R. L., I.C.F. 130
Shields, J., Y.C.L. 117
Sims, George, C.L.C. 29; S.D.P. 29; I.L.P. 29
Simon, Sir John, Vice-Pres. of I.P.S. 106
Simpson, A. Noel, E.C. of N.M.W.M. 105
Simpson, R., E.C. of I.P.S. 107
Sinn Fein, 71
Skinner, J. Allen, 96
Slesser, Sir Henry, 132; L.K.G. 131; E.C. of I.C.F. (1924)
Smarodin, Y.C.L. 116
Smart, Russell, B.S.P. 33
Smillie, Robert (M.F.G.B.) 62; I.L.P. 21; N.C.C.L. 36; H.O.R.C. 64
Smith, Adolphe, 13, 43, 45, 68; S.D.F. 16; B.S.P. 33; N.S.P. 33
Smith, Constance, I.C.F. 130
Smith, Edward J., L.P.F. 35
Smith, Herbert (M.F.G.B.) 79, 90, 95; delegate to Russia 1924 88
Smith, H., Y.C.L. 117
Smythe, Nora, 69
Sneevliet, H., C.P. of Holland 51
Snowden, Philip, 17; I.L.P. 21; N.C.F. 35; C.W.S.D. 62, 63; Vice-Pres. of I.P.S. 106; and N.C.P.W. 108
Snowden, Mrs. Philip, W.I.L. 35; W.P.C. 35; 1917 Club 37; U.D.C. 104; and N.C.P.W. 108
Sorel, Georges, 28
Sorge, S. A., 14, 17
Spiridinova, Maria, 40
Spoke, Father John Corner, 131
Spooner. Lysander. 26
Spoor, Ben, H.O.R.C. 64; E.C. of I.P.S. 107; L.P., U.D.C., 1917 Club, Sec. N.P.C.
Stacy, Rev. Paul, L.K.G. 130
Stamm-Ponsen, Mrs., C.P. (Hol.) 51

Stang, Emil, 53
Starr, Kathleen, P.L. 93; E.C. of W.I.R. 99
Starr, Mark, E.C. of P.L. 93; E.C. of N.C.L.C. 93; 1917 Club, Brit. League Esperantist Socialists
Steinhardt, K., 46
Steinhart, 52
Stephen, Adrian, 36
Sterringa, C.P. of Holland, 51
Stewart, James, 117; S.L.P., C.P.G.B., E.C. of Y.C.L., Edit. *Young Rebel, Young Communist*
Stewart, Robert, E.C. of C.P.G.B. 67, 95, 102; E.C. of W.I.R. 99; Hon. Sec. of Irish branch of W.I.R.
Stilson, I., 56
Stocker, R., I.C.W.P.A. 100
Stockton, Sir Edwin, I.C.F. 130
Stokes, John, N.S.P. 33
Stokes, Rose Pastor, 55; W.P.A. 59; F.S.R. 61
Stoklitzky, Alexander, C.P. of America, 44, 56; A.C.P. 55; R.S.F. M.F.G.B.
Straker, W., Vice-Pres. W.I.R. 99; M.F.G.B.
Strickland, Sir Walter, F.G. 70
Stromer, R.
Sturgkh, Count, 52
Swales, A. B. (A.E.U.), 96; C. of A. 78; T.U.C. (President), 88, 90; I.L.P.
Swann, N. E. Egerton, L.K.G. 130
Swanwick, Mrs. H. M.; E.C. of U.D.C. 34, 104; Pres. W.I.L. 35; 1917 Club 36; and N.C.P.W. 108

Tagore, Rabindranath, K.K. 124
Tanner, Jack (A.E.U.), 44; B.B. of R.I.L.U. 84; I.W.W.
Tapsell, W., Y.C.L. 117
Taylor, Mrs. G. R. S., G.S. 30
Taylor, Helen, D.F. 16
Tawney, R. H., E.C. of Fab. 101; S.C.R. 101; W.E.A.
Tcheidze, 41
Tchernov, 40
Tetley, Arthur, 119
Thomas, Albert, S.P. (Fr.) 33
Thomas, J. H. (N.U.R.), 128; Pres. I.F.T.U. 78, 80, 87; L.S.I.
Thomas, Rev. Norman, F.O.R. 38
Thorn, J. D., N.M.M. 86; I.C.W.P.A. 100
Thorne, Will, S.D.F. 16; 68; N.S.P. 33; Gen. Council Brit. T.U.C. 90; indicts E. D. Morel 34
Thorndike, Sybil, S.C.R. 101
Tillett, Ben, 96; S.D.F. 16; founder of Labour Union of Bradford 20;

INDEX OF PERSONS

stood for Bradford 21; delegate to Russia 1924 88, 89; Gen. Council Brit. T.U.C. 90
Tinkler, Ida J., Sec. N.M.W.M. 105
Tolain, 11
Toller, W.I.R. 99
Tolstoi, 40
Toman, K., 46
Tomski, Michael (Joseph Izbitsky), 92; A.R.C.C.T.U. (Pres.) 81, 88, 89, 90; led delegation to England in 1925 91; presented with gold watch by T.U.C. 91
Townsend, D.F. 16
Townshend, Mrs., G.S. 30
Tranmael, Martin, Sec. L.P. (Nor.) 52
Treint, C.P. (Fr.) 49
Trepoff, General, 25
Trevelyan, Charles, 63; I.L.P. 34; E.C. of U.D.C. 34, 104; 1917 Club 36; and N.C.P.W. 108
Trevelyan, Mrs. C. P., E.C. of W.I.L. 35
Troelstra, S.D.A.P. of Holland 50
Trotsky (Lev Davidovitch Bronstein), 25, 41, 42, 44, 46, 48, 49, 52, 54; H.O.R.C. 63; and A.A. 54
Truro, Bishop of, Vice-Pres. of I.P.S. 106
Tschaikowsky, 40
Tucker, Benjamin R., 26, 27
Turati, S.P. (It.) 25, 50
Turner, Ben., 90; Vice-Pres. Int. Peace Scouts 107
Turner, Mrs. Beth, E.C. of C.P.G.B. 95
Turner, John, delegate to Russia 1924 89
Tywerowsky, Oscar, Russ. S.F. 55

Van der Glas, C.P. of Holland 51
Vandervelde, Belg. L.P. 33, 50
Van Lakerveld, C.P. of Holland 51
Van Leuven, 46
Van Overstraeten, Will, Belg. C.P. 50
Van Ravestyn, S.D.P. of Holland 50; C.P. of Holland 51
Varga, 46
Varley, Julia, Gen. Council Brit. T.U.C. 90
Vaughan, George, Left Wing S.P. of America 55
Villard, Mrs. Henry, First Am. C.D.T.P. 38
Vincent, Charles R., 113
Visser, L. L. H., C.P. of Holland 51
Viviani, 25
Vorovsky, V., 44

Vrooman, Walter, R.Col. 29

Wagenknecht, A., Ex. Sec. C.L.P. of America 57
Wake, Egerton, I.L.P. 34
Wakeman, John, F.G. 70
Walcher, J., 46
Wales, Archbishop of, Pres. of I.C.F. 129
Walker, R. B., Gen. Council Brit. T.U.C. 90; C. of A. 78
Wallas, Graham, Fab. 18
Walsh, Frank P. 110
Ward, Albert, E.C. of B.S.P. 33
Wardman, G. W., 131
Watering, E. V., E.C. of N.M.W.M. 105
Watkins, Nat, 91; R.I.L.U. 81, 102; Organising Secretary N.M.M. 85, 86, 87; E.C. of C.P.G.B. 95
Watson, W. F., H.O.R.C. 65
Watts, A. A., 113; E.C. of B.S.P. 33; E.C. of C.P.G.B. 67; Originator of S.S.S. Movement
Watts, F. C., 23
Watts, Hunter, B.S.P. 33; N.S.P. 33
Weardale, Lord, N.P.C. 32
Webb, Sidney, 30, 32; Fab. 18; F.R.D. 18, 19
Webb, Mrs., F.R.D. 18, 19; S.C.R. 101; Fab.
Webster, J. G., N.S.P. 33
Wedgwood, Josiah, 1917 Club 37; H.O.R.C. 64; C. of A. 78; I.L.P., T.U.C.
Wegner, Arnim T., 121
Weinstein, Gregory, 55
Weiss, Charles, L.P.F. 35
Wellcock, Wilfred, E.C. of N.M.W.M. 105
Wells, H. G., Fab. 18; S.C.R. 101; K.K. 124; 1917 Club
Welsh, Francis Ralston, 111
West, Julius, Secretary F.R.D. 18
Westminster Abbey, Canon of, 106
Weston, 11
Wheatley, John, 95; L.P., I.L.P.
Wheeler, George, N.U.W.C.M. 96
Whitehead, Edgar T., Sec. W.I.R. 98; Sec. 1st British Communist Party
Whitehouse, J. Howard, K.K. 124
Whiting, Councillor A., N.S.P. 33
Wicks, H. M., C.P. (Am.) 56
Wilker, Karl, 121
Wilkinson, Ellen, 84; B.B. of R.I.L.U. 84; P.L. 93; E.C. of W.I.R. 99; C.P.G.B., Workers C'tee. of R.I.L.U. in Moscow, returns from Moscow in 1921 81

INDEX OF PERSONS

Williams, Dr. Ethel, E.C. of W.I.L. 104
Williams, John, D.F. 16
Williams, Robert (N.T.W.F.), 62, 64, 79, 81, 96, 128; N.C.C.L. 36; C. of A. 78; B.B. of R.I.L.U. 84; I.L.P., H.O.R.C., Dir. *Daily Herald*
Williams, V., B. B. of R.I.L.U. 84
Willis, F., H.O.R.C. 65; E.C. of C.P.G.B. 67
Wilson, D., Y.C.L. 117
Wilson, Havelock, 63
Wilson, J. H., M.P. for Middlesbrough, 21
Wilson, Theodora Wilson, E.C. of N.M.W.M. 105; I.L.P., W.I.L.
Windsor, Walter, E.C. of I.P.S. 107; Vice-Pres. of Int. Peace Scouts 107
Winberg, 46
Winitsky, Harry M., C.P. of America 56; arrest of 58
Winston, James, H.O.R.C. 64
Wintringham —, C.P.G.B. 101
Wise, E. F., 132; S.C.R. 101
Wise, Mrs., S.C.R. 101
Wise, Rabbi Stephen, E.C. of A.N.C. 38
Wolfe, Bertram D., C.P. (Am.) 56
Wolfe, L. L., Left Wing S.P. (Am.) 55
Wolff, 12
Wolfstein, R., 46

Woodifield, Robert, and C.C. 12,
Woolf, Leonard S., F.R.D. 19; 1917 Club 37; S.C.R. 101
Woolley, E., Y.C.L. 117
Woolwich, Bishop of, I.C.F. 130
Wright, W., E.C. of I.P.S. 107; Vice-Pres. Int. Peace Scouts 107
Wyneken, Gustave, 121
Wynkoop, D., 46; D.C. 44; S.D.P. of Holland 50; C.P. of Holland 51
Wyonopsky, S., 82

Yarotsky, V. Y., A.R.C.C.T.U. 89
York, Archbishop of, Pres. of I.C.F. 129
Young, George, Gen. Council Brit. T.U.C. 90
Young, H., Y.C.L. 117

Zaaier, De, 51, 114
Zalewsky. See Abramovitch
Zalkind, Dr. M., F.G. 70
Zangwill, Israel, 64; U.D.C. 34
Zassulitch, Vera, 25
Zetkine, Clara, 49; Spart. 48; W.I.R. 97, 99; E.C. of 3rd Internationale
Zinoviev, G. E. (Ovse Gershon Aronovitch Radomisilsky), 41, 44, 46, 47, 53, 68, 75, 99; letter to I.W.W. 58, 73; overtures to I.W.W. 74; Pres. of I.K.K.I. 74, 96

Note.—The real names of Parvus, Trotsky and Zinoviev are given correctly in brackets in above Index and not quite correctly in Text, pages 41 and 44. Apfelbaum is one of Zinoviev's pseudonyms.

On page 113 reference is made to Bristol Socialist Sunday Society. This should read Bristol Socialist Society.

GENERAL INDEX

"Adamites," 121
Allgemeiner Deutscher Arbeiter Verein, 14
Allgemeine Deutsche gewerkschaftbund, 89
Alliance Sociale Démocratique. See Social Democratic Alliance
All Power, organ of B.B. of R.I.L.U., 85
All Russian Central Council of Trade Unions, 88, 89, 90; conference of, in Moscow, 81
All Russian Congress of Peasants, 41
All Russian Congress of Trade Unions, 81
All Russian Co-operative Society (Arcos), 98, 101
Amalgamated Clothing Workers' Union (Amer.), 82
Amalgamated Textile Workers (Amer.), 82
America, early Socialism in, 13
American Anarchist Federated Commune Soviets, 54
American Association for the Recognition of the Irish Republic, 72
American Civil Liberties Union, 110, 119
American Federation of Labour, 28, 44, 74, 82; Left Wing of, 76
American Labor Alliance, 58
American League to Limit Armaments, 37, 110
American Neutral Conference, 38
American Peace Society, 37
American Socialist Society, 15
American Union Against Militarism, 37, 110
Amsterdam Internationale. See International Federation of Trade Unions
Anarchism, 12; chap. iii; origin of, 26; in America, 26; in England, 27; spirit of, 27
Anarchist Communism, in England, 27, 69; in America, 54
Anarchists, French, 26; Russian, 26, 42; Italian, 26; American, 26, 53; English, 27

Anarchist Soviet Bulletin, 54
Anarcho-Syndicalism, 82
Anglo-Russian Trade Union Unity Committee, 89
Anti-Parliamentary Communist Federation, 69, 71
Anti-War Council of Holland, 37
Arbeiderbladet, organ of Communists of Norway, 53
Arbitrate First Bureau, 109
Austria, Bolshevism in, 52
Avanti, organ of It. S.P., 50
Awakening Magyars, 52

Babouvistes, 10
Bakunin House, 69
Balkan Socialist Federation, 44
Band of Peace Union, Comrades of Peace, 32, 107
Belgian Labour Party, 33, 44
Belgium, Bolshevism in, 50
"Black Friday," 79
Blast, The, organ of A.A., 54
Bolsheviks, 10, 25, 40
Bolshevik Consul (John Maclean), 64
Bolshevism, chap. vi, 62; in Great Britain, 62; in France, 48; in Germany, 48; world, 48; in Italy, 49; in Holland, 50; in Belgium, 50; in Switzerland, 51; in Austria, 52; in Hungary, 52; in Scandinavia, 52; in America, 53; in Ireland, 71
Bond en Kommunistische Stryd en Propaganda Clubs, 51
Bridgman Convention, 83
Bristol Socialist Society, 113
British Boys' and Girls' Peace Scouts, 107
British Communist Party, 1st, 66
British delegation to Russia, 1924. See Russia.
British National Peace Congress, 32
British Socialist Party, 33, 62, 66
British Socialist Sunday School Committee, 113
British Socialist Sunday School Union, 113
Brotherhood Church, 116

156

GENERAL INDEX

Broussistes, 25
Buford, the "Soviet Ark," 58
Building Workers' Minority Movement, 85

Cabet's Community, 10
Call, The, organ of B.S.P., 33, 65, 68
Cambridge University War and Peace Society, 32
Catholic Crusade, foundation of, 127, 128
Catholic Peace Society, 32
Central Executive Committee of the Russian Soviet Republic. See TS.I.K.
Central Labour College, 29
Chartist riots, 15
Christian Internationale. See Fellowship of Reconciliation, 106
Christian Order of Politics, Economics, and Citizenship (Copec), 132
Christian Social Union, 127, 128
Christian Socialists, 15, 16, 127
Christian World, The, 131
Church of England Peace League, 32, 108
Church Socialist League, 127, 130
Civil Service and Fabian Society, 18
Clan-na-gael, 72
"Clarté," 99; joins up with F.C.P., 103
Class Struggle, The, organ of S.P. of America, 54
Clyde Workers' Committee, 62
Clyde Workers' Propaganda Defence Committee, 65
Cobden Club and N.C.P.W., 108
Code of Criminal Laws, 70
Committee of International Relations, 132
Commonwealth, The, organ of L.K.G., 131
Commune, organ of Communist Fed., 70
Communism, early ideas on, 10; aim of British Socialist bodies, 20; theory of, 42
Communist, The, organ of S.L., 17; organ of C.P. (Am.), 56, 58; organ of C.P.G.B., 68
Communist Council of Action, 69
Communist Federation, 69
Communist Internationale (see Internationale, the 3rd)
Communist Labor, organ of C.L.P. (Am.), 57
Communist Labour Party of America, 44, 57, 58
Communist League of Youth, 116

Communist Party of America, 44, 55, 58, 76
Communist Party of Austria, 52
Communist Party of Belgium, 3rd Int., 50
Communist Party of France, foundation of, 49; Clarté joins up with, 104
Communist Party of Great Britain, 66, 67, 71, 87, 95, 101
Communist Party of Holland, 51
Communist Party of Hungary, 45, 52
Communist Party of Ireland, 71
Communist Party of Russia, 44
Communist Party of Switzerland, 52
Communist Propaganda Groups, 27
Communist Rules, 118
Communist Workers' Party of Holland, 51
Communist World, organ of C.P. (Am.), 56
Communist Workers' Party, 71
Communist Youth International. See Young Communist Int.
Confédération générale du Travail, 27, 74, 82
Confédération générale du Travail Unitaire, 82
Co-operative Holidays' Association and N.C.P.W., 108
Co-operative movement, 15, 91
Co-operative Society, 77, 78
Co-operative Union, 77; and N.C.P.W., 108
Co-Partnership, 91
Council of Action, 77, 91
Council for Civil Liberties, 62
Councils of Workmen's and Soldiers' Delegates, in England, 62; in Russia, 109
Crusader, The, organ of Soc. of Socialist Christians, 131
Crusaders of Peace, 107

Daily Herald, 62, 66, 97
Democratic Federation, foundation of, 16, 126
Der Arbeiter Freind, London Yiddish revolutionary paper, 27, 70
Der Kampf, 56
Distributionists, 9
Drapeau Rouge, organ of Belg. C.P., 50
Dutch East Indies, revolutionary organisations in, 51

Eenheit (Unity), 51
Emergency Peace Federation, 37, 110

GENERAL INDEX

Fabian Research Department, foundation of, 18; changes name to Lab. Res. Dept., 30, 130
Fabian Society, 93; foundation of, 17; and Civil Service, 18; programme of, 18
Fascists, British, 118, 129
Federation of British Youth Movements, 120, 122; and K.K., 123
Federazione Italiano Operai Metallurgichi (F.I.O.M.), 50
Fellowship of Reconciliation, 35, 62, 106, 119, 123, 132; in America, 38, 110
Fellowship of Youth for Peace, 119
Fenians and Karl Marx, 24; and 1st International, 24
Ferens, T. R., Vice-Pres. of I.P.S., 106
Feu, Le, 103
First American Conference for Democracy and Terms of Peace, 38, 109
Flame, The, 119
Foreign Affairs, organ of U.D.C., 104
Foreign Jews' Protection Committee, 62
Foreign Languages Federations of America, 55
Forward, 63
Fourierists in America, 14
France, Utopian Socialists of, 10; Marxian Socialists of, 25. See also Communist Party of France
France Libre, La, organ of F.S.P., 49
Freedom Group, 27, 70
Freiheit, paper of Johann Most, 27
French Unified Socialist Party, 3rd Int., 49; = French Communist Party, 49
Friends' Council for International Service, 109
Friends' Peace Committee and N.C.P.W., 108
Friends of Soviet Russia (America), 60

Garton Foundation, 32
General Strike. See Strike, General
General Workers' Minority movement, 85
German Independent Party, 46
German Social Democratic Party, 41, 48, 114
Germany, early Socialism in, 25
Glasgow Anarchist Group, 69
Glasgow Communist Group defeated Anarchist Group, 27, 68
Glasgow Socialist Sunday Schools, 113

Group for the Emancipation of Labour, 25, 40
Guild of Citizens of To-morrow, 122
Guild of St. Matthew, 127
Guild Socialism, 30; and L.K.G., 130

Hague Congress for Women, 35, 37
Hands Off Russia Committee, 63, 64
Hearst Press, 111
Herald, The (original name of *Daily Herald*),
Herald League, 62
Herald of Peace, The, organ of Peace Society, 107
Herald of Revolt, 27
Holland, Bolshevism in, 50; Social Democratic Party of, 50 (S.D.P.); Social Democratic Labour Party of, 50 (S.D.A.P.); Communist Workers' Party of, 51 (C.A.P.); Union of Fight and Propaganda Clubs of, 51 (B.K.S.P.)
Humanité, L', organ of C.P. (Fr.), 49
Hungary, Bolshevism in, 52
Hunger marches, 96
Hyde Park Socialist Club, 71

Icarian communities in America, 14
I.K.K.I. (Executive Committee of Communist International), 44, 47, 56
I.L.P. Guild of Youth, foundation of, 118
Independent Labour Party, 33, 34, 62, 95, 132; foundation of, 19; inspired by Engels, 19; programme of, 20; Left Wing of, 67
Industrial Christian Fellowship, 127, 128, 129, 130
Industrial Syndicalist League, 29
Industrial Workers of the World, 28, 57, 75, 86; of America, 75, 110; of Great Britain, 75; of Australia, 75
Intercollegiate Socialist Society, 15
Internationale, the 1st, foundation of, 11; end of, 12
Internationale, the 2nd, 43; foundation of, 12; Conference at Amsterdam (1919), 45; Conference at Lucerne (1919), 45; Conference at Geneva (1919), 45; headquarters of, 50; Congress in Paris (1900), 114
Internationale, the 3rd, 70, 71; foundation of, 43; West European Secretariat of, 47; Third Congress of, 58; and Youth Movement, 115

GENERAL INDEX

Internationale, the 4th, 69
International, organ of W.I.C.P.P., 38
International Arbitration and Peace Association, 32
International Class War Prisoners' Aid (I.C.W.P.A.), 99, 102
International Committee of Women for Permanent Peace, 35
International Communist School Movement, 116
International Council of Trade and Industrial Unions, 81
International Federation of Trade Unions or Amsterdam International, 28, 73, 78, 87; and May 1, 1921, Manifesto, 79; refuses to affiliate with R.I.L.U., 87
International Fellowship of Reconciliation, 106
International Ladies' Garment Workers' Union of America, 54, 82
International League of Youth for Peace, 122, 123
International League of Youth, 120
International Peace Brethren, 37
International Peace Scouts, 107
International Peace Society, 106
International Red Aid. See Intern. Class War Pris. Aid
International Revolutionary Congress (1881), 26
International Socialist Club, 66
International of Socialist Youth, foundation of, 114
International Suffrage Alliance, 37
International Syndicalist Congress in America, 28
International Union of Socialist Workers, 118
International Union of Unemployed, 96
International of Working Class Youth, the, 118
International of Youth, The, 115
International Youth, 117
International Workingmen's Association in New York, 14
Ireland, Bolshevism in, 71
Irish Communist Brotherhood, 72
Irish Nationalist Movement, 71
Irish Peace Society, 32
Irish Republican Brotherhood, 24, 71, 72
Irish Socialist Republican Party, 24, 71
Irish Transport and General Workers' Union led by James Larkin, 24, 71
Irish Workers' League, 71
Irish Workers' Union, 71

Iron and Steel Trades Confederation and N.C.P.W., 108
Italian Federation of Labour, 81
Italian Socialists' Union, 33
Italy, Socialism in, 25; Bolshevism in, 50

Jacobin Club, 9
Jewish Peace Society, 109
Joint Manifesto of British Socialist Bodies, 20
Joint Provisional Committee for the Communist Party of Great Britain, 66
Joint Research Department of the T.U.C. and Lab. Party, 93
Jugendbewegung, 123
Justice, organ of B.S.P., 33; organ of N.S.P., 33; organ of S.D.F., 68, 113; organ of I.L.G.W.U. (Amer.), 82

Kibbo Kift, 124; foundation of, 123
Klassenstryd, De, organ of C.P. (Hol.), 51
Komsomol. See Young Communist League
Kropotkine Anarchists, 27, 70

Labour Colleges, 29
Labour Leader, edited by Keir Hardie, 19; organ of I.L.P., 21
Labour Monthly (Communist), 77
Labour Party, origins of, 21; aim of (1906), 21; conference at Liverpool, 92
Labour Party of Illinois, 14
Labour Party of Norway, 45, 53
Labour Research Department, 95; formerly Fabian Research Dept., 19, 90, 93
Labour Representation Committee, 21
Labour Socialist International, 89
Labour Union of Bradford, 20
Language Federations, 57
Lauensteiner Kreis, formed by I.L.Y., 120
League to Abolish War, 109
League of Amnesty of Political Prisoners in America, 54
League of Communist Youth, 124
League for Industrial Democracy, 15
League of the Kingdom of God, the, 130, 132
League of Nations Union, foundation of, 108; and I.L.Y., 120
League of Peace and Freedom, 35
Leeds Conference, 62
Left Wing, 102
Left Wing Movements, 102

GENERAL INDEX

Left Wing Section of the Socialist Party of America, 57
Letchworth Garden City, 131
Liberty, organ of American Anarchists, 26; started by Benjamin R. Tucker, 26
London Labour College, 94

Majority Socialists of Sweden, 52
Marxian Socialism, chap. ii.
Mask, The, 123
Massachusetts Public Interests League, 119
Masses, 54
Men of the Trees, 125
Mensheviks, 33, 42
Meshrabpom. See Workers' International Relief, 97
Metal Workers' Minority Movement, 85
Mine Worker, The, organ of National Minority Movement, 86
Miner, The, edited by Keir Hardie, 21
Miners' Federation of Great Britain, 30, 79
Miners' Minority Movement (M.M.M.), 85
Miners' Next Step, The, 30
Miners' Reform Movement, 30, 86
Mines for the Miners' Movement, 30, 73, 85
M.O.P.R. See International Class War Pris. Aid
Mot Dag, 53
Mother Earth, official organ of A.A., 54
Move, the. See Awakening Magyars

National Association of Schoolmasters and N.C.P.W., 108
National Brotherhood Council and N.C.P.W., 108
National Building Guild, 30
National Council against Conscription, 36
National Council for Civil Liberties, 36
National Council of Labour Colleges, 93, 94
National Council for the Prevention of War, 107; in America, 111
National Council for the Reduction of Armaments (America), 111
National Free Church Council and N.C.P.W., 108
National Guilds Council, 30
National Guilds League, 30
National Joint Council of T.U.C. and L.P., 74, 87

National Labor Union of New York, 14
National League of Women Voters of America, 111
National Minority Movement (N.M.M.), 85, 86, 87, 117
National Peace Council. See National Council for the Prevention of War
National Peace Federation, 37
National Reform Union and N.C.P.W., 108
National Socialist Party, 33, 68
National Union of Railwaymen, 79
National Unemployed Workers' Committee Movement, 96
National Workers' Committee Organisation, 66
Navvy Mission, 128
New Gymnosophical Society, 122
New Harmony, 10
New International, The, organ of S.P. of America, 54
New Leader, organ of I.L.P., 21
New Solidarity, organ of I.W.W., 75
New Standards : a Journal of Workers' Control, 92
New Student, The, 121
News from Nowhere, 17
Nihilists, 26
Nineteen Seventeen Club, 36
No Conscription Fellowship, 62, 103
No Conscription League (of America), 34, 54
Nomad, The, organ of K.K., 123, 124
No More War, 105
No More War Committee. See N.M.W.M.
No More War Movement, 104, 105, 132; Youth Section, 105, 121; and N.C.P.W., 108
Norwegian Left Wing Socialists, 53
Novy Mir, organ, R.S.F., 55, 56
Nudity Movement, 121

One Big Union, idea of A.C.W.U. and of I.W.W., 75, 82; adopted by Bolsheviks, 86; adopted by Brit. T.U.C., 91
One Big Union Monthly, organ of I.W.W., 74, 75
Order of the Round Table, T.S. group, 122
Out of Work, organ of N.U.W.C.M., 97
Owenites in America, 14

Pacifism, during War, chap. iv
Pacifism, post-War, chap. xi
Pacifist Youth International. See I.L.Y.

GENERAL INDEX

Parliamentary Labour Party, 77
Parliamentarianism, 46
Patriot, The, 72, 127, 129; and I.C.F., 129
Peace Conference at Berne, 69
Peace Society, foundation of, 30
People's Council of America, 54, 109
People's Freedom Union (Am.), 109, 110
People's Social Party of Russia, 40
Plebs League, 29, 93, 95
Plebs, organ of " Plebs League," 29
Poland, 77
Polit-Bureau, 47
Profintern. See Red Int. of Lab. Unions
Proletarian Sunday School Movement, 65, 118
Proletcult, 118
Provisional International Council of Trade and Industrial Unions, British Bureau of, 84
Public Ownership League, 110

Quakers, 120

Railwaymen, patriotism of, in 1921, 79
Rationalist Peace Society, 32
" Réconciliation, La," 106
Red Army, 70
Red Catechism, 118
Red Dawn, The, 116
" Red Flag," 114
Red Flag, The, 116
Red International of Labour Unions (" Profintern "), 83, 86, 95, 96; British Bureau of, 84; of Moscow, 81; First Congress of, 81
Reds in America, 60, 61, 76, 83
Red Trade Union International of Moscow, 81; campaign against I.F.T.U., 82
Religion, opposed by S.P.G.B., 23
Revolutionary Age, The, 55
Revolutionary Socialists of Russia, 26, 33, 40
Roode Vaan, organ of Belg. C.P., 50
Rose Street Club in Soho, 16
Rothe Fahne, Die, organ of German Communists, 48
Ruskin College, 29
Russia, Revolution in, chap. v; early Socialism in, 25; Anarchism in, 25, 40; Trade Unions in, 80; British Delegation to (1924), 88, 89
Russian-American Industrial Corporation, 110
Russian Anarchists. See Anarchists, Russian

Russian delegation to England, 1925, members of, 89
Russian Democratic Party, led by Plekhanov, 25
Russian Revolution, chap. v
Russian Social Democratic Party, 40
Russian Socialist Federation, 55, 56
Russian Trade Delegation to England in 1920, 78; financing propaganda in 1920, 78

Scarborough Conference, 91
Scandinavia, Bolshevism in, 52
Scottish Labour Party, 19
Secours Rouge International, 99
Servers' Group of Young Theosophists, 122
Shakers in America, 13
Social Democrat, The, organ of S.D.F., 68
Socialdemokrat, organ of L.P. (Nor.), 53
Social Democratic Alliance, 12
Social Democratic Federation, 27, 68, 113; foundation of, 16
Social Democratic Labour Party of Austria, 52
Social Democratic Labour Party of Holland, 50
Social Democratic Party, 33
Social Democratic Party of America, 14
Social Democratic Party of Austria, 33
Social Democratic Party of Germany, 25
Social Democratic Party of Holland, 50, 114
Social Democratic Party of Switzerland, 45, 51
Social Democratic Workingmen's Party of North America, 14
Social Democratic Young Workers' International, 118
Social Party of New York, 14
Socialist, The, organ of, S.L.P., 67
Socialist Labour Party, 33, 67; foundation of, 22
Socialist Labor Party of America, 22, 29, 54
Socialist Labor Party of North America, 14
Socialist Labour Press, 22
Socialist League, foundation of, 16; Manifesto of, 17; collapse of, 17
Socialist Party of America, 46, 54, 55
Socialist Party of France, 33, 44, 46, 48, 49
Socialist Party of Great Britain, 33; foundation of, 23; objects of, 23

GENERAL INDEX

Socialist Party of Ireland, 24, 71
Socialist Party of Italy, 3rd Int., 45, 50
Socialist Party of Sweden, 53
Socialist Party of Switzerland, 44
Socialist Propaganda League of America, 54
Socialist Review, organ of I.L.P., 21
Socialist Standard, organ of S.L.P. 23
Socialist Sunday School Movement, 113
Socialist Youth Internationale, 120 ; Congress of, 119
Society for Cultural Relations Between the Peoples of the British Commonwealth and the Union of Socialist Soviet Republics (S.C.R.), 101
Society of Friends' Peace Committee, 109
Society for the Promotion of Permanent and Universal Peace. See Peace Society.
Society of Socialist Christians, 131
Socio-Political Labor Unions of Cincinnati, 14
South German Social Democrats, 37
South Wales Miners' Federation, 29
South Wales Socialist Society, 66
Soviet Russia, organ of F.S.R. (Am.), 61
Soviet Russia Pictorial, organ of F.S.R. of America, 61 ; organ of W.I.R., 98
Soviet of Soldiers', Workmen's and Sailors' Deputies in Russia, 41, 62
Spartacists, 48
Steinerites, 122
Stormvogels, K.K. in Holland, 124
Strike, General, 46, 77, 78 ; plan of Syndicalists, 28 ; weapon of Syndicalists, 74 ; of 1921, 78 ; of 1926, 135
Strike, railway, of 1919, 76
Sunday Worker, The, 89
Swedish Left Socialist Party, 53
Switzerland, Bolshevism in, 51
Syndicalism, chap. iii ; in America, 28 ; Book "Syndicalism," by Ramsay Macdonald, 28 ; and Parliamentarianism, 75 ; and Communism, 73
Syndicalist, The, 29

Theosophical Society, 122
Torch, The, organ of I.C.F., 128
Tours Congress, 49
Trades Union Congress Parliamentary Committee, 77

Trade Union Congress, 30, 73, 77, 96 ; foundation of, 28 ; in 1895, 28 ; personnel in 1925, 88 ; Scarborough Conference, 91
Trade Union Educational League of America, 76, 82
Trade Union Internationale, 80
Trade Union Movement, 15
Trade Union Unity, 90
Trade Union Unity Movement, 89
Transport Workers' Minority Movement, 85
Transport Workers' Union of Ireland, 71
Tribune, De, organ of C.P. of Holland, 51
Triple Alliance, The, 78 ; Manifesto of, 79
TS.I.K. = Central Executive Committee of U.S.S.R., 47, 88, 90

Unemployed Committees, 96
Unemployed Workers' Organisation, 69
"Unemployment Sunday," 96
Unified Socialist Party, French = French Communist Party
Union of Democratic Control, 34, 37, 62, 103, 104, 132 ; and N.C.P.W., 108
Union of Russian Workers, 58
United Communist Party of America, 58
United Garment Workers of America, 82
United Irishmen, 24
United Peace Fellowship of the Churches, 107
Universal Republican Alliance, 16
Utopian Socialism, 10

Versöhnungsbund, 106, 119
Vorwärts, 48

War and Peace Societies of Oxford and Cambridge, 32
War Resisters' Internationale, 105, 119
West European Secretariat of the I.K.K.I., 47
Western Federation of Miners in America, 28
Women's Committee for World Disarmament (in America), 111
Women's Co-operative Guild, and N.C.P.W., 108

GENERAL INDEX

Women's International Committee for Permanent Peace, 37; Conference of, at Zurich, 110
Women's International League, 35, 38, 62; and N.C.P.W., 108
Women's International League for Peace and Freedom, 104, 110; in America, 111
Women's Peace Crusade, 35
Women's Peace Party of America, 37
Women's Suffrage Federation, 66
Women's Union for Peace, 109
Woodcraft League in Poland, 124
Worker, The, organ of W.P.A., 59; organ of B.B. of R.I.L.U., 85, 89, 97; organ of N.M.M., 86
Workers' Communist Movement, 69
Workers' Defence Corps, 91
Workers' Defence Union (America), 82
Workers' Dreadnought, 66, 68
Workers' Educational Association, 94
Workers' International Industrial Union (America), 29, 75
Workers' International Pictorial, organ of W.I.R., 98
Workers' International Relief (W.I.R.), "Meshrabpom," 61, 97, 98; Irish Committee of, 99
Workers' International Russian Relief (W.I.R.R.). See Workers' International Relief
Workers' and Soldiers' Council of Russia, 54, 63
Workers' Party of America, 59, 60, 76
Workers' Peace Council, 36
Workers' Republic, The, organ of C.P.I., 71
Workers' Socialist Federation, 66

Workers' Suffrage Federation. See Workers' Socialist Federation
Workers' Weekly, The, 100; organ of C.P.G.B., 89
Workingmen's Association, 11
Workingmen's Party of the United States, 14
World Council, 123; world survey, 124
World Federation of Young Theosophists, 122
World of Labour, by G. D. H. Cole, 30

Young Communist International, 115; affiliated to 3rd Internationale, 115; publications of, 115; in Berlin, 116
Young Communist League, 115, 116, 119
Young Communist, The, 116, 117
Young Communist Review, 117
Young Comrade, The, 117
Young Comrades' League, 117
Young Friends' Movement, 123
Young Pioneers, 116, 117
Young Rebel, The, 117
Young Socialist, The, organ of S.S.S., 113
Young Socialist International, 118
Young Socialist League, 116
Young Winkle, by John Hargrave, 123
The Young Worker, 117
Young Workers of Austria, 118
Young Workers' League, 116, 117
Youth, 121, 123; organ of I.L.Y., 120

Zimmerwald Congress, 39, 51
Zurich Congress (1893), 13